D1331572

RED EMMA SPEAKS

BOOKS BY ALIX KATES SHULMAN

Bosley on the Number Line

Awake or Asleep

To The Barricades:
The Anarchist Life of Emma Goldman

Finders Keepers

Red Emma Speaks (editor)

Memoirs of an Ex-Prom Queen

RED EMMA SPEAKS

Selected Writings and Speeches

by EMMA GOLDMAN

Compiled and Edited

by ALIX KATES SHULMAN

 VINTAGE BOOKS

A Division of Random House / New York

PERSONAL ACKNOWLEDGMENTS

My thanks to Judy Goldberg and Dorothy Swanson
of the Tamiment Library for their help in locating documents of the Mother Earth Group; to the staff of the
Manuscript Division of the New York Public Library;
and to Martin Shulman for his invaluable suggestions.

VINTAGE BOOKS EDITION, FEBRUARY 1972

First Edition

ISBN: 0-394-71172-6

Library of Congress Catalog Card Number: 77-37077

Acknowledgment is gratefully extended to Ian Ballantine
for permission to reprint copyrighted materials.

Manufactured in the United States of America by
H. Wolff, New York

For the Barbaras

Contents

RED EMMA SPEAKS

Introduction by Alix Shulman

I.

Until somewhere toward the end of the 1960's, anarchism and feminism seemed irrelevant anachronisms to most Americans, each an old joke which in one version had Emma Goldman as the punch line. Like the punch line of other passé stories, Goldman's name, if remembered at all, was slightly offensive, flat, recalling a style that had long since passed. Even among radicals, in the last few decades, few have shared her disgust with the regimented centralization and mechanization that characterize modern life. Her libertarian vision was derided as hopelessly utopian and laughably naive. In 1969 almost every word she wrote had long been out of print and her life—which Theodore Dreiser once described as "the richest of any woman's of the century"—all but forgotten. Even her vigorous and lucid autobiography, *Living My Life,* went out of print.

Now, as everyone knows, things have changed. Old punch lines are new slogans. "Anarchism," proclaims an article in a recent literary journal, "was dead and is alive." Likewise, feminism. And likewise, the anomalously named

"Anarchist Queen," Emma Goldman. In 1970 Goldman's books were all suddenly reissued, not only for the libraries, but in paperback. Her style of theater is being reenacted on street corners, and nowadays there is likely to be someone with her implacable commitment on trial for conspiracy or being hunted by the FBI. The revolutionary Goldman is back in her old haunts, up to her old tricks. "For further information [about me]," she advises her readers, "consult . . . any police department in America or Europe."

Watch her defending herself at her conspiracy trial, solemnly refusing to rise when *The Star-Spangled Banner* is played. There she is, thumbing her nose at a congressman. She is eluding her police captors long enough to make one last speech before going to prison for "inciting to riot," or skillfully slipping into the country under the noses of the very immigration officials assigned to keep her out. She is living now in a commune, now in solitary confinement. See her carrying the red flag, leading women strikers to a May Day rally. She has gone underground for a while (alias E. G. Smith). She is writing a new manifesto, invading an all-male club, outwitting the vigilantes. She is flaunting the contraceptive laws and obstructing the draft, despite certain arrest, then serving time in prison for both. In fact, she never makes a speech without taking a good book with her to read in jail in case she is arrested.

The story is no longer stale. Her vision is current again. Her witty antics and petulant style, the gesture of defiance and the ferocious glower, her fanatical integrity, are suddenly immensely interesting. Someone is writing a play about Goldman, someone else is making a movie. In an East Village coffee house in New York City, only a few blocks from where she once lived, there is a blow-up of an old poster announcing her Sunday-night lectures. Her picture is on the cover of *Rat* and *Off Our Backs*. In the first mass demonstration of the new feminists on August 26, 1970, a vociferous group called the Emma Goldman

Brigade marched down New York's Fifth Avenue behind a
huge red-and-black banner bearing her name; militant
young women passed out handbills with quotes from Goldman's speeches, all the while chanting

> Emma said it in 1910,
> Now we're going to say it again . . .

and few onlookers snickered. On the contrary, it seemed
that everyone lining the avenue was straining to hear. That
we may have heard the punch line before only makes us
want to hear the story again.

II.

Emma Goldman was born into a Jewish family of changing
fortunes in czarist Russia, on June 27, 1869. Her childhood
seems to have served her as an object lesson in the brutaliz-
ing effects of capriciously exercised authority. In the remote
village of Popelan, where Goldman's parents ran a small
government inn, young Emma's sensibilities were steadily
assaulted by the spectacle of wives and children being
beaten, peasants whipped, pregnant girls ostracized, Jews
outcast, and even the poorest peasant shaken down by an
endless stream of corrupt petty officials.

She was the middle child between two older half-sisters
and two younger brothers. Her despotic father, whom she
remembered as "the nightmare of my childhood," evidently
singled her out as the special object of his frequent rages,
insuring that from the very beginning her development was,
as she later summed it up, "largely in revolt."

She had four years of Jewish elementary schooling in her
grandmother's city of Koenigsberg, where she mastered
German and excelled academically, but failed in deport-
ment. Her religious instructor gave her a public tongue-
lashing instead of the recommendation that would have got
her into the *Gymnasium,* thus effectively squelching the

child's academic ambitions. Then, at thirteen, she moved with her family to the St. Petersburg ghetto. It was 1882; Czar Alexander II had been assassinated less than a year before. Revolution was in the air; the teeming Russian capital, alive with the libertarian and egalitarian ideas the populists had been spreading for decades, was suddenly in a state of terror. That year brought one of the worst political repressions (and worst waves of pogroms) Russia had yet suffered. Emma managed to squeeze in only six months of school in St. Petersburg before the family's poverty forced her to take a full-time factory job. But six months was long enough to fire the impressionable girl with the populist ideas being whispered everywhere.

She began devouring the forbidden novels and tracts—of Chernechevsky and Turgenev—that were passing secretly from hand to hand; and she began to revere revolutionary women like young Vera Zasulich, who had shot the police chief of St. Petersburg, or Sophia Perovskaya, who had been martyred for conspiring against the czar. With such models before her, she soon began to question everything, rejecting for herself the restricted ghetto life of her family. When her father tried to marry her off at fifteen, she was ready to do anything to prevent it. She pleaded with him, protesting that she wanted to study and travel instead of marrying. Her father, in a characteristic rage, grabbed her French grammar and threw it into the fire. "Girls do not have to learn much," he screamed; only how to "prepare minced fish, cut noodles fine, and give the man plenty of children!"

Her father's threat precipitated her flight with a sister the following year to America, where their other sister had already settled. Emma Goldman arrived in New York in 1886, at the age of seventeen, full of golden images and dreams.

Like so many other immigrants from Eastern Europe, she came seeking freedom and opportunity, only to find instead repression, squalor, and hard times. In Rochester, New York, where she settled with her sisters, ghetto and factory life seemed not much different from what she had left behind in the land of the czars. Her first job, making overcoats for ten hours a day, paid $2.50 a week; it was a statistic she would never stop citing. Before long, lonely and defeated, she married a fellow Russian immigrant named Jacob Kershner, and almost immediately the marriage fell apart.

When Goldman learned of the political trial and conviction of eight Chicago anarchists—whose ideals were similar to those of the Russian populists she revered—it seemed to her that "free" America was not only as exploitative as czarist Russia but as repressive too. The Chicago anarchists had been convicted on the flimsiest evidence of throwing a bomb into a crowd of police at a rally in Chicago's Haymarket Square. The explosion had crowned days of tension growing out of labor agitation for the eight-hour day—agitation led mainly by anarchists. In the ensuing panic, a nationwide anarchist hunt was launched, followed by the 1886 Chicago conspiracy trial, and eventually the hanging of four of the convicted anarchists in 1887. These events influenced a whole generation; yet young Goldman, raptly following the trial from Rochester, reading everything on anarchism she could lay her hands on, was more deeply affected than most. On that Black Friday the Haymarket martyrs were hanged—a day from which she would ever after date the beginning of her life—she underwent a profound conversion. Thereafter she was no longer content to sympathize with the revolution; she determined to become a revolutionary.

I had a distinct sensation that something new and wonderful had been born in my soul [she wrote of that night in her memoirs]. A great ideal, a burning faith, a determination to dedicate myself to the memory of my martyred comrades, to make their cause my own. . . . My mind was made up. I would go to New York . . . [and] prepare myself for my new task.

She divorced her husband and, at age twenty, went to New York to begin her radical life. Her only assets were a sewing machine with which to make her way, five dollars (borrowed), and a passion to join the revolutionary anarchists whose scathing tracts she had read so avidly in Rochester.

In New York she quickly became the protégée of the movement's veteran spokesman, Johann Most, editor of the German-language anarchist paper *Freiheit*. Under his tutelage, Goldman studied political theory and began to organize and speak, at first addressing only small groups of immigrant workers in German, Yiddish, Russian. Before her first New York winter was out, she was living in a commune with several other young Russian-born anarchist revolutionaries, including her first great love, Alexander Berkman, the "Sasha" of her memoirs, with whom her entire life would be meshed. And after only six months she set off on her first independent speaking tour. With the success of that tour, Goldman launched a career which would eventually make her one of the most charismatic and volatile speakers in the history of the stump. Returning to Rochester during the tour, she later recalled, "Something strange happened. . . . Words I had never heard myself utter before came pouring forth, faster and faster. They came with passionate intensity. . . . The audience had vanished, the hall itself had disappeared; I was conscious only of my own words, of my ecstatic song." With that initial triumph, she abandoned Johann Most's direction, and from then on she was no one's protégée.

Earning her living as a seamstress or a factory hand, Goldman plunged into the work of the movement. She was the leading organizer of women in the 1889 cloak-maker's strike. Carrying the red flag, she led the anarchists in the

1891 May Day demonstrations, from which the socialists had tried to ban them. But organizing, leafletting, demonstrating were not enough for the passionately committed woman, impatient for revolution. Like other Russian anarchists in New York at the time, unaware of the differences between European and American traditions, she believed that if only the working masses could be aroused to action by some dazzling or polarizing event, the revolution against the capitalist masters might commence. All that was lacking was the right opportunity.

For a while the little anarchist commune moved to New Haven to organize. When illness broke it up, Goldman, Berkman, and their artist comrade Fedya formed a commune of their own, where they lived as a *ménage à trois*. ("I believe in your freedom to love," said the principled Berkman, giving Emma's and Fedya's love his blessing; jealousy, he maintained, deserved no place in an anarchist's heart. And Goldman, who had nothing but contempt for the demeaning notion that a woman must belong to one man as a piece of property, admired Berkman all the more for his largeness of spirit.) Together the three lovers made a solemn pact: to dedicate themselves "to the Cause in some supreme deed; to die if necessary, or to continue to live and work for the ideal for which one of us might have to give his life."

Very soon their "supreme deed" presented itself. In Homestead, Pennsylvania, in 1892, a strike of steelworkers against the Carnegie Steel Corporation was suppressed by armed Pinkertons. A dozen died and hundreds were injured. When the three comrades learned of it, they decided it was time for their own political deed of violence. With the nation's attention focused on the violence at Homestead, they thought it the perfect psychological moment for an *attentat:* a violent deed of propaganda, in the anarchist tradition, that would arouse the people against their capitalist oppressors. As their Russian idols had assassinated the

czar, they would assassinate the man responsible for the
bloodshed at Homestead, the chairman of the company,
Henry Clay Frick. "Human life is indeed sacred and inviolate," wrote Berkman. "But the killing of a tyrant, an
enemy of the People, is in no way to be considered the
taking of a life."[1] Goldman's tasks were to raise the money
for the gun and afterward to explain the deed to the world.
Berkman was to pull the trigger, sacrificing his own life in
the process. Desperate to get the necessary funds, Goldman
even tried whoring on Fourteenth Street, but in the end she
had to borrow the money. On July 23, 1892, Berkman
invaded Frick's Pittsburgh office, aimed at the tycoon's
head, and shot him twice before being knocked to the
ground by onlookers and carried off by the police. Record-
ing the event in his *Memoirs,* Berkman illuminates the
doubt so often at the center of the conspirator's consciousness. Frick's face, he writes,

> is ashen grey, the black beard is streaked with red and
> blood is oozing from his neck. For an instant a strange
> feeling, as of shame, comes over me; but the next moment
> I am filled with anger at the sentiment, so unworthy of a
> revolutionist.[2]

The fact that Frick recovered quickly—in time to direct
the crushing of the union with the aid of the National
Guard—rendered Berkman's crime punishable by a maximum of seven years; but the charges against the anarchist
were compounded, and he was sentenced to twenty-two
years, of which he ultimately served fourteen. His act did
little but confuse the issues in the strike and reawaken a
nationwide fear of anarchism. The Homestead strikers in-

[1] Alexander Berkman, *Prison Memoirs of an Anarchist,* New York,
Mother Earth Publishing Association, 1912, p. 7.
[2] *Ibid.,* p. 35.

stantly repudiated the deed; the rest of the country dismissed Berkman as a lunatic. Not that the American landscape hadn't long been littered with violent deeds, not the least of which was the company violence at Homestead; but in the United States there was no precedent to make Berkman's political *attentat* comprehensible to the public. Though Goldman applied her considerable powers of oratory to the task of explaining and defending their act, few people even understood their motives, much less approved their deed. Even Johann Most himself—long a leading proponent of the *attentat,* having at one time gone so far as to publish instructions in bomb-making—repudiated Berkman's act, claiming that the American proletariat was not nearly ready for such a deed, and insinuating that Berkman may have intended to do no more than wound Frick. This charge so incensed the hot-tempered Goldman, who had counted on Most to join her in Berkman's defense, that at a large meeting where Most was to speak, from the front row where she sat next to Fedya, she demanded that Most withdraw his slurs on Berkman. After he refused, mumbling something about a "hysterical woman," she leaped to the stage, drew a long horsewhip from under her cloak, and subjected Most to a fierce public lashing. When she had finished, she snapped the whip in two across her knee, flung the pieces at Most's feet, and stalked from the hall.

The episode marked the beginning of a permanent rift in the U.S. anarchist movement, and of a new phase in Goldman's career. Her demonic legend was launched. Her own trial and conviction the following year, for delivering a speech that allegedly incited the New York unemployed to riot (though no riot occurred), was, predictably, sensational news. To a reporter Goldman predicted her own one-year sentence, "Not because my offense deserves it, but because I am an anarchist." When she emerged from prison a year later, she found herself a notorious celebrity. "Red Emma," she was called, enemy of God, law, marriage, the State. There was no one else like her in America.

Dedication to her vision kept Goldman traveling and speaking in the succeeding years, participating in each radical crisis as it came up, while her mounting reputation packed in the audiences. At a time when the lecture circuit was big business, "Red Emma," with her legendary gifts of speech, was one of the star performers of the continent. Generous and loyal almost to a fault, she moved back and forth across the country collecting funds and supporters for every movement cause, large or small. Frequently she supported herself with odd jobs to avoid charging admission so that the poor she most wanted to reach could attend her meetings. In prison in 1894 she had mastered English in order to reach the American "natives"; now thousands of new people, many of whom went to her lectures to be scandalized and titillated, fell under the spell of her idealism —or, at the least, came away impressed by her integrity. The veteran civil libertarian Roger Baldwin, for example, describes the kind of response Goldman's presence frequently inspired:

> When I was a youngster just out of Harvard, Emma Goldman came to town to lecture. I was asked to hear her. I was indignant at the suggestion that I could be interested in a woman firebrand reputed to be in favor of assassination, free love, revolution, and atheism; but curiosity got me there. It was the eye-opener of my life. Never before had I heard such social passion, such courageous exposure of basic evils, such electric power behind words, such a sweeping challenge to all values I had been taught to hold highest. From that day forth I was her admirer.[3]

    [3] *New York Herald Tribune* (Oct. 25, 1931), as quoted by Joseph Ishill in *Emma Goldman: A Challenging Rebel,* Berkeley Heights, N.J., Oriole Press, 1957, pp. 22–23.

After two trips to Europe (1895 and 1899), during which she studied nursing and midwifery in Vienna, lectured in London, and attended clandestine anarchist meetings in Paris, she began to build an international reputation in revolutionary circles. Such celebrated European anarchists as Peter Kropotkin, Errico Malatesta, and the veteran of the Paris Commune, Louise Michel, came to know and admire her.

Then suddenly, in 1901, Goldman's public organizing came to an abrupt halt. President William McKinley was assassinated by a young man, Leon Czolgosz, who claimed to be an anarchist. As the most notorious anarchist in America, whom Czolgosz even confessed to having met at a lecture, Goldman was immediately arrested as an accomplice. It was one of the many ironies of her life that while her complicity in the attempt on Frick's life had gone unapprehended, she should be arrested in connection with an assassination of which she openly disapproved and at a time when, having reexamined individual acts of terror, she no longer even condoned such deeds. From jail she shocked the public by offering to nurse the dying McKinley. ("You were splendid, dear," wrote Berkman from prison, learning of the offer. "How impossible such [an offer] would have been to us in the days of a decade ago! We should have considered it treason to the spirit of revolution; it would have outraged all our traditions even to admit the humanity of an official representative of capitalism."[4]) But her expression of sympathy for the defenseless assassin Czolgosz brought on her such an avalanche of public wrath that long after she was set free for lack of any evidence against her, and long after Czolgosz had been electrocuted, she had to stay underground for her safety. The repression of anarchists that followed McKinley's death was so extreme that it was several years before she could again appear in public under

[4] Berkman, op. cit., p. 413.

her own name. As the unknown E. G. Smith, she lived alternately by nursing, sewing, running a massage parlor, and managing a visiting troupe of Russian actors.

Goldman returned to full public life in 1906 as the publisher of a new radical monthly, *Mother Earth*. Berkman, released from prison that same year, joined her as coeditor of the journal, and together with a coterie of friends they kept it running for twelve years, with only occasional lapses due to police interference. Van Wyck Brooks described "the tumultuous office of *Mother Earth*" as "one of the lively centers of thinking New York" at a time when Greenwich Village "swarmed with the movers and shakers who were expressing a new insurgent spirit." The Goldman flat at 210 East Thirteenth Street was a place, said Big Bill Haywood, where one could always get a cup of coffee "black as the night, strong as the revolutionary ideal, sweet as love."

In Europe in 1895 Goldman had fallen under the spell of such writers as Ibsen, Strindberg, Shaw, Hauptmann, Nietzsche. She wanted *Mother Earth* to be a forum for discussing their ideas and presenting "socially significant" art, as well as a platform for her own circle's anarchist commentary. "My great faith in the wonder worker, the spoken word, is no more," she wrote in 1910 as preface to her only published volume of essays, *Anarchism and Other Essays*. "The very fact that most people attend meetings only if aroused by newspaper sensations, or because they expect to be amused, is proof that they really have no inner urge to learn. It is altogether different with the written mode of human expression." Her own book contained essays on anarchism, education, prisons, political violence, and five pieces on the oppression of women, always one of her major concerns. Besides the journal and her own book, her Mother Earth Publishing Association published Ibsen's plays, poems of Oscar Wilde, anarchist classics by Kropotkin, Bakunin and Thoreau, books on sex and birth control, and Berkman's revolutionary gem, *Prison Memoirs of an Anarchist*.

Despite her swing to print, in the following years Goldman pursued her own characteristic mode, continuing to speak out against the system, both in regular Sunday-night lectures and discussions in ebullient New York, and on grand cross-country lecture tours, where she was regularly arrested. Wherever her intervention was needed, she showed up. After she took on as manager the dashing Dr. Ben L. Reitman, Chicago's "King of the Hobos," with whom she had fallen in love in 1908, she reached some of her largest audiences. On their 1910 tour, she reports speaking 120 times in thirty-seven cities in twenty-five states to 25,000 paying, and even more nonpaying, listeners.

Wanting to change the world and reach audiences for whom anarchism was a new idea, sometimes she avoided arrest by such ruses as lecturing on the seemingly innocent topic, the modern drama. (Her drama lectures, which always turned on social problems, were published in 1914 as *The Social Significance of the Modern Drama*.) But, combative by nature, she also presented the most provocative topics in the most dangerous places, thus feeding her legend. She talked up free love to puritans, atheism to churchmen, revolution to reformers; she denounced the ballot to suffragists, patriotism to soldiers and patriots. "The more opposition I encountered," she boasted, "the more I was in my element." With her libertarian vision always hovering just before her eyes, she was impatient of compromise and intolerant of any hint of equivocation.

Finally, in 1917, her habit of opposition went too far. For setting up No-Conscription Leagues and organizing antiwar rallies all over the East even after the United States had entered the war, she and Berkman were arrested and charged with "conspiracy" to obstruct the draft. Though they defended themselves admirably at their trial ("In the conduct of this case," said the presiding judge, "the defendants have shown . . . an ability which might have been utilized for the great benefit of this country, had they seen fit to employ themselves in behalf of it rather than against it."), they were convicted, fined, and imprisoned for the maximum two years. "For such people as would nullify our laws," said the judge, recommending that they be deported when their sentences were up, "we have no place in our country."

The judge's recommendation was followed. To render Goldman eligible for deportation, the government revoked her acquired citizenship by the device of stripping her long-missing former husband of his. J. Edgar Hoover himself directed her deportation hearing. In 1919, on the crest of one of the worst repressions in American history, Goldman, Berkman, and 247 other "Reds" were marched at dawn onto a retired army transport, the *Buford,* and deported under the 1918 Alien Exclusion Act to the newly created Soviet Union. As the "Red Ark" prepared to leave New York harbor, the fifty-year-old Goldman made a final statement to the American press: "I consider it an honor to be the first political agitator to be deported from the United States." The story is reported that a watching congressman shouted, "Merry Christmas, Emma!" and Goldman, spinning around to confront him with her famous glower, raised her hand and thumbed her nose at him as her final gesture on American soil.

The cargo of the *Buford,* after being rushed across Finland in sealed trains guarded by soldiers with fixed bayonets, were jubilantly welcomed in Soviet Russia. Unlike many another anarchist—as wary of the socialist State as of any capitalist one—Goldman fully expected to find in Russia the revolution of her dreams. Despite its being under a strong central authority, she was prepared to switch her enormous energies from opposing the institutions of society, as she had always done in the United States, to supporting them. But almost from the beginning, she found herself again in opposition. Her first impressions:

> Nothing was of moment compared with the supreme need of giving one's all to safeguard the Revolution and its gains. . . . Yet I could not entirely free myself from an undercurrent of uneasiness one often feels when left alone in the dark. . . . The gagging of free speech at the session of the Petro-Soviet that we had attended, the discovery that better and more plentiful food was served Party members at the Smolny dining-room and many similar injustices had attracted my attention.

Lenin himself assured her that the revolution was facing too many counterrevolutionary threats to allow of such a "bourgeois luxury" as free speech. Eager to get to work for the revolution, despite their uneasiness, Goldman and Berkman took the assignment of traveling over the vast country collecting documents for the revolutionary archives. But as they witnessed widespread privilege, forced labor, bureaucracy, and political persecution—particularly of anarchists—their travels became for them an experience of steady, agonizing disillusionment.

In March 1921 a series of strikes erupted in Petrograd, supported by the sailors of Kronstadt, whom Trotsky himself had once called the "pride and glory of the Revolution." Led by anarchists, the workers and sailors submitted to the government a list of demands, such as election to the Soviets, freedom of speech for left groups, and equalization of rations. Goldman and Berkman supported them. The government, refusing even to consider their grievances, and calling their strike a mutiny, moved an army on Kronstadt; in the ensuing battle, thousands of people were slaughtered. At that moment, Goldman and Berkman vowed to leave the country, even though, wrote Goldman, "the idea that I might want to leave Russia had never before entered my mind." That she had stayed so long was ample evidence of her good will; but after Kronstadt she was convinced that "the triumph of the State meant the defeat of the Revolution." The two anarchists applied for passports immediately, and when they came through in December of 1921, exactly two years after their deportation from the United States, they left Soviet Russia, "desolate and denuded of dreams."

From Russia the pair went into an exile that would lead them on a succession of temporary visas all over Europe. Eventually, Berkman settled in France, and Goldman in England. They each earned a meager living by writing and lecturing, either unheeded or hated by almost the entire left for criticizing the Bolshevik regime. Though in her criticism Goldman always defended the revolution, while denouncing Bolshevik tyranny, she was airily accused of betraying the revolution. In his autobiography Bertrand Russell described her initial reception by London radicals in 1924:

> A dinner was given in her honor. When she rose to speak she was welcomed enthusiastically; but when she sat down there was dead silence. This was because almost the whole of her speech was against the Bolsheviks.[5]

She wrote a series of articles for the *New York World* and then a book, *My Disillusionment in Russia* (1923, 1924), on her Russian experiences; she was denounced for these publications by some of the very radicals who a decade later in face of the Moscow trials turned against not only Bolshevism but the revolution itself.

Being an outcast among friends, however, was nothing new to Goldman. Almost alone among anarchists she had defended Czolgosz; almost alone among feminists she had exposed the illusions about woman's suffrage; now almost alone among revolutionaries she denounced Bolshevism,

[5] *The Autobiography of Bertrand Russell, 1914–1944*, New York, Bantam, 1969, p. 168.

without ever forsaking her revolutionary vision. "Censorship from comrades," she once said, "had the same effect on me as police persecution; it made me surer of myself." In exile she lost none of her tenacity or her willingness to stand "in revolt."

In 1925, in order to become a British subject and thereby obtain a valid passport, she married an old anarchist miner from Wales named James Colton. Goldman had long been an outspoken enemy of the institution of marriage, and though the ceremony was purely formal—she was careful to pay Colton for his fare to and from London and his lost days' wages—it created a minor scandal. With her new passport she left on a tour of Canada; then, joining Berkman in the South of France, where she lived on funds donated by American friends, she settled down to write her astonishing autobiography, *Living My Life*.

The book, published by Knopf in 1931, was well received, but the world it evoked was gone. The thirties had no patience with anarchist solutions to economic and social problems; by then all was centralism. In the early thirties, despite various government obstacles and censorship, Goldman traveled around Europe denouncing "Hitler and his gang," watching with horror as one country after another gave way to state centralism and dictatorship, and anarchism appeared increasingly irrelevant. In 1934 her once-dangerous views seemed sufficiently benign for distinguished American friends to arrange a ninety-day lecture tour for her in the United States. Except for an angry and predictable boycott by the American Communist party, her return was relatively uneventful. Fifteen years after she had been sent into exile described by J. Edgar Hoover as one of the most dangerous women in America, whose "return to the community will result in undue harm," her ideas of decentralization and libertarianism were in such eclipse that they no longer posed any threat; the choice had become fascism or communism. (In a recent introduction to the

Catholic Worker, Dwight Macdonald writes: "anarchism [was] an eccentricity, almost a solipsism, in the Marxian Thirties," adding that it has "become the norm of radical behavior in the Sixties.") Goldman returned to France fearful that she was fighting a losing battle.

When Berkman committed suicide in 1936, Goldman might have succumbed to despondency and old age but for the sudden outbreak of revolution and civil war in Spain. In response to a summons from the Spanish anarchists in control of Barcelona, she rushed to the barricades, once again daring to imagine that the revolution of her dreams was coming true. "The crushing weight that was pressing down on my heart since Sasha's death left me as by magic," she wrote in a letter, as she saw anarchist-organized farm and factory collectives, schools, utilities, and militia all operating on libertarian principles. At sixty-seven she threw herself back into active struggle, directing the Spanish anarchists' press and propaganda effort in England, with the energy and spirit of youth.

Watching the anarchists lose ground to Franco's fascists on the one hand and to Stalinist-led communists on the other, seeing them make fatal compromises with the coalition Republican government for the sake of the war effort, forced her to ponder the same agonizing dilemmas she had earlier faced in Russia. Still, she refused to abandon her vision or admit defeat. Even after it became obvious that Franco was the victor she went to Canada to try to raise money for Spain.

There, on February 17, 1940, the seventy-year-old Goldman suffered a stroke, and died three months later on May 14. Her body was shipped to Chicago for burial among the Haymarket martyrs to whose memory she had dedicated her life that Black Friday more than fifty years before. The monument raised to the martyred anarchists in Chicago's Waldheim Cemetery—a monument before which Goldman

had laid many wreaths and shed many tears—thereafter
served to honor her, too.

III.

If Goldman seems, in Richard Drinnon's phrase, "larger
than life,"[6] it is partly because she was always, with her
fanatical courage, idealism, and energy, lunging into the
action. It is hard to imagine someone of ordinary dimen-
sions attacking the system on so many fronts at once, and
with such persistence and ferocity as Emma Goldman. She
was an activist, not a theoretician. The libertarian vision
she began with at twenty served for theory, and from it,
together with her large emotional resources, flowed her
commitment to action. "She has warmed both hands at the
fire of life," wrote Frank Harris. Unlike so many other
radicals who, in the pages of leftist journals, argued endlessly over the niceties of "correct" interpretation of events,
she wanted to do something about them. Direct action—
now. She was impatient with anyone less courageous than
she, even people on her own side. She was supercritical of
anyone, including radicals, workers, and women, who lived
with less integrity than she demanded of herself. She was
hot-tempered, stubborn, passionate; sufficiently provoked,
she was given to violent tantrums and elitist tirades; when
something caught her imagination she was all aflame, burning like a fuse to some climactic showdown. But she always
had her eye on her ultimate ideal, and frequently the
"action" she took was directed toward preventing violence
or avoiding a losing confrontation with the powers, particularly if comrades other than she would be taking the rap.
Prevented from speaking in an American town, she would
gather her forces about her and fight back with a ven-

---

[6] See Drinnon's pioneer biography of Goldman, *Rebel in Paradise,*
Chicago, University of Chicago Press, 1961.

geance, frequently leaving in her wake a permanent branch
of the Free Speech League (the forerunner and inspiration
for the later American Civil Liberties Union). When the
anarcho-syndicalist union the International Workers of the
World (I.W.W.) was under brutal attack in the West by
local vigilante bands who beat, jailed, and even lynched
I.W.W. organizers, predictably Goldman went West. When
the laws against disseminating birth-control information
needed challenging, it was she who courted arrest by giving
the first public instruction on the use of contraceptives—
and after being tried and jailed, went right back to deliver
the same lecture again and again in other communities.
And even after her deportation to Russia, where she was
honored with one of the rare audiences with Lenin himself,
she audaciously took advantage of the interview to protest
to him about the treatment of anarchists and the general
abridgment of free speech under the Bolshevik regime.

But Goldman did more than, in the words of Floyd Dell,
"hold before our eyes the ideal of freedom . . . [and]
taunt us with our moral cowardice." She was an indefati-
gable organizer struggling to bring about fundamental
change. "Revolution is but thought carried into action," she
wrote in the essay "Anarchism," and in that sense she was
constantly trying to make the revolution by inventing new
ways to carry her thought into action. She derided those she
called "philosophical anarchists" precisely because they did
not attempt to carry out their ideas, however consonant
with her own.

In reading over nowadays her clear, simple lectures advocating fundamental change or a new spirit, one wonders
why some of them should have created such an uproar.
True, each of them carries at its heart at least one stick of
pure dynamite. (From "The Social Importance of the Modern School," for example: "[School] is for the child what
the prison is for the convict and the barracks for the
soldier—a place where everything is being used to break

the will of the child, and then to pound, knead, and shape it into a being utterly foreign to itself." From "The Traffic in Women": "Nowhere is woman treated according to the merit of her work, but rather as a sex. It is therefore almost inevitable that she should pay for her right to exist, to keep a position in whatever line, with sex favors. Thus it is merely a question of degree whether she sells herself to one man, in or out of marriage, or to many men.") But still, one guesses they could have been written by other iconoclasts of the time without creating so much of a stir. They are provocative but not particularly original. The best are reasonable, concrete arguments for a new consciousness, demanding a reconsideration. The worst harangues are strident and rhetorical, but do not advocate violence or stir people to wanton acts of rebellion or riot. Yet as often as not, Goldman was arrested or run out of town for delivering them, sometimes, as one policeman told her, "just on general principles," because "you're Emma Goldman." Even the Socialist party at one time found it expedient to forbid its members to debate her publicly. Part of the fearful effect of her speeches must have stemmed from their having been composed and delivered by her: it was always feared that Red Emma would indeed carry "thought into action"; and almost all of her essays could be footnoted with reports of their sensational consequences, reports that might be considerably more shocking than the essays themselves. Many such stories—from false arrest to near-riot (riot often averted by Goldman's quick-witted mastery of the mob) to outright assault—fill the two fat volumes of Goldman's much-trimmed autobiography, and still there are more.

To give the reader some impression of Goldman's style of politics and her running battle with the system, I have included in this anthology several sections from her rich autobiography, *Living My Life*. A number of essays from *Anarchism and Other Essays*, as well as the conclusion to

My Disillusionment in Russia, are included because they seem to me to represent Goldman's fullest statement on their particular subjects. But most of the selections in this volume have never before been available in book form, and four of them, taken from drafts of speeches in the New York Public Library and slightly edited, have never before been published.

As to Goldman's thought and preoccupations, the essays, magazine pieces, pamphlets and speeches (including, besides propaganda speeches, a trial defense speech and an address to her comrades in the Spanish Civil War) collected here speak for themselves. I have divided the writings into four sections, presenting Goldman's views on (1) the political and economic organization of society; (2) social institutions; (3) violence, both individual and institutional; and (4) the two revolutions in which she was involved, the Russian and the Spanish. But there is really no dividing her thought, as it is all illuminated by her single vision.

To these pieces I would like to add an account of one more speech with the Goldman touch, hardly her least effective, though certainly her shortest. She delivered it on September 11, 1917, at a mass New York rally for Berkman, then fighting extradition from New York to California on a trumped-up murder charge. It was at a time when Goldman herself was out on bail pending a Supreme Court review of her antidraft conspiracy conviction, and her bail was subject to revocation.

She arrived at the auditorium ready to speak in Berkman's behalf just in time to be told by a federal marshal that unless she promised not to speak he would lock the audience out of the hall. Ordinarily, Goldman would simply have disregarded such an ultimatum, but feeling the urgency of this particular rally, she reluctantly gave the marshal her promise, then took a seat in the auditorium.

When the preliminaries were over and several speeches had been delivered, the time came for Goldman's speech.

As the chairman began explaining her regrettable absence, out onto the stage strode Red Emma, a large handkerchief stuffed in her mouth. There she stood facing her audience without a word, as she had promised. It brought down the house.

The writings collected here span the genres, decades, and continents, but they reflect a single awareness. From the time Goldman burst onto the New York radical scene at twenty, all energy and anticipation, until she died fighting at seventy, what changed was the context, not the content, of her struggle. Beginning with her earliest credo, "What I Believe" (1908), published originally in the *New York World* for a large and hostile American audience, and ending with another credo, "Was My Life Worth Living?" (1934), published in *Harper's Magazine* toward the end of her life for a large American audience of a different generation and bent, one can see the unity in her activities and sympathies. Through all of them one can sense the discrepancy between Emma Goldman the demon of the legend and Emma Goldman the idealistic revolutionary who from the age of twenty wished for nothing less than to free the world. Between the two personae is a courageous if egotistical, a dedicated if cantankerous woman, a veritable "mountain of integrity" as the novelist Rebecca West described her, an unmovable visionary, but one whose tongue and passion no one could tame.

PART ONE

ORGANIZATION
OF SOCIETY

PREFACE TO PART ONE

In this section are five essays in which Emma Goldman explains her vision (or, to use her phrase, her "beautiful ideal") of the political and economic organization of society under anarchism. As commentators have had to point out repeatedly ever since the misleading name became attached to this movement, anarchism, while utterly libertarian, is not a doctrine of chaos and destruction but one of order based on freely undertaken cooperation, mutual aid, and improvisation. It is founded on the insight that people left to their own devices cooperate—that in the end what keeps the world running is people working freely together at the tasks of daily life, and what messes up the world is regulation of and interference with them by the people and institutions in authority.

Like Bakunin's, Goldman's vision was powered by a fanatic love of liberty and hatred of authority. Very early in her career she told a reporter: "I am really too much of an anarchist to bother about all the trifling details [of a program]; all I want is freedom, perfect, unrestricted liberty for myself and others."[1] But by the time she wrote her essays on anarchism, she had already become sufficiently involved in the detail work of trying to change society to be concerned with its organization. Her

[1] Quoted by Richard Drinnon in *Rebel in Paradise*, Chicago, University of Chicago Press, 1961, p. 102.

program, like Bakunin's and Kropotkin's, was anarcho-communist, but like them she was convinced that any organization must be strictly voluntary.

In a recent essay describing the anarchist view of the organization of society, Noam Chomsky writes:

> The consistent anarchist . . . should be a socialist, but a socialist of a particular sort. He will not only oppose alienated and specialized labor and look forward to the appropriation of capital by the whole body of workers, but he will also insist that this appropriation be direct, not exercised by some elite force acting in the name of the proletariat. . . . Some sort of council communism is the natural form of revolutionary socialism in an industrial society. It reflects the intuitive understanding that democracy is largely a sham when the industrial system is controlled by any form of autocratic elite, whether of owners, managers, and technocrats, a "vanguard" party, or a State bureaucracy.[2]

Thus we find Goldman describing syndicalism (a basis for what Chomsky calls "council communism") as "in essence, the economic expression of anarchism"; we find her lashing out at the American "vanguard" socialist party for participating in electoral politics, though she frequently worked with individual socialists on particular causes; we find her arguing that we cannot "cure the evils of [State] democracy with more democracy."

The brief credo "What I Believe" was first published in the *New York World* in 1908, when the assassination of McKinley was still in the public mind, as a corrective to some of the widespread public misconceptions of anarchism. Reissued by Goldman as a pamphlet, it became at once her record-breaking best seller. Viewing anarchism as a theory of organic growth, Goldman reflects the strong influence of Peter Kropotkin, whose central metaphor for society was the living organism.

"Anarchism: What It Really Stands For," which Goldman

---

[2] Noam Chomsky, "Notes on Anarchism," *New York Review of Books* (May 21, 1970), Vol. XIV, no. 10, pp. 31–35.

published in *Anarchism and Other Essays* in 1911, gives a fuller
description of the vision and attempts to answer certain frequent
objections to it. In her preface to that volume, she wrote:

> "Why do you not say how things will be operated under Anarchism?" is a question I have had to meet thousands of times. Because I believe that Anarchism can not consistently impose an iron-clad program or method on the future. The things every new generation has to fight, and which it can least overcome, are the burdens of the past, which hold us all as in a net. Anarchism, at least as I understand it, leaves posterity free to develop its own particular systems, in harmony with its needs. Our most vivid imagination can not foresee the potentialities of a race set free from external restraints. How, then, can any one assume to map out a line of conduct for those to come? We, who pay dearly for every breath of pure, fresh air, must guard against the tendency to fetter the future. If we succeed in clearing the soil from the rubbish of the past and present, we will leave to posterity the greatest and safest heritage of all ages.

Accordingly, her vision is of a living process of imaginative improvisation, and not a specific theory of social change. She has
a good nose for the rubbish.

In the next two essays, Goldman examines two aspects of the
process. "Syndicalism: Its Theory and Practice," probably composed as a lecture, was published as an essay in the January–
February 1913 *Mother Earth* and issued as a pamphlet the same
year. The lecture entitled "Socialism: Caught in the Political
Trap," though never published (the version printed here, possibly incomplete, is from a typescript in the New York Public
Library's manuscript collection), was probably written around
the same time, when socialist candidates were polling substantial
numbers of votes.

The final piece in this section, "The Individual, Society and
the State," was published as a pamphlet entitled "The Place of
the Individual in Society" by the Chicago anarchist Free Society
Forum around 1940 (it is undated). It is probably Goldman's
last published piece. Addressing herself to the question of the

legitimacy of any external authority, she reaffirms the anarchist position that there is no legitimate authority outside the individual.[3] In the essay, though she remains uncompromisingly collectivist, clearly distinguishing her position from that of economic laissez-faire libertarians who, like the recent self-styled anarchists of the New Right, would retain private ownership of property, Goldman reasserts her faith in the bedrock value of the individual.

Through all the essays in this section runs what Richard Drinnon called Goldman's "attempted spiritualization of politics," an effort once again recognizable among the radical young. In the early essay, "Anarchism," she wrote:

> While all anarchists agree . . . that the main evil today is an economic one, they maintain that the solution of that evil can be brought about only through consideration of every phase of life—individual as well as the collective, the internal as well as the external phases.

In "The Individual, Society and the State," written almost three decades later at a time when the entire West, left and right, was surrendering to a deadening and dehumanizing centralization, mechanization, and regimentation in every aspect of social and

---

[3] Robert Paul Wolff, in the essay *In Defense of Anarchism* (New York, Harper & Row, 1970), defines the "fundamental problem of political philosophy" as "how the moral autonomy of the individual can be made compatible with the legitimate authority of the state" and concludes that

> there can be no resolution of the conflict between the autonomy of the individual and the putative authority of the state. Insofar as a man fulfills his obligation to make himself the author of his decisions, he will resist the state's claim to have authority over him. That is to say, he will deny that he has a duty to obey the laws of the state *simply because they are the laws*. In that sense, it would seem that anarchism is the only political doctrine consistent with the virtue of autonomy [p. 18]. . . . States achieve their legitimacy only by means of the citizens' forfeit of their autonomy, and hence are not solutions to the fundamental problem of political philosophy. . . . Whatever else may be said for a majoritarian democracy, it does not appear to be true that the minority remain free and self-ruled while submitting to the majority [p. 70].

political life, Goldman continued her quarrel with Marxist economic reductionism that "overlooked the human element."

In an essay analyzing the new-style anarchist radicalism among the youth of the sixties, Emile Capouya writes:

> What more than anything else united the young militants on campuses halfway round the world—and many of their fellow-students who were not radical in the least—was an instinctive revulsion to the way of life bequeathed them by their elders and its characteristic social structures and ideology. And in their eyes, communism in all its forms was a kind of postgraduate capitalism, rationalized still further in the interests of a religion of accumulation, dehumanized still further by the absence of amenity and civil liberty. The bureaucratic forms of organization shared by communism and capitalism were embodiments of insult to the ideals of individualism, spontaneity, mutual trust, and generosity that are the dominant themes of the new sensibility.[4]

It is Goldman's commitment to those same themes—her emphasis on what she called "the human element," her insistence that "society exists for man, not man for society"—that puts her close to the radical sensibility of our own time.

[4] "The Red Flag and the Black," *New American Review #6* (April 1969), p. 188.

What I Believe

"What I believe" has many times been the target of hack writers. Such blood-curdling and incoherent stories have been circulated about me, it is no wonder that the average human being has palpitation of the heart at the very mention of the name Emma Goldman. It is too bad that we no longer live in the times when witches were burned at the stake or tortured to drive the evil spirit out of them. For, indeed, Emma Goldman is a witch! True, she does not eat little children, but she does many worse things. She manufactures bombs and gambles in crowned heads. B-r-r-r!

Such is the impression the public has of myself and my beliefs. It is therefore very much to the credit of *The World* that it gives its readers at least an opportunity to learn what my beliefs really are.

The student of the history of progressive thought is well aware that every idea in its early stages has been misrepresented, and the adherents of such ideas have been maligned and persecuted. One need not go back two thousand years to the time when those who believed in the gospel of Jesus were thrown into the arena or hunted into dungeons to realize how little great beliefs or earnest believers are understood. The history of progress is written in the blood of men and women who have dared to espouse an unpopular cause, as, for instance, the black man's right to his body, or woman's right to her soul. If, then, from time immemorial, the New has met with opposition and condemnation, why should my beliefs be exempt from a crown of thorns?

"What I believe" is a process rather than a finality. Finalities are for gods and governments, not for the human intellect. While it may be true that Herbert Spencer's formulation of liberty is the most important on the subject, as a political basis of society, yet life is something more than formulas. In the battle for freedom, as Ibsen has so well pointed out, it is the *struggle* for, not so much the attainment of, liberty, that develops all that is strongest, sturdiest and finest in human character.

Anarchism is not only a process, however, that marches on with "sombre steps," coloring all that is positive and constructive in organic development. It is a conspicuous protest of the most militant type. It is so absolutely uncompromising, insisting and permeating a force as to overcome the most stubborn assault and to withstand the criticism of those who really constitute the last trumpets of a decaying age.

Anarchists are by no means passive spectators in the theatre of social development; on the contrary, they have some very positive notions as regards aims and methods.

That I may make myself as clear as possible without using too much space, permit me to adopt the topical mode of treatment of "What I Believe":

I. AS TO PROPERTY

"Property" means dominion over things and the denial to others of the use of those things. So long as production was not equal to the normal demand, institutional property may have had some *raison d'être*. One has only to consult economics, however, to know that the productivity of labor within the last few decades has increased so tremendously as to exceed normal demand a hundred-fold, and to make property not only a hindrance to human well-being, but an obstacle, a deadly barrier, to all progress. It is the private dominion over things that condemns millions of people to be mere nonentities, living corpses without originality or power of initiative, human machines of flesh and blood, who pile up mountains of wealth for others and pay for it with a gray, dull and wretched existence for themselves. I believe that there can be no real wealth, social wealth, so long as it rests on human lives—young lives, old lives and lives in the making.

It is conceded by all radical thinkers that the fundamental cause of this terrible state of affairs is (1) that man must sell his labor; (2) that his inclination and judgment are subordinated to the will of a master.

Anarchism is the only philosophy that can and will do away with this humiliating and degrading situation. It differs from all other theories inasmuch as it points out that man's development, his physical well-being, his latent qualities and innate disposition alone must determine the character and conditions of his work. Similarly will one's physical and mental appreciations and his soul cravings decide how much he shall consume. To make this a reality will, I believe, be possible only in a society based on voluntary co-operation of productive groups, communities and societies loosely federated together, eventually developing into a free communism, actuated by a solidarity of interests. There can be no freedom in the large sense of the word, no harmonious development, so long as mercenary and commercial considerations play an important part in the determination of personal conduct.

II. AS TO GOVERNMENT

I believe government, organized authority, or the State is necessary *only* to maintain or protect property and monopoly. It has proven efficient in that function only. As a promoter of individual liberty, human well-being and social harmony, which alone constitute real order, government stands condemned by all the great men of the world.

I therefore believe, with my fellow-Anarchists, that the statutory regulations, legislative enactments, constitutional provisions, are invasive. They never yet induced man to do anything he could and would not do by virtue of his intellect or temperament, nor prevented anything that man was impelled to do by the same dictates. Millet's pictorial description of "The Man with the Hoe," Meunier's masterpieces of the miners that have aided in lifting labor from its degrading position, Gorki's descriptions of the underworld, Ibsen's psychological analysis of human life, could never have been induced by government any more than the spirit which impels a man to save a drowning child or a crippled woman from a burning building has ever been called into operation by statutory regulations or the policeman's club. I believe—indeed, I know—that whatever is fine and beautiful in the human expresses and asserts itself in spite of government, and not because of it.

The Anarchists are therefore justified in assuming that Anarchism—the absence of government—will insure the widest and greatest scope for unhampered human development, the cornerstone of true social progress and harmony.

As to the stereotyped argument that government acts as a check on crime and vice, even the makers of law no longer believe it. This country spends millions of dollars for the maintenance of her "criminals" behind prison bars, yet crime is on the increase. Surely this state of affairs is not owing to an insufficiency of laws! Ninety per cent of all crimes are property crimes, which have their root in our economic iniquities. So long as these latter continue to exist we might convert every lamp-post into a gibbet without having the least effect on the crime in our midst. Crimes resulting from heredity can certainly never be cured by law. Surely we are learning even to-day that such crimes can effectively be treated only by the best modern medical methods at our command, and, above all, by the spirit of a deeper sense of fellowship, kindness and understanding.

III. AS TO MILITARISM

I should not treat of this subject separately, since it belongs to the paraphernalia of government, if it were not for the fact that those who are most vigorously opposed to my beliefs on the ground that the latter stand for force are the advocates of militarism.

The fact is that Anarchists are the only true advocates of peace, the only people who call a halt to the growing tendency of militarism, which is fast making of this erstwhile free country an imperialistic and despotic power.

The military spirit is the most merciless, heartless and brutal in existence. It fosters an institution for which there is not even a pretense of justification. The soldier, to quote Tolstoi, is a professional man-killer. He does not kill for the love of it, like a savage, or in a passion, like a homicide. He is a cold-blooded, mechanical, obedient tool of his military superiors. He is ready to cut throats or scuttle a ship at the command of his ranking officer, without knowing or, perhaps, caring how, why or wherefore. I am supported in this contention by no less a military light than Gen. Funston. I quote from the latter's communication to the New York *Evening Post* of June 30, dealing with the case of Private William Buwalda, which caused such a stir all through the

Northwest.* "The first duty of an officer or enlisted man," says our noble warrior, "is unquestioning obedience and loyalty to the government to which he has sworn allegiance; it makes no difference whether he approves of that government or not."

How can we harmonize the principle of "unquestioning obedience" with the principle of "life, liberty and the pursuit of happiness"? The deadly power of militarism has never before been so effectually demonstrated in this country as in the recent condemnation by court-martial of William Buwalda, of San Francisco, Company A, Engineers, to five years in military prison. Here was a man who had a record of fifteen years of continuous service. "His character and conduct were unimpeachable," we are told by Gen. Funston, who, in consideration of it, reduced Buwalda's sentence to three years. Yet the man is thrown suddenly out of the army, dishonored, robbed of his chances of a pension and sent to prison. What was his crime? Just listen, ye free-born Americans! William Buwalda attended a public meeting, and after the lecture he shook hands with the speaker. Gen. Funston, in his letter to the *Post,* to which I have already referred above, asserts that Buwalda's action was a "great military offense, infinitely worse than desertion." In another public statement, which

---

* Editor's note: William Buwalda was an army private who, for shaking Emma Goldman's hand following a lecture she delivered on patriotism in San Francisco in 1908, was arrested, court-martialed, dishonorably discharged, and sentenced to five years of hard labor in Alcatraz. The general who presided at the trial named his crime "shaking hands with that dangerous anarchist woman." Buwalda, a soldier for fifteen years, once decorated for "faithful service," had known nothing about anarchism at the time, but had attended Goldman's lecture out of sheer curiosity. Ten months after his sentence, he was pardoned by President Theodore Roosevelt. Upon his release from prison he sent his medal back to the army with a letter explaining he had "no further use for such baubles. . . . Give it to some one who will appreciate it more than I do." Then he joined the anarchist movement.

the General made in Portland, Ore., he said that "Buwalda's was a serious crime, equal to treason."

It is quite true that the meeting had been arranged by Anarchists. Had the Socialists issued the call, Gen. Funston informs us, there would have been no objection to Buwalda's presence. Indeed, the General says, "I would not have the slightest hesitancy about attending a Socialist meeting myself." But to attend an Anarchist meeting with Emma Goldman as speaker—could there be anything more "treasonable"?

For this horrible crime a man, a free-born American citizen, who has given this country the best fifteen years of his life, and whose character and conduct during that time were "unimpeachable," is now languishing in a prison, dishonored, disgraced and robbed of a livelihood.

Can there be anything more destructive of the true genius of liberty than the spirit that made Buwalda's sentence possible—the spirit of unquestioning obedience? Is it for this that the American people have in the last few years sacrificed four hundred million dollars and their hearts' blood?

I believe that militarism—a standing army and navy in any country—is indicative of the decay of liberty and of the destruction of all that is best and finest in our nation. The steadily growing clamor for more battleships and an increased army on the ground that these guarantee us peace is as absurd as the argument that the peaceful man is he who goes well armed.

The same lack of consistency is displayed by those peace pretenders who oppose Anarchism because it supposedly teaches violence, and who would yet be delighted over the possibility of the American nation soon being able to hurl dynamite bombs upon defenseless enemies from flying machines.

I believe that militarism will cease when the liberty-loving spirits of the world say to their masters: "Go and do your own killing. We have sacrificed ourselves and our loved ones long enough fighting your battles. In return you have made parasites and criminals of us in times of peace and brutalized us in times of war. You have separated us from our brothers and have made of the world a human slaughterhouse. No, we will not do your killing or fight for the country that you have stolen from us."

Oh, I believe with all my heart that human brotherhood and solidarity will clear the horizon from the terrible red streak of war and destruction.

IV. AS TO FREE SPEECH AND PRESS

The Buwalda case is only one phase of the larger question of free speech, free press and the right of free assembly.

Many good people imagine that the principles of free speech or press can be exercised properly and with safety within the limits of constitutional guarantees. That is the only excuse, it seems to me, for the terrible apathy and indifference to the onslaught upon free speech and press that we have witnessed in this county within the last few months.

I believe that free speech and press mean that I may say and write what I please. This right, when regulated by constitutional provisions, legislative enactments, almighty decisions of the Postmaster General or the policeman's club, becomes a farce. I am well aware that I will be warned of consequences if we remove the chains from speech and press. I believe, however, that the cure of consequences resulting from the unlimited exercise of expression is to allow more expression.

Mental shackles have never yet stemmed the tide of progress, whereas premature social explosions have only too often been brought about through a wave of repression.

Will our governors never learn that countries like England, Holland, Norway, Sweden and Denmark, with the largest freedom of expression, have been freest from "consequences"? Whereas Russia, Spain, Italy, France and, alas! even America, have raised these "consequences" to the most pressing political factor. Ours is supposed to be a country ruled by the majority, yet every policeman who is not vested with power by the majority can break up a meeting, drag the lecturer off the platform and club the audience out of the hall in true Russian fashion. The Postmaster General, who is not an elective officer, has the power to suppress publications and confiscate mail. From his decision there is no more appeal than from that of the Russian Czar. Truly, I believe we need a new Declaration of Independence. Is there no modern Jefferson or Adams?

V. AS TO THE CHURCH

At the recent convention of the political remnants of a once revolutionary idea it was voted that religion and vote getting have nothing to do with each other. Why should they? So long as man is willing to delegate to the devil the care of his soul, he might, with the same consistency, delegate to the politician the care of his rights. That religion is a private affair has long been settled by the Bis-Marxian Socialists of Germany. Our American Marxians, poor of blood and originality, must needs go to Germany for their wisdom. That wisdom has served as a capital whip to lash the several millions of people into the well-disciplined army of Socialism. It might do the same here. For goodness' sake, let's not offend respectability, let's not hurt the religious feelings of the people.

Religion is a superstition that originated in man's mental inability to solve natural phenomena. The Church is an organized institution that has always been a stumbling block to progress.

Organized churchism has stripped religion of its naïveté and primitiveness. It has turned religion into a nightmare that oppresses the human soul and holds the mind in bondage. "The Dominion of Darkness," as the last true Christian, Leo Tolstoi, calls the Church, has been a foe of human development and free thought, and as such it has no place in the life of a truly free people.

VI. AS TO MARRIAGE AND LOVE

I believe these are probably the most tabooed subjects in this country. It is almost impossible to talk about them without scandalizing the cherished propriety of a lot of good folk. No wonder so much ignorance prevails relative to these questions. Nothing short of an open, frank, and intelligent discussion will purify the air from the hysterical, sentimental rubbish that is shrouding these vital subjects, vital to individual as well as social well-being.

Marriage and love are not synonymous; on the contrary, they are often antagonistic to each other. I am aware of the fact that some marriages are actuated by love, but the narrow, material confines of marriage, as it is, speedily crush the tender flower of affection.

Marriage is an institution which furnishes the State and Church with a tremendous revenue and the means of prying into that phase of life which refined people have long considered their own, their very own most sacred affair. Love is that most powerful factor of human relationship which from time immemorial has defied all man-made laws and broken through the iron bars of conventions in Church and morality. Marriage is often an economic arrangement purely, furnishing the woman with a life-long life insurance policy and the man with a perpetuator of his kind or a pretty toy. That is, marriage, or the training thereto, prepares the woman for the life of a parasite, a dependent, helpless servant, while it furnishes the man the right of a chattel mortgage over a human life.

How can such a condition of affairs have anything in

common with love?—with the element that would forego
all the wealth of money and power and live in its own world
of untrammeled human expression? But this is not the age of
romanticism, of Romeo and Juliet, Faust and Marguerite,
of moonlight ecstasies, of flowers and songs. Ours is a
practical age. Our first consideration is an income. So much
the worse for us if we have reached the era when the soul's
highest flights are to be checked. No race can develop
without the love element.

But if two people are to worship at the shrine of love,
what is to become of the golden calf, marriage? "It is the
only security for the woman, for the child, the family, the
State." But it is no security to love; and without love no
true home can or does exist. Without love no child should
be born; without love no true woman can be related to a
man. The fear that love is not sufficient material safety for
the child is out of date. I believe when woman signs her
own emancipation, her first declaration of independence
will consist in admiring and loving a man for the qualities
of his heart and mind and not for the quantities in his
pocket. The second declaration will be that she has the right
to follow that love without let or hindrance from the outside
world. The third and most important declaration will be the
absolute right to free motherhood.

In such a mother and an equally free father rests the
safety of the child. They have the strength, the sturdiness,
the harmony to create an atmosphere wherein alone the
human plant can grow into an exquisite flower.

VII. AS TO ACTS OF VIOLENCE

And now I have come to that point in my beliefs about
which the greatest misunderstanding prevails in the minds
of the American public. "Well, come, now, don't you
propagate violence, the killing of crowned heads and Presi-
dents?" Who says that I do? Have you heard me, has any-

one heard me? Has anyone seen it printed in our literature? No, but the papers say so, everybody says so; consequently it must be so. Oh, for the accuracy and logic of the dear public!

I believe that Anarchism is the only philosophy of peace, the only theory of the social relationship that values human life above everything else. I know that some Anarchists have committed acts of violence, but it is the terrible economic inequality and great political injustice that prompt such acts, not Anarchism. Every institution to-day rests on violence; our very atmosphere is saturated with it. So long as such a state exists we might as well strive to stop the rush of Niagara as hope to do away with violence. I have already stated that countries with some measure of freedom of expression have had few or no acts of violence. What is the moral? Simply this: No act committed by an Anarchist has been for personal gain, aggrandizement or profit, but rather a conscious protest against some repressive, arbitrary, tyrannical measure from above.

President Carnot, of France, was killed by Caserio in response to Carnot's refusal to commute the death sentence of Vaillant, for whose life the entire literary, scientific and humanitarian world of France had pleaded.

Bresci went to Italy on his own money, earned in the silk weaving mills of Paterson, to call King Humbert to the bar of justice for his order to shoot defenseless women and children during a bread riot. Angelino executed Prime Minister Canovas for the latter's resurrection of the Spanish inquisition at Montjuich Prison. Alexander Berkman attempted the life of Henry C. Frick during the Homestead strike only because of his intense sympathy for the eleven strikers killed by Pinkertons and for the widows and orphans evicted by Frick from their wretched little homes that were owned by Mr. Carnegie.

Every one of these men not only made his reasons known to the world in spoken or written statements, showing the cause that led to his act, proving that the unbearable economic and political pressure, the suffering and despair of their fellow-men, women and children prompted the acts, and not the philosophy of Anarchism. They came openly, frankly and ready to stand the consequences, ready to give their own lives.

In diagnosing the true nature of our social disease I cannot condemn those who, through no fault of their own, are suffering from a wide-spread malady.

I do not believe that these acts can, or ever have been intended to, bring about the social reconstruction. That can only be done, first, by a broad and wide education as to man's place in society and his proper relation to his fellows; and, second, through example. By example I mean the actual living of a truth once recognized, not the mere theorizing of its life element. Lastly, and the most powerful weapon, is the conscious, intelligent, organized, economic protest of the masses through direct action and the general strike.

The general contention that Anarchists are opposed to organization, and hence stand for chaos, is absolutely groundless. True, we do not believe in the compulsory, arbitrary side of organization that would compel people of antagonistic tastes and interests into a body and hold them there by coercion. Organization as the result of natural blending of common interests, brought about through voluntary adhesion, Anarchists do not only not oppose, but believe in as the only possible basis of social life.

It is the harmony of organic growth which produces variety of color and form—the complete whole we admire in the flower. Analogously will the organized activity of free human beings endowed with the spirit of solidarity result in the perfection of social harmony—which is Anarchism. Indeed, only Anarchism makes non-authoritarian organization a reality, since it abolishes the existing antagonism between individuals and classes.

Anarchism: What It Really Stands For

ANARCHY

Ever reviled, accursed, ne'er understood,
   Thou art the grisly terror of our age.
"Wreck of all order," cry the multitude,
   "Art thou, and war and murder's endless rage."
O, let them cry. To them that ne'er have striven
   The truth that lies behind a word to find,
To them the word's right meaning was not given.
   They shall continue blind among the blind.
But thou, O word, so clear, so strong, so pure,
   Thou sayest all which I for goal have taken.
I give thee to the future! Thine secure
   When each at least unto himself shall waken.
Comes it in sunshine? In the tempest's thrill?
   I cannot tell—but it the earth shall see!
I am an Anarchist! Wherefore I will
   Not rule, and also ruled I will not be!

JOHN HENRY MACKAY

The history of human growth and development is at the same time the history of the terrible struggle of every new idea heralding the approach of a brighter dawn. In its tenacious hold on tradition, the Old has never hesitated to make use of the foulest and cruelest means to stay the advent of the New, in whatever form or period the latter may have asserted itself. Nor need we retrace our steps into the distant past to realize the enormity of opposition, difficulties, and hardships placed in the path of every progressive idea. The rack, the thumbscrew, and the knout are still with us; so are the convict's garb and the social wrath, all conspiring against the spirit that is serenely marching on.

Anarchism could not hope to escape the fate of all other ideas of innovation. Indeed, as the most revolutionary and uncompromising innovator, Anarchism must needs meet with the combined ignorance and venom of the world it aims to reconstruct.

To deal even remotely with all that is being said and done against Anarchism would necessitate the writing of a whole volume. I shall therefore meet only two of the principal objections. In so doing, I shall attempt to elucidate what Anarchism really stands for.

The strange phenomenon of the opposition to Anarchism is that it brings to light the relation between so-called intelligence and ignorance. And yet this is not so very strange when we consider the relativity of all things. The ignorant mass has in its favor that it makes no pretense of knowledge or tolerance. Acting, as it always does, by mere impulse, its reasons are like those of a child. "Why?" "Because." Yet the opposition of the uneducated to Anarchism deserves the same consideration as that of the intelligent man.

What, then, are the objections? First, Anarchism is impractical, though a beautiful ideal. Second, Anarchism stands for violence and destruction, hence it must be repudiated as vile and dangerous. Both the intelligent man and the ignorant mass judge not from a thorough knowledge of the subject, but either from hearsay or false interpretation.

A practical scheme, says Oscar Wilde, is either one already in existence, or a scheme that could be carried out under the existing conditions; but it is exactly the existing conditions that one objects to, and any scheme that could accept these conditions is wrong and foolish. The true criterion of the practical, therefore, is not whether the latter can keep intact the wrong or foolish; rather is it whether the scheme has vitality enough to leave the stagnant waters of the old, and build, as well as sustain, new life. In the light of this conception, Anarchism is indeed practical. More than any other idea, it is helping to do away with the wrong and foolish; more than any other idea, it is building and sustaining new life.

The emotions of the ignorant man are continuously kept at a pitch by the most blood-curdling stories about Anarchism. Not a thing is too outrageous to be employed against this philosophy and its exponents. Therefore Anarchism represents to the unthinking what the proverbial bad man does to the child—a black monster bent on swallowing everything; in short, destruction and violence.

Destruction and violence! How is the ordinary man to know that the most violent element in society is ignorance; that its power of destruction is the very thing Anarchism is combating? Nor is he aware that Anarchism, whose roots, as it were, are part of nature's forces, destroys, not healthful tissue, but parasitic growths that feed on the life's essence of society. It is merely clearing the soil from weeds and sagebrush, that it may eventually bear healthy fruit.

Someone has said that it requires less mental effort to condemn than to think. The widespread mental indolence, so prevalent in society, proves this to be only too true. Rather than to go to the bottom of any given idea, to examine into its origin and meaning, most people will either condemn it altogether, or rely on some superficial or prejudicial definition of non-essentials.

Anarchism urges man to think, to investigate, to analyze

every proposition; but that the brain capacity of the average reader be not taxed too much, I also shall begin with a definition, and then elaborate on the latter.

> ANARCHISM: The philosophy of a new social order based on liberty unrestricted by man-made law; the theory that all forms of government rest on violence, and are therefore wrong and harmful, as well as unnecessary.

The new social order rests, of course, on the materialistic basis of life; but while all Anarchists agree that the main evil today is an economic one, they maintain that the solution of that evil can be brought about only through the consideration of *every phase* of life—individual, as well as the collective; the internal, as well as the external phases.

A thorough perusal of the history of human development will disclose two elements in bitter conflict with each other; elements that are only now beginning to be understood, not as foreign to each other, but as closely related and truly harmonious, if only placed in proper environment: the individual and social instincts. The individual and society have waged a relentless and bloody battle for ages, each striving for supremacy, because each was blind to the value and importance of the other. The individual and social instincts—the one a most potent factor for individual endeavor, for growth, aspiration, self-realization; the other an equally potent factor for mutual helpfulness and social well-being.

The explanation of the storm raging within the individual, and between him and his surroundings, is not far to seek. The primitive man, unable to understand his being, much less the unity of all life, felt himself absolutely dependent on blind, hidden forces ever ready to mock and taunt him. Out of that attitude grew the religious concepts of man as a mere speck of dust dependent on superior powers on high, who can only be appeased by complete surrender. All the early sagas rest on that idea, which continues to be the *Leitmotiv* of the biblical tales dealing with the relation of man to God, to the State, to society. Again and again the same motif, *man is nothing, the powers are everything*. Thus Jehovah would only endure man on condition of complete surrender. Man can have all the glories of the earth, but he must not become conscious of himself. The State, society, and moral laws all sing the same refrain: Man can have all the glories of the earth, but he must not become conscious of himself.

Anarchism is the only philosophy which brings to man the consciousness of himself; which maintains that God, the State, and society are non-existent, that their promises are null and void, since they can be fulfilled only through man's subordination. Anarchism is therefore the teacher of the unity of life; not merely in nature, but in man. There is no conflict between the individual and the social instincts, any more than there is between the heart and the lungs: the one the receptacle of a precious life essence, the other the repository of the element that keeps the essence pure and strong. The individual is the heart of society, conserving the essence of social life; society is the lungs which are distributing the element to keep the life essence—that is, the individual—pure and strong.

"The one thing of value in the world," says Emerson, "is the active soul; this every man contains within him. The soul active sees absolute truth and utters truth and creates." In other words, the individual instinct is the thing of value in the world. It is the true soul that sees and creates the truth alive, out of which is to come a still greater truth, the re-born social soul.

Anarchism is the great liberator of man from the phantoms that have held him captive; it is the arbiter and pacifier of the two forces for individual and social harmony. To accomplish that unity, Anarchism has declared war on the pernicious influences which have so far prevented the harmonious blending of individual and social instincts, the individual and society.

Religion, the dominion of the human mind; Property, the dominion of human needs; and Government, the dominion of human conduct, represent the stronghold of man's enslavement and all the horrors it entails. Religion! How it dominates man's mind, how it humiliates and degrades his soul. God is everything, man is nothing, says religion. But out of that nothing God has created a kingdom so despotic, so tyrannical, so cruel, so terribly exacting that naught but gloom and tears and blood have ruled the world since gods began. Anarchism rouses man to rebellion against this black monster. Break your mental fetters, says Anarchism to man, for not until you think and judge for yourself will you get rid of the dominion of darkness, the greatest obstacle to all progress.

Property, the dominion of man's needs, the denial of the right to satisfy his needs. Time was when property claimed a divine right, when it came to man with the same refrain, even as religion, "Sacrifice! Abnegate! Submit!" The spirit of Anarchism has lifted man from his prostrate position. He now stands erect, with his face toward the light. He has learned to see the insatiable, devouring, devastating nature of property, and he is preparing to strike the monster dead.

"Property is robbery," said the great French Anarchist Proudhon. Yes, but without risk and danger to the robber. Monopolizing the accumulated efforts of man, property has robbed him of his birthright, and has turned him loose a pauper and an outcast. Property has not even the time-worn excuse that man does not create enough to satisfy all needs. The ABC student of economics knows that the productivity of labor within the last few decades far exceeds normal demand. But what are normal demands to an abnormal institution? The only demand that property recognizes is its own gluttonous appetite for greater wealth, because wealth means power; the power to subdue, to crush, to exploit, the power to enslave, to outrage, to degrade. America is particularly boastful of her great power, her enormous national wealth. Poor America, of what avail is all her wealth, if the individuals comprising the nation are wretchedly poor? If they live in squalor, in filth, in crime, with hope and joy gone, a homeless, soilless army of human prey.

It is generally conceded that unless the returns of any business venture exceed the cost, bankruptcy is inevitable. But those engaged in the business of producing wealth have not yet learned even this simple lesson. Every year the cost of production in human life is growing larger (50,000 killed, 100,000 wounded in America last year); the returns to the masses, who help to create wealth, are ever getting smaller. Yet America continues to be blind to the inevitable bankruptcy of our business of production. Nor is this the only crime of the latter. Still more fatal is the crime of turning the producer into a mere particle of a machine, with less will and decision than his master of steel and iron. Man is being robbed not merely of the products of his labor, but of the power of free initiative, of originality, and the interest in, or desire for, the things he is making.

Real wealth consists in things of utility and beauty, in things that help to create strong, beautiful bodies and surroundings inspiring to live in. But if man is doomed to wind cotton around a spool, or dig coal, or build roads for thirty years of his life, there can be no talk of wealth. What he gives to the world is only gray and hideous things, reflecting a dull and hideous existence—too weak to live, too cowardly to die. Strange to say, there are people who extol this deadening method of centralized production as the proudest achievement of our age. They fail utterly to realize that if we are to continue in machine subserviency, our slavery is more complete than was our bondage to the King. They do not want to know that centralization is not only the death-knell of liberty, but also of health and beauty, of art and science, all these being impossible in a clocklike, mechanical atmosphere.

Anarchism cannot but repudiate such a method of production: its goal is the freest possible expression of all the latent powers of the individual. Oscar Wilde defines a perfect personality as "one who develops under perfect conditions, who is not wounded, maimed, or in danger." A perfect personality, then, is only possible in a state of society where man is free to choose the mode of work, the conditions of work, and the freedom to work. One to whom the making of a table, the building of a house, or the tilling of the soil is what the painting is to the artist and the discovery to the scientist—the result of inspiration, of intense longing, and deep interest in work as a creative force. That being the ideal of Anarchism, its economic arrangements must consist of voluntary productive and distributive associations, gradually developing into free communism, as the best means of producing with the least waste of human energy. Anarchism, however, also recognizes the right of the individual, or numbers of individuals, to arrange at all times for other forms of work, in harmony with their tastes and desires.

Such free display of human energy being possible only under complete individual and social freedom, Anarchism directs its forces against the third and greatest foe of all social equality; namely, the State, organized authority, or statutory law—the dominion of human conduct.

Just as religion has fettered the human mind, and as property, or the monopoly of things, has subdued and stifled man's needs, so has the State enslaved his spirit, dictating every phase of conduct. "All government in essence," says Emerson, "is tyranny." It matters not whether it is government by divine right or majority rule. In every instance its aim is the absolute subordination of the individual.

Referring to the American government, the greatest American Anarchist, David Thoreau, said: "Government, what is it but a tradition, though a recent one, endeavoring to transmit itself unimpaired to posterity, but each instance losing its integrity; it has not the vitality and force of a single living man. Law never made man a whit more just; and by means of their respect for it, even the well disposed are daily made agents of injustice."

Indeed, the keynote of government is injustice. With the arrogance and self-sufficiency of the King who could do no wrong, governments ordain, judge, condemn, and punish the most insignificant offenses, while maintaining themselves by the greatest of all offenses, the annihilation of individual liberty. Thus Ouida is right when she maintains that "the State only aims at instilling those qualities in its public by which its demands are obeyed, and its exchequer is filled. Its highest attainment is the reduction of mankind to clockwork. In its atmosphere all those finer and more delicate liberties, which require treatment and spacious expansion, inevitably dry up and perish. The State requires a taxpaying machine in which there is no hitch, an exchequer in which there is never a deficit, and a public, monotonous, obedient, colorless, spiritless, moving humbly like a flock of sheep along a straight high road between two walls."

Yet even a flock of sheep would resist the chicanery of the State, if it were not for the corruptive, tyrannical, and oppressive methods it employs to serve its purposes. Therefore Bakunin repudiates the State as synonymous with the surrender of the liberty of the individual or small minorities —the destruction of social relationship, the curtailment, or complete denial even, of life itself, for its own aggrandizement. The State is the altar of political freedom and, like the religious altar, it is maintained for the purpose of human sacrifice.

In fact, there is hardly a modern thinker who does not

agree that government, organized authority, or the State is necessary *only* to maintain or protect property and monopoly. It has proven efficient in that function only.

Even George Bernard Shaw, who hopes for the miraculous from the State under Fabianism, nevertheless admits that "it is at present a huge machine for robbing and slave-driving of the poor by brute force." This being the case, it is hard to see why the clever prefacer wishes to uphold the State after poverty shall have ceased to exist.

Unfortunately there are still a number of people who continue in the fatal belief that government rests on natural laws, that it maintains social order and harmony, that it diminishes crime, and that it prevents the lazy man from fleecing his fellows. I shall therefore examine these contentions.

A natural law is that factor in man which asserts itself freely and spontaneously without any external force, in harmony with the requirements of nature. For instance, the demand for nutrition, for sex gratification, for light, air, and exercise, is a natural law. But its expression needs not the machinery of government, needs not the club, the gun, the handcuff, or the prison. To obey such laws, if we may call it obedience, requires only spontaneity and free opportunity. That governments do not maintain themselves through such harmonious factors is proven by the terrible array of violence, force, and coercion all governments use in order to live. Thus Blackstone is right when he says, "Human laws are invalid, because they are contrary to the laws of nature."

Unless it be the order of Warsaw after the slaughter of thousands of people, it is difficult to ascribe to governments any capacity for order or social harmony. Order derived through submission and maintained by terror is not much of a safe guaranty; yet that is the only "order" that governments have ever maintained. True social harmony grows naturally out of solidarity of interests. In a society where those who always work never have anything, while those who never work enjoy everything, solidarity of interests is non-existent; hence social harmony is but a myth. The only way organized authority meets this grave situation is by extending still greater privileges to those who have already monopolized the earth, and by still further enslaving the disinherited masses. Thus the entire arsenal of government —laws, police, soldiers, the courts, legislatures, prisons—is strenuously engaged in "harmonizing" the most antagonistic elements in society.

The most absurd apology for authority and law is that they serve to diminish crime. Aside from the fact that the State is itself the greatest criminal, breaking every written and natural law, stealing in the form of taxes, killing in the form of war and capital punishment, it has come to an absolute standstill in coping with crime. It has failed utterly to destroy or even minimize the horrible scourge of its own creation.

Crime is naught but misdirected energy. So long as every institution of today, economic, political, social, and moral, conspires to misdirect human energy into wrong channels; so long as most people are out of place doing the things they hate to do, living a life they loathe to live, crime will be inevitable, and all the laws on the statutes can only increase, but never do away with, crime. What does society, as it exists today, know of the process of despair, the poverty, the horrors, the fearful struggle the human soul must pass on its way to crime and degradation. Who that knows this terrible process can fail to see the truth in these words of Peter Kropotkin:

"Those who will hold the balance between the benefits thus attributed to law and punishment and the degrading effect of the latter on humanity; those who will estimate the torrent of depravity poured abroad in human society by the informer, favored by the Judge even, and paid for in clinking cash by governments, under the pretext of aiding to unmask crime; those who will go within prison walls and there see what human beings become when deprived of liberty, when subjected to the care of brutal keepers, to coarse, cruel words, to a thousand stinging, piercing humiliations, will agree with us that the entire apparatus of prison and punishment is an abomination which ought to be brought to an end."

The deterrent influence of law on the lazy man is too absurd to merit consideration. If society were only relieved of the waste and expense of keeping a lazy class, and the equally great expense of the paraphernalia of protection this lazy class requires, the social tables would contain an abundance for all, including even the occasional lazy individual. Besides, it is well to consider that laziness results either from special privileges, or physical and mental abnormalities. Our present insane system of production fosters both, and the most astounding phenomenon is that people should want to work at all now. Anarchism aims to strip labor of its deadening, dulling aspect, of its gloom and compulsion. It aims to make work an instrument of joy, of strength, of color, of real harmony, so that the poorest sort of a man should find in work both recreation and hope.

To achieve such an arrangement of life, government, with its unjust, arbitrary, repressive measures, must be done away with. At best it has but imposed one single mode of life upon all, without regard to individual and social variations and needs. In destroying government and statutory laws, Anarchism proposes to rescue the self-respect and independence of the individual from all restraint and invasion by authority. Only in freedom can man grow to his full stature. Only in freedom will he learn to think and move, and give the very best in him. Only in freedom will he realize the true force of the social bonds which knit men together, and which are the true foundation of a normal social life.

But what about human nature? Can it be changed? And if not, will it endure under Anarchism?

Poor human nature, what horrible crimes have been committed in thy name! Every fool, from king to policeman, from the flatheaded parson to the visionless dabbler in science, presumes to speak authoritatively of human nature. The greater the mental charlatan, the more definite his insistence on the wickedness and weaknesses of human nature. Yet, how can any one speak of it to-day, with every soul in a prison, with every heart fettered, wounded, and maimed?

John Burroughs has stated that experimental study of animals in captivity is absolutely useless. Their character, their habits, their appetites undergo a complete transformation when torn from their soil in field and forest. With human nature caged in a narrow space, whipped daily into submission, how can we speak of its potentialities?

Freedom, expansion, opportunity, and, above all, peace and repose, alone can teach us the real dominant factors of human nature and all its wonderful possibilities.

Anarchism, then, really stands for the liberation of the human mind from the dominion of religion; the liberation of the human body from the dominion of property; liberation from the shackles and restraint of government. Anarchism stands for a social order based on the free grouping of individuals for the purpose of producing real social wealth; an order that will guarantee to every human being free access to the earth and full enjoyment of the necessities of life, according to individual desires, tastes, and inclinations.

This is not a wild fancy or an aberration of the mind. It is the conclusion arrived at by hosts of intellectual men and women the world over; a conclusion resulting from the close and studious observation of the tendencies of modern society: individual liberty and economic equality, the twin forces for the birth of what is fine and true in man.

As to methods. Anarchism is not, as some may suppose, a theory of the future to be realized through divine inspiration. It is a living force in the affairs of our life, constantly creating new conditions. The methods of Anarchism therefore do not comprise an iron-clad program to be carried out under all circumstances. Methods must grow out of the economic needs of each place and clime, and of the intellectual and temperamental requirements of the individual. The serene, calm character of a Tolstoy will wish different methods for social reconstruction than the intense, overflowing personality of a Michael Bakunin or a Peter Kropotkin. Equally so it must be apparent that the economic and political needs of Russia will dictate more drastic measures than would England or America. Anarchism does not stand for military drill and uniformity; it does, however, stand for the spirit of revolt, in whatever form, against everything that hinders human growth. All Anarchists agree in that, as they also agree in their opposition to the political machinery as a means of bringing about the great social change.

"All voting," says Thoreau, "is a sort of gaming, like checkers, or backgammon, a playing with right and wrong; its obligation never exceeds that of expediency. Even voting for the right thing is doing nothing for it. A wise man will not leave the right to the mercy of chance, nor wish it to prevail through the power of the majority." A close examination of the machinery of politics and its achievements will bear out the logic of Thoreau.

What does the history of parliamentarism show? Nothing but failure and defeat, not even a single reform to ameliorate the economic and social stress of the people. Laws have been passed and enactments made for the improvement and protection of labor. Thus it was proven only last year that

Illinois, with the most rigid laws for mine protection, had the greatest mine disasters. In States where child labor laws prevail, child exploitation is at its highest, and though with us the workers enjoy full political opportunities, capitalism has reached the most brazen zenith.

Even were the workers able to have their own representatives, for which our good Socialist politicians are clamoring, what chances are there for their honesty and good faith? One has but to bear in mind the process of politics to realize that its path of good intentions is full of pitfalls: wire-pulling, intriguing, flattering, lying, cheating; in fact, chicanery of every description, whereby the political aspirant can achieve success. Added to that is a complete demoralization of character and conviction, until nothing is left that would make one hope for anything from such a human derelict. Time and time again the people were foolish enough to trust, believe, and support with their last farthing aspiring politicians, only to find themselves betrayed and cheated.

It may be claimed that men of integrity would not become corrupt in the political grinding mill. Perhaps not; but such men would be absolutely helpless to exert the slightest influence in behalf of labor, as indeed has been shown in numerous instances. The State is the economic master of its servants. Good men, if such there be, would either remain true to their political faith and lose their economic support, or they would cling to their economic master and be utterly unable to do the slightest good. The political arena leaves one no alternative, one must either be a dunce or a rogue.

The political superstition is still holding sway over the hearts and minds of the masses, but the true lovers of liberty will have no more to do with it. Instead, they believe with Stirner that man has as much liberty as he is willing to take. Anarchism therefore stands for direct action, the open defiance of, and resistance to, all laws and restrictions, economic, social, and moral. But defiance and resistance are illegal. Therein lies the salvation of man. Everything illegal necessitates integrity, self-reliance, and courage. In short, it calls for free, independent spirits, for "men who are men, and who have a bone in their backs which you cannot pass your hand through."

Universal suffrage itself owes its existence to direct action. If not for the spirit of rebellion, of the defiance on the part of the American revolutionary fathers, their posterity would still wear the King's coat. If not for the direct action of a John Brown and his comrades, America would still trade in the flesh of the black man. True, the trade in white flesh is still going on; but that, too, will have to be abolished by direct action. Trade-unionism, the economic arena of the modern gladiator, owes its existence to direct action. It is but recently that law and government have attempted to crush the trade-union movement, and condemned the exponents of man's right to organize to prison as conspirators. Had they sought to assert their cause through begging, pleading, and compromise, trade-unionism would today be a negligible quantity. In France, in Spain, in Italy, in Russia, nay even in England (witness the growing rebellion of English labor unions), direct, revolutionary, economic action has become so strong a force in the battle for industrial liberty as to make the world realize the tremendous importance of labor's power. The General Strike, the supreme expression of the economic consciousness of the workers, was ridiculed in America but a short time ago. Today every great strike, in order to win, must realize the importance of the solidaric general protest.

Direct action, having proven effective along economic lines, is equally potent in the environment of the individual. There a hundred forces encroach upon his being, and only persistent resistance to them will finally set him free. Direct action against the authority in the shop, direct action against the authority of the law, direct action against the invasive, meddlesome authority of our moral code, is the logical, consistent method of Anarchism.

Will it not lead to a revolution? Indeed, it will. No real social change has ever come about without a revolution. People are either not familiar with their history, or they have not yet learned that revolution is but thought carried into action.

Anarchism, the great leaven of thought, is today permeating every phase of human endeavor. Science, art, literature, the drama, the effort for economic betterment, in fact every individual and social opposition to the existing disorder of things, is illumined by the spiritual light of Anarchism. It is the philosophy of the sovereignty of the individual. It is the theory of social harmony. It is the great, surging, living truth that is reconstructing the world, and that will usher in the Dawn.

Syndicalism: Its Theory
and Practice

In view of the fact that the ideas embodied in Syndicalism
have been practised by the workers for the last half century,
even if without the background of social consciousness; that
in this country five men had to pay with their lives because
they advocated Syndicalist methods as the most effective in
the struggle of labor against capital; and that, furthermore,
Syndicalism has been consciously practised by the workers
of France, Italy and Spain since 1895, it is rather amusing
to witness some people in America and England now
swooping down upon Syndicalism as a perfectly new and
never before heard-of proposition.

It is astonishing how very naïve Americans are, how
crude and immature in matters of international importance.
For all his boasted practical aptitude, the average American
is the very last to learn of the modern means and tactics
employed in the great struggles of his day. Always he lags
behind in ideas and methods that the European workers
have for years past been applying with great success.

It may be contended, of course, that this is merely a sign
of youth on the part of the American. And it is indeed

beautiful to possess a young mind, fresh to receive and perceive. But unfortunately the American mind seems never to grow, to mature and crystallize its views.

Perhaps that is why an American revolutionist can at the same time be a politician. That is also the reason why leaders of the Industrial Workers of the World continue in the Socialist party, which is antagonistic to the principles as well as to the activities of the I.W.W. Also why a rigid Marxian may propose that the Anarchists work together with the faction that began its career by a most bitter and malicious persecution of one of the pioneers of Anarchism, Michael Bakunin. In short, to the indefinite, uncertain mind of the American radical the most contradictory ideas and methods are possible. The result is a sad chaos in the radical movement, a sort of intellectual hash, which has neither taste nor character.

Just at present Syndicalism is the pastime of a great many Americans, so-called intellectuals. Not that they know anything about it, except that some great authorities—Sorel, Bergson and others—stand for it: because the American needs the seal of authority, or he would not accept an idea, no matter how true and valuable it might be.

Our bourgeois magazines are full of dissertations on Syndicalism. One of our most conservative colleges has even gone to the extent of publishing a work of one of its students on the subject, which has the approval of a professor. And all this, not because Syndicalism is a force and is being successfully practiced by the workers of Europe, but because—as I said before—it has official authoritative sanction.

As if Syndicalism had been discovered by the philosophy of Bergson or the theoretic discourses of Sorel and Berth, and had not existed and lived among the workers long before these men wrote about it. The feature which distinguishes Syndicalism from most philosophies is that it represents the revolutionary philosophy of labor conceived and born in the actual struggle and experience of the workers themselves—not in universities, colleges, libraries, or in the brain of some scientists. *The revolutionary philosophy of labor,* that is the true and vital meaning of Syndicalism.

Already as far back as 1848 a large section of the workers realized the utter futility of political activity as a means of helping them in their economic struggle. At that time already the demand went forth for direct economic measures, as against the useless waste of energy along political lines. This was the case not only in France, but even prior to that, in England, where Robert Owen, the true revolutionary Socialist, propagated similar ideas.

After years of agitation and experiment the idea was incorporated by the first convention of the *Internationale* in 1867, in the resolution that the economic emancipation of the workers must be the principal aim of all revolutionists, to which everything else is to be subordinated.

In fact, it was this determined radical stand which eventually brought about the split in the revolutionary movement of that day, and its division into two factions: the one, under Marx and Engels, aiming at political conquest; the other, under Bakunin and the Latin workers, forging ahead along industrial and Syndicalist lines. The further development of those two wings is familiar to every thinking man and woman: the one has gradually centralized into a huge machine, with the sole purpose of conquering political power within the existing capitalist State; the other is becoming an ever more vital revolutionary factor, dreaded by the enemy as the greatest menace to its rule.

It was in the year 1900, while a delegate to the Anarchist Congress in Paris, that I first came in contact with Syndicalism in operation. The Anarchist press had been discussing the subject for years prior to that; therefore we Anarchists knew something about Syndicalism. But those of us who lived in America had to content ourselves with the theoretic side of it.

In 1900, however, I saw its effect upon labor in France: the strength, the enthusiasm and hope with which Syndicalism inspired the workers. It was also my good fortune to learn of the man who more than anyone else had directed Syndicalism into definite working channels, Fernand Pelloutier. Unfortunately, I could not meet this remarkable young man, as he was at that time already very ill with cancer. But wherever I went, with whomever I spoke, the love and devotion for Pelloutier was wonderful, all agreeing that it was he who had gathered the discontented forces in the French labor movement and imbued them with new life and a new purpose, that of Syndicalism.

On my return to America I immediately began to propagate Syndicalist ideas, especially Direct Action and the General Strike. But it was like talking to the Rocky Mountains—no understanding, even among the more radical elements, and complete indifference in labor ranks.

In 1907 I went as a delegate to the Anarchist Congress at Amsterdam and, while in Paris, met the most active Syndicalists in the *Confédération Générale du Travail:* Pouget, Delesalle, Monate, and many others. More than that, I had the opportunity to see Syndicalism in daily operation, in its most constructive and inspiring forms.

I allude to this to indicate that my knowledge of Syndicalism does not come from Sorel, Bergson or Berth, but from actual contact with and observation of the tremendous work carried on by the workers of Paris within the ranks of the Confédération. It would require a volume to explain in detail what Syndicalism is doing for the French workers. In the American press you read only of its resistive methods, of strikes and sabotage, of the conflicts of labor with capital. These are no doubt very important matters, and yet the chief value of Syndicalism lies much deeper. It lies in the constructive and educational effect upon the life and thought of the masses.

The fundamental difference between Syndicalism and the

old trade methods is this: while the old trade unions, without exception, move within the wage system and capitalism, recognizing the latter as inevitable, Syndicalism repudiates and condemns present industrial arrangements as unjust and criminal, and holds out no hope to the worker for lasting results from this system.

Of course Syndicalism, like the old trade unions, fights for immediate gains, but it is not stupid enough to pretend that labor can expect humane conditions from inhuman economic arrangements in society. Thus it merely wrests from the enemy what it can force him to yield; on the whole, however, Syndicalism aims at, and concentrates its energies upon, the complete overthrow of the wage system. Indeed, Syndicalism goes further: it aims to liberate labor from every institution that has not for its object the free development of production for the benefit of all humanity. In short, the ultimate purpose of Syndicalism is to reconstruct society from its present centralized, authoritative and brutal state to one based upon the free, federated grouping of the workers along lines of economic and social liberty.

With this object in view, Syndicalism works in two directions: first, by undermining the existing institutions; secondly, by developing and educating the workers and cultivating their spirit of solidarity, to prepare them for a full, free life, when capitalism shall have been abolished.

Syndicalism is, in essence, the economic expression of Anarchism. That circumstance accounts for the presence of so many Anarchists in the Syndicalist movement. Like Anarchism, Syndicalism prepares the workers along direct economic lines, as conscious factors in the great struggles of to-day, as well as conscious factors in the task of reconstructing society along autonomous industrial lines, as against the paralyzing spirit of centralization with its bureaucratic machinery of corruption, inherent in all political parties.

Realizing that the diametrically opposed interests of capital and labor can never be reconciled, Syndicalism must needs repudiate the old, rusticated, worn-out methods of trade unionism, and declare for an open war against the capitalist régime, as well as against every institution which to-day supports and protects capitalism.

As a logical sequence Syndicalism, in its daily warfare against capitalism, rejects the contract system, because it does not consider labor and capital equals, hence cannot consent to an agreement which the one has the power to break, while the other must submit to without redress.

For similar reasons Syndicalism rejects negotiations in labor disputes, because such a procedure serves only to give the enemy time to prepare his end of the fight, thus defeating the very object the workers set out to accomplish. Also, Syndicalism stands for spontaneity, both as a preserver of the fighting strength of labor and also because it takes the enemy unawares, hence compels him to a speedy settlement or causes him great loss.

Syndicalism objects to a large union treasury, because money is as corrupting an element in the ranks of labor as it is in those of capitalism. We in America know this to be only too true. If the labor movement in this country were not backed by such large funds, it would not be as conservative as it is, nor would the leaders be so readily corrupted. However, the main reason for the opposition of Syndicalism to large treasuries consists in the fact that they create class distinctions and jealousies within the ranks of labor, so detrimental to the spirit of solidarity. The worker whose organization has a large purse considers himself superior to his poorer brother, just as he regards himself better than the man who earns fifty cents less per day.

The chief ethical value of Syndicalism consists in the stress it lays upon the necessity of labor's getting rid of the element of dissension, parasitism and corruption in its ranks. It seeks to cultivate devotion, solidarity and enthusiasm, which are far more essential and vital in the economic struggle than money.

As I have already stated, Syndicalism has grown out of the disappointment of the workers with politics and parliamentary methods. In the course of its development Syndicalism has learned to see in the State—with its mouthpiece, the representative system—one of the strongest supports of capitalism; just as it has learned that the army and the church are the chief pillars of the State. It is therefore that Syndicalism has turned its back upon parliamentarism and political machines, and has set its face toward the economic arena wherein alone gladiator Labor can meet his foe successfully.

Historic experience sustains the Syndicalists in their uncompromising opposition to parliamentarism. Many had entered political life and, unwilling to be corrupted by the atmosphere, withdrew from office, to devote themselves to the economic struggle—Proudhon, the Dutch revolutionist Nieuwenhuis, Johann Most and numerous others. While those who remained in the parliamentary quagmire ended by betraying their trust, without having gained anything for labor. But it is unnecessary to discuss here political history. Suffice to say that Syndicalists are anti-parliamentarians as a result of bitter experience.

Equally so has experience determined their anti-military attitude. Time and again has the army been used to shoot down strikers and to indicate the sickening idea of patriotism, for the purpose of dividing the workers against themselves and helping the masters to the spoils. The inroads that Syndicalist agitation has made into the superstition of patriotism are evident from the dread of the ruling class for the loyalty of the army, and the rigid persecution of the anti-militarists. Naturally, for the ruling class realizes much better than the workers that when the soldiers will refuse to obey their superiors, the whole system of capitalism will be doomed.

Indeed, why should the workers sacrifice their children that the latter may be used to shoot their own parents? Therefore Syndicalism is not merely logical in its anti-military agitation; it is most practical and far-reaching, inasmuch as it robs the enemy of his strongest weapon against labor.

Now, as to the methods employed by Syndicalism—Direct Action, Sabotage, and the General Strike.

> DIRECT ACTION: Conscious individual or collective effort to protest against, or remedy, social conditions through the systematic assertion of the economic power of the workers.

Sabotage has been decried as criminal, even by so-called revolutionary Socialists. Of course, if you believe that property, which excludes the producer from its use, is justifiable, then sabotage is indeed a crime. But unless a Socialist continues to be under the influence of our bourgeois morality—a morality which enables the few to monopolize the earth at the expense of the many—he cannot consistently maintain that capitalist property is inviolate. Sabotage undermines this form of private possession. Can it therefore be considered criminal? On the contrary, it is ethical in the best sense, since it helps society to get rid of its worst foe, the most detrimental factor of social life.

Sabotage is mainly concerned with obstructing, by every possible method, the regular process of production, thereby demonstrating the determination of the workers to give according to what they receive, and no more. For instance, at the time of the French railroad strike of 1910, perishable goods were sent in slow trains, or in an opposite direction from the one intended. Who but the most ordinary philistine will call that a crime? If the railway men themselves go hungry, and the "innocent" public has not enough feeling of solidarity to insist that these men should get enough to live on, the public has forfeited the sympathy of the strikers and must take the consequences.

Another form of sabotage consisted, during this strike, in placing heavy boxes on goods marked "Handle with care," cut glass and china and precious wines. From the standpoint of the law this may have been a crime, but from the standpoint of common humanity it was a very sensible thing. The same is true of disarranging a loom in a weaving mill, or living up to the letter of the law with all its red tape, as the Italian railway men did, thereby causing confusion in the railway service. In other words, sabotage is merely a weapon of defense in the industrial warfare, which is the more effective, because it touches capitalism in its most vital spot, the pocket.

By the General Strike, Syndicalism means a stoppage of work, the cessation of labor. Nor need such a strike be postponed until all the workers of a particular place or country are ready for it. As has been pointed out by Pelloutier, Pouget, as well as others, and particularly by recent events in England, the General Strike may be started by one industry and exert a tremendous force. It is as if one man suddenly raised the cry "Stop the thief!" Immediately others will take up the cry, till the air rings with it. The General Strike, initiated by one determined organization, by one industry or by a small, conscious minority among the workers, is the industrial cry of "Stop the thief," which is soon taken up by many other industries, spreading like wildfire in a very short time.

One of the objections of politicians to the General Strike is that the workers also would suffer for the necessaries of life. In the first place, the workers are past masters in going hungry; secondly, it is certain that a General Strike is surer of prompt settlement than an ordinary strike. Witness the transport and miner strikes in England: how quickly the lords of State and capital were forced to make peace. Besides, Syndicalism recognizes the right of the producers to the things which they have created; namely, the right of the workers to help themselves if the strike does not meet with speedy settlement.

When Sorel maintains that the General Strike is an inspiration necessary for the people to give their life meaning, he is expressing a thought which the Anarchists have never tired of emphasizing. Yet I do not hold with Sorel that the General Strike is a "social myth," that may never be realized. I think that the General Strike will become a fact the moment labor understands its full value—its destructive as well as constructive value, as indeed many workers all over the world are beginning to realize.

These ideas and methods of Syndicalism some may consider entirely negative, though they are far from it in their effect upon society to-day. But Syndicalism has also a directly positive aspect. In fact, much more time and effort is being devoted to that phase than to the others. Various forms of Syndicalist activity are designed to prepare the workers, even within present social and industrial conditions, for the life of a new and better society. To that end the masses are trained in the spirit of mutual aid and brotherhood, their initiative and self-reliance developed, and an *esprit de corps* maintained whose very soul is solidarity of purpose and the community of interests of the international proletariat.

Chief among these activities are the *mutualitées,* or mutual aid societies, established by the French Syndicalists. Their object is, foremost, to secure work for unemployed members, and to further that spirit of mutual assistance which rests upon the consciousness of labor's identity of interests throughout the world.

In his "The Labor Movement in France," Mr. L. Levine states that during the year 1902 over 74,000 workers, out of a total of 99,000 applicants, were provided with work by these societies, without being compelled to submit to the extortion of the employment bureau sharks.

These latter are a source of the deepest degradation, as well as of most shameless exploitation, of the worker. Especially does it hold true of America, where the employment agencies are in many cases also masked detective agencies, supplying workers in need of employment to strike regions, under false promises of steady, remunerative employment.

The French Confédération had long realized the vicious rôle of employment agencies as leeches upon the jobless worker and nurseries of scabbery. By the threat of a General Strike the French Syndicalists forced the government to abolish the employment bureau sharks, and the workers' own *mutualitées* have almost entirely superseded them, to the great economic and moral advantage of labor.

Besides the *mutualitées,* the French Syndicalists have established other activities tending to weld labor in closer bonds of solidarity and mutual aid. Among these are the efforts to assist workingmen journeying from place to place. The practical as well as ethical value of such assistance is inestimable. It serves to instill the spirit of fellowship and gives a sense of security in the feeling of oneness with the large family of labor. This is one of the vital effects of the Syndicalist spirit in France and other Latin countries. What a tremendous need there is for just such efforts in this country! Can anyone doubt the significance of the consciousness of workingmen coming from Chicago, for instance, to New York, sure to find there among their comrades welcome lodging and food until they have secured employment? This form of activity is entirely foreign to the labor bodies of this country, and as a result the traveling workman in search of a job—the "blanket stiff"— is constantly at the mercy of the constable and policeman, a victim of the vagrancy laws, and the unfortunate material whence is recruited, through stress of necessity, the army of scabdom.

I have repeatedly witnessed, while at the headquarters of the Confédération, the cases of workingmen who came with their union cards from various parts of France, and even from other countries of Europe, and were supplied with meals and lodging, and encouraged by every evidence of brotherly spirit, and made to feel at home by their fellow workers of the Confédération. It is due, to a great extent, to these activities of the Syndicalists that the French government is forced to employ the army for strikebreaking, because few workers are willing to lend themselves for such service, thanks to the efforts and tactics of Syndicalism.

No less in importance than the mutual aid activities of the Syndicalists is the cooperation established by them between the city and the country, the factory worker and the peasant or farmer, the latter providing the workers with food supplies during strikes, or taking care of the strikers' children. This form of practical solidarity has for the first time been tried in this country during the Lawrence strike, with inspiring results.

And all these Syndicalist activities are permeated with the spirit of educational work, carried on systematically by evening classes on all vital subjects treated from an un-biased, libertarian standpoint—not the adulterated "knowl-edge" with which the minds are stuffed in our public schools. The scope of the education is truly phenomenal, including sex hygiene, the care of women during pregnancy and confinement, the care of home and children, sanitation and general hygiene; in fact, every branch of human knowl-edge—science, history, art—receives thorough attention, together with the practical application in the established workingmen's libraries, dispensaries, concerts and festivals, in which the greatest artists and littérateurs of Paris consider it an honor to participate.

One of the most vital efforts of Syndicalism is to prepare

the workers, *now,* for their role in a free society. Thus the
Syndicalist organizations supply its members with textbooks
on every trade and industry, of a character that is calcu-
lated to make the worker an adept in his chosen line, a
master of his craft, for the purpose of familiarizing him with
all the branches of his industry, so that when labor finally
takes over production and distribution, the people will be
fully prepared to manage successfully their own affairs.

A demonstration of the effectiveness of this educational
campaign of Syndicalism is given by the railroad men of
Italy, whose mastery of all the details of transportation is so
great that they could offer to the Italian government to take
over the railroads of the country and guarantee their operation with greater economy and fewer accidents than is at
present done by the government.

Their ability to carry on production has been strikingly
proved by the Syndicalists, in connection with the glass
blowers' strike in Italy. There the strikers, instead of remaining idle during the progress of the strike, decided
themselves to carry on the production of glass. The wonderful spirit of solidarity resulting from the Syndicalist propaganda enabled them to build a glass factory within an
incredibly short time. An old building, rented for the purpose and which would have ordinarily required months to
be put into proper condition, was turned into a glass factory
within a few weeks, by the solidaric efforts of the strikers
aided by their comrades who toiled with them after working
hours. Then the strikers began operating the glass-blowing
factory, and their cooperative plan of work and distribution
during the strike has proved so satisfactory in every way
that the experimental factory has been made permanent
and a part of the glass-blowing industry in Italy is now in
the hands of the cooperative organization of the workers.

This method of applied education not only trains the
worker in his daily struggle, but serves also to equip him for
the battle royal and the future, when he is to assume his

place in society as an intelligent, conscious being and useful producer, once capitalism is abolished.

Nearly all leading Syndicalists agree with the Anarchists that a free society can exist only through voluntary association, and that its ultimate success will depend upon the intellectual and moral development of the workers who will supplant the wage system with a new social arrangement, based on solidarity and economic well-being for all. That is Syndicalism, in theory and practice.

Socialism: Caught in the Political Trap

Legend tells us that healthy newborn infants aroused the envy and hatred of evil spirits. In the absence of the proud mothers, the evil ones stole into the houses, kidnapped the babies, and left behind them deformed, hideous-looking monsters.

Socialism has met with such a fate. Young and lusty, crying out defiance to the world, it aroused the envy of the evil ones. They stole near when Socialism least expected and made off with it, leaving behind a deformity which is now stalking about under the name of Socialism.

At its birth, Socialism declared war on all constituted institutions. Its aim was to fell every injustice to the ground and replace it with economic and social well-being and harmony.

Two fundamental principles gave Socialism its life and strength: the wage system and its master, private property. The cruelty, criminality, and injustice of these principles were the enemies against which Socialism hurled its bitterest attacks and criticisms. Private property and the wage system being the staunchest pillars of society, everyone who dared expose their cruelty was denounced as an enemy of society, a dangerous character, a revolutionist. Time was when Socialism carried these epithets with head erect, feeling that the hatred and persecution of its enemies were its greatest attributes.

Not so the Socialism that has been caught in the trap of the evil ones, of the political monsters. This sort of Socialism has either given up altogether the unflinching attacks against the bulwarks of the present system, or has weakened and changed its form to an unrecognizable extent.

The aim of Socialism today is the crooked path of politics as a means of capturing the State. Yet it is the State which represents the mightiest weapon sustaining private property and our system of wrong and inequality. It is the power which protects the system against every rebellious, determined revolutionary attack.

The State is organized exploitation, organized force, and crime. And to the hypnotic manipulation of this very monster, Socialism has become a willing prey. Indeed, the representatives of Socialism are more devout in their religious faith in the State than the most conservative statists.

The Socialist contention is that the State is not half centralized enough. The State, they say, should not only control the political phase of society, it should become the arch manager, the very fountain-head, of the industrial life of the people as well, since that alone would do away with special privileges, with trusts and monopolies. Never does it occur to these abortionists of a great idea that the State is the coldest, most inhuman monopolist, and if once economic dictatorship were added to the already supreme political power of the State, its iron heel would cut deeper into the flesh of labor than that of capitalism today.

Of course, I will be told that Socialism does not aim for such a State, that it wants a true, just, democratic, real State. Alas, the true, real, and just State is like the true, real, just God, who has never yet been discovered. The real

God, according to our good Christians, is kind and loving, just and fair. But what has he proven to be in reality? A God of tyranny, of war and bloodshed, of crime and injustice. The same is the case with the State, whether of Republican, Democratic, or Socialist color. Always and everywhere it has and must stand for *supremacy,* hence for slavery, submission, and dependency.

How the political scene-shifters must grin when they see the rush of the people to the newest attraction in the political moving-picture show. The poor, deluded, childish people, who are forever fed on the political patent medicine, either of the Republican elephant, the Democratic cow, or the Socialist mule, the grunting of each merely representing a new ragtime from the political music box.

The muddy waters of the political life run high for a time, while underneath moves the giant beast of greed and strife, of corruption and decay, mercilessly devouring its victims. All politicians, no matter how sincere (if such an anomaly is at all thinkable), are but petty reformers, hence the perpetuators of the present system.

Socialism in its inception was absolutely and irrevocably opposed to this system. It was anti-authoritarian, anti-capitalistic, anti-religious; in short, it could not and would not make peace with a single institution of today. But since it was led astray by the evil spirit of politics, it landed in the trap and has now but one desire—to adjust itself to the narrow confines of its cage, to become part of the authority, part of the very power that has slain the beautiful child Socialism and left behind a hideous monster.

Since the days of the old *Internationale,* since the strife between Bakunin, Marx and Engels, Socialism has slowly but surely been losing its fighting plumes—its rebellious spirit and its strong revolutionary tendencies—as more and more it has allowed itself to be deceived by political gains and government offices. And more and more, Socialism has grown powerless to arouse itself from the political hypnosis, thereby spreading apathy and passivity in proportion to its political successes.

The masses are being drilled and canned for the political cold storage of Socialist campaigns. Every direct, independent, and courageous attack on capitalism and the State is being discouraged or tabooed. The stupid voters wait patiently from one political performance to another for the comrade actors in the theater of representation to give a show, and perhaps perform a new stunt. Meanwhile, the Socialist congressman introduces yard upon yard of resolutions for the waste basket, proposing the perpetuation of the very things Socialism once set out to overthrow. And the Socialist mayors are busy assuring the business interests of their towns that they may rest in peace, no harm will ever come to them from a Socialist mayor. And if such Punch-and-Judy shows are criticised, the good Socialist adherents grow indignant and say that we must wait until the Socialists have the majority.

The political trap has transferred Socialism from the proud, uncompromising position of a revolutionary minority, fighting fundamentals and undermining the strongholds of wealth and power, to the camp of the scheming, compromising, inert political majority, busying itself with non-essentials, with things that barely touch the surface, measures that have been used as political bait by the most lukewarm reformers: old age pensions, initiative and referendum, the recall of judges, and other such very startling and terrible things.

In order to achieve these "revolutionary" measures, the elite in the Socialist ranks go down on their knees to the majority, holding out the palm leaf of compromise, catering to every superstition, every prejudice, every silly tradition. Even the Socialist politicians know that the voting majority is intellectually steeped in ignorance, that it does not know as much as the ABC of Socialism. One would therefore assume that the aim of these "scientific" Socialists would be to lift the mass up to its intellectual heights. But no such thing. That would hurt the feelings of the majority too much. Therefore the leaders must sink to the low level of their constituency, therefore they must cater to the ignorance and prejudice of the voters. And that is precisely what Socialism has been doing since it was caught in the political trap.

One of the commonplaces of Socialism today is the notion of evolution. For heaven's sake, let's have nothing of revolution, we are peace-loving people, we want evolution. I shall not now attempt to prove that evolution must mean growth from a lower to a higher state of mind, and that thus Socialists, from their own evolutionary standpoint, have failed miserably, since they have gone back on every one of their original principles. I only wish to examine into this wonderful thing, Socialist evolution.

Thanks to Karl Marx and Engels we are assured that Socialism has developed from a Utopia to a science. Softly, gentlemen, Utopian Socialism is not the kind that would allow itself to be caught in the political trap, it is the kind that will never make peace with our murderous system, it is the kind that has inspired and still inspires enthusiasm, zeal, courage, and idealism. It is the kind of Socialism that will have none of the disgustingly cringing compromise of a Berger, a Hillquit, a Ghent, and other such "scientific" gentlemen.

Every daring attempt to make a great change in existing conditions, every lofty vision of new possibilities for the human race, has been labeled Utopian. If "scientific" Socialism is to substitute stagnation for activity, cowardice for courage, acquiescence for daring, submission for defiance, then Marx and Engels might never have lived, for all the service they have done to Socialism.

But I deny that so-called scientific Socialism has proven its superiority to Utopian Socialism. Certainly, if we examine into the failure of some of the predictions the great prophets have made, we will see how arrogant and over-bearing the scientific contentions are. Marx was determined that the middle class would get off the scene of action, leaving but two fighting forces, the capitalistic and prole-tarian classes. But the middle class has had the impudence not to oblige comrade Marx.

The middle class is growing everywhere, and is indeed the strongest ally of capitalism. In fact, the middle class was never more powerful than it is today, as can be adduced by a thousand facts, but mainly by the very gentlemen in the Socialist ranks—the lawyers, ministers, and small business-men—who infest the movement. They are making of Social-ism a respectable, middle-class, law-abiding issue because they themselves represent that very tendency. It is inevi-table that they should espouse methods of propaganda to fit everybody's taste and strengthen the system of robbery and exploitation.

Marx prophesied that the workers would grow poorer in proportion to the increase of wealth. That did not come to pass, either, in the way Marx hoped. The masses of workers are really getting poorer, but that has not prevented the rise of an aristocracy of labor in the very ranks of labor. A class of snobs who—because of superior wages and more re-spected positions, but mainly because they have saved a little or acquired some property—have lost sympathy with their own kind, and are now the loudest proclaimers against revolutionary means. Truth is, the entire Socialist Party of today is recruited from these very aristocrats of labor; that's why they will have nothing to do with those who stand for revolutionary, anti-political methods. The possibility of be-coming mayor, congressman, or some other high official is too alluring to allow these upstarts to do anything that would jeopardize such a glorious chance.

But what about the much-extolled class consciousness of the workers which is to act as such leaven? Where and how does it assert itself? Surely, if it were an innate quality the workers would long since have demonstrated this fact, and their first act would have been to sweep clean from the Socialist ranks lawyers, ministers, and real-estate sharks, the most parasitic types in society.

Class consciousness can never be demonstrated in the political arena, for the interests of the politician and the voter are not identical. The one aims for office while the other must stand the cost. How then can there be a fellow-feeling between them?

Solidarity of interests develops class consciousness, as is demonstrated in the Syndicalist and every other revolutionary movement, in the determined effort to overthrow the present system, in the great war that is being waged against every institution of today in behalf of a new edifice.

The political Socialists care nothing at all for such a class consciousness. On the contrary, they fight it tooth and nail. In Mexico, class consciousness is being demonstrated as it has not been since the great French Revolution. The real and true proletarians, the robbed and enslaved peons, are fighting for land and liberty. It is true they know nothing of the theory of scientific Socialism, nor yet of the materialistic interpretation of history, as laid down in Marx's *Das Kapital,* but they know with mathematical accuracy that they have been sold into slavery. They also know that their interests are inimical to the interests of the land robbers, and they have risen in revolt against that class, against those interests.

How do the class-conscious monopolists of scientific Socialism meet this wonderful uprising? With the cries of "bandits, filibusters, anarchists, ignoramuses"—unfit to understand or interpret economic necessity. And predictably, the paralysing effect of the political trap does not permit of sympathy with the sublime wrath of the oppressed. It must move in straight-laced legal bounds, while the Indian Yaquis, the Mexican peons have broken all laws, all propriety, they have even had the impudence to expropriate the land from the expropriators, they have driven back their tyrants and tormentors. How then can peaceful aspirants for political jobs approve such conduct? Trying hard for the fleshpots of the State, which is the staunchest protector of property, the Socialist cannot possibly affiliate with any movement that so brazenly attacks property. On the other hand, it is quite consistent with the political aims of the party to oblige those who might add to the voting strength of class-conscious Socialism. Witness how tenderly religion is treated, how prohibition is patted on the back, how the anti-Asiatic and Negro question is met with, in short how every spook prejudice is treated with kid gloves so as not to hurt its sensitive souls.

The Individual, Society and the State

The minds of men are in confusion, for the very foundations of our civilization seem to be tottering. People are losing faith in the existing institutions, and the more intelligent realize that capitalist industrialism is defeating the very purpose it is supposed to serve.

The world is at a loss for a way out. Parliamentarism and democracy are on the decline. Salvation is being sought in Fascism and other forms of "strong" government.

The struggle of opposing ideas now going on in the world involves social problems urgently demanding a solution. The welfare of the individual and the fate of human society depend on the right answer to those questions. The crises of unemployment, war, disarmament, international relations, etc., are among those problems.

The State, government with its functions and powers, is now the subject of vital interest to every thinking man. Political developments in all civilized countries have brought the questions home. Shall we have a strong government? Are democracy and parliamentary government to be preferred, or is Fascism of one kind or another, dictatorship—monarchical, bourgeois or proletarian—the solution of the ills and difficulties that beset society today?

In other words, shall we cure the evils of democracy by more democracy, or shall we cut the Gordian knot of popular government with the sword of dictatorship?

My answer is neither the one nor the other. I am against dictatorship and Fascism as I am opposed to parliamentary regimes and so-called political democracy.

Nazism has been justly called an attack on civilization. This characterization applies with equal force to every form of dictatorship; indeed, to every kind of suppression and coercive authority. For what is civilization in the true sense? All progress has been essentially an enlargement of the liberties of the individual with a corresponding decrease of the authority wielded over him by external forces. This holds good in the realm of physical as well as of political and economic existence. In the physical world man has progressed to the extent in which he has subdued the forces of nature and made them useful to himself. Primitive man made a step on the road to progress when he first produced fire and thus triumphed over darkness, when he chained the wind or harnessed water.

What role did authority or government play in human endeavor for betterment, in invention and discovery? None whatever, or at least none that was helpful. It has always been the individual that has accomplished every miracle in that sphere, usually in spite of the prohibition, persecution and interference by authority, human and divine.

Similarly, in the political sphere, the road of progress lay in getting away more and more from the authority of the tribal chief or of the clan, of prince and king, of government, of the State. Economically, progress has meant greater well-being of ever larger numbers. Culturally, it has signified the result of all the other achievements—greater independence, political, mental and psychic.

Regarded from this angle, the problem of man's relation

to the State assumes an entirely different significance. It is no more a question of whether dictatorship is preferable to democracy, or Italian Fascism superior to Hitlerism. A larger and far more vital question poses itself: Is political government, is the State, beneficial to mankind, and how does it affect the individual in the social scheme of things?

The individual is the true reality in life. A cosmos in himself, he does not exist for the State, nor for that abstraction called "society," or the "nation," which is only a collection of individuals. Man, the individual, has always been and necessarily is the sole source and motive power of evolution and progress. Civilization has been a continuous struggle of the individual or of groups of individuals against the State and even against "society," that is, against the majority subdued and hypnotized by the State and State worship. Man's greatest battles have been waged against man-made obstacles and artificial handicaps imposed upon him to paralyse his growth and development. Human thought has always been falsified by tradition and custom, and perverted false education in the interests of those who held power and enjoyed privileges. In other words, by the State and the ruling classes. This constant incessant conflict has been the history of mankind.

Individuality may be described as the consciousness of the individual as to what he is and how he lives. It is inherent in every human being and is a thing of growth. The State and social institutions come and go, but individuality remains and persists. The very essence of individuality is expression; the sense of dignity and independence is the soil wherein it thrives. Individuality is not the impersonal and mechanistic thing that the State treats as an "individual." The individual is not merely the result of heredity and environment, of cause and effect. He is that and a great deal more, a great deal else. The living man cannot be defined; he is the fountain-head of all life and all values; he is not a part of this or of that; he is a whole, an individual whole, a growing, changing, yet always constant whole.

Individuality is not to be confused with the various ideas and concepts of Individualism; much less with that "rugged individualism" which is only a masked attempt to repress and defeat the individual and his individuality. So-called Individualism is the social and economic *laissez-faire:* the exploitation of the masses by the classes by means of legal trickery, spiritual debasement and systematic indoctrination of the servile spirit, which process is known as "education." That corrupt and perverse "individualism" is the straitjacket of individuality. It has converted life into a degrading race for externals, for possession, for social prestige and supremacy. Its highest wisdom is "the devil take the hindmost."

This "rugged individualism" has inevitably resulted in the greatest modern slavery, the crassest class distinctions, driving millions to the breadline. "Rugged individualism" has meant all the "individualism" for the masters, while the people are regimented into a slave caste to serve a handful of self-seeking "supermen." America is perhaps the best representative of this kind of individualism, in whose name political tyranny and social oppression are defended and held up as virtues; while every aspiration and attempt of man to gain freedom and social opportunity to live is denounced as "un-American" and evil in the name of that same individualism.

There was a time when the State was unknown. In his natural condition man existed without any State or organized government. People lived as families in small communities; they tilled the soil and practiced the arts and crafts. The individual, and later the family, was the unit of social life where each was free and the equal of his neighbor. Human society then was not a State but an association; a voluntary association for mutual protection and benefit. The elders and more experienced members were the guides and advisers of the people. They helped to manage the affairs of the life, not to rule and dominate the individual.

Political government and the State were a much later development, growing out of the desire of the stronger to take advantage of the weaker, of the few against the many. The State, ecclesiastical and secular, served to give an appearance of legality and right to the wrong done by the few to the many. That appearance of right was necessary the easier to rule the people, because no government can exist without the consent of the people, consent open, tacit or assumed. Constitutionalism and democracy are the modern forms of that alleged consent; the consent being inoculated and indoctrinated by what is called "education," at home, in the church, and in every other phase of life.

That consent is the belief in authority, in the necessity for it. At its base is the doctrine that man is evil, vicious, and too incompetent to know what is good for him. On this all government and oppression is built. God and the State exist and are supported by this dogma.

Yet the State is nothing but a name. It is an abstraction. Like other similar conceptions—nation, race, humanity—it has no organic reality. To call the State an organism shows a diseased tendency to make a fetish of words.

The State is a term for the legislative and administrative machinery whereby certain business of the people is transacted, and badly so. There is nothing sacred, holy or mysterious about it. The State has no more conscience or moral mission than a commercial company for working a coal mine or running a railroad.

The State has no more existence than gods and devils have. They are equally the reflex and creation of man, for man, the individual, is the only reality. The State is but the shadow of man, the shadow of his opaqueness, of his ignorance and fear.

Life begins and ends with man, the individual. Without him there is no race, no humanity, no State. No, not even "society" is possible without man. It is the individual who lives, breathes and suffers. His development, his advance, has been a continuous struggle against the fetishes of his own creation and particularly so against the "State."

In former days religious authority fashioned political life in the image of the Church. The authority of the State, the "rights" of rulers came from on high; power, like faith, was divine. Philosophers have written thick volumes to prove the sanctity of the State; some have even clad it with infallibility and with god-like attributes. Some have talked themselves into the insane notion that the State is "super-human," the supreme reality, "the absolute."

Enquiry was condemned as blasphemy. Servitude was the highest virtue. By such precepts and training certain things came to be regarded as self-evident, as sacred of their truth, but because of constant and persistent repetition.

All progress has been essentially an unmasking of "divin-ity" and "mystery," of alleged sacred, eternal "truth"; it has been a gradual elimination of the abstract and the substitu-tion in its place of the real, the concrete. In short, of facts against fancy, of knowledge against ignorance, of light against darkness.

That slow and arduous liberation of the individual was not accomplished by the aid of the State. On the contrary, it was by continuous conflict, by a life-and-death struggle with the State, that even the smallest vestige of independence and freedom has been won. It has cost mankind much time and blood to secure what little it has gained so far from kings, czars and governments.

The great heroic figure of that long Golgotha has been Man. It has always been the individual, often alone and singly, at other times in unity and co-operation with others of his kind, who has fought and bled in the age-long battle against suppression and oppression, against the powers that enslave and degrade him.

More than that and more significant: It was man, the

individual, whose soul first rebelled against injustice and degradation; it was the individual who first conceived the idea of resistance to the conditions under which he chafed. In short, it is always the individual who is the parent of the liberating thought as well as of the deed.

This refers not only to political struggles, but to the entire gamut of human life and effort, in all ages and climes. It has always been the individual, the man of strong mind and will to liberty, who paved the way for every human advance, for every step toward a freer and better world; in science, philosophy and art, as well as in industry, whose genius rose to the heights, conceiving the "impossible," visualizing its realization and imbuing others with his enthusiasm to work and strive for it. Socially speaking, it was always the prophet, the seer, the idealist, who dreamed of a world more to his heart's desire and who served as the beacon light on the road to greater achievement.

The State, every government whatever its form, character or color—be it absolute or constitutional, monarchy or republic, Fascist, Nazi or Bolshevik—is by its very nature conservative, static, intolerant of change and opposed to it. Whatever changes it undergoes are always the result of pressure exerted upon it, pressure strong enough to compel the ruling powers to submit peaceably or otherwise, generally "otherwise"—that is, by revolution. Moreover, the inherent conservatism of government, of authority of any kind, unavoidably becomes reactionary. For two reasons: first, because it is in the nature of government not only to retain the power it has, but also to strengthen, widen and perpetuate it, nationally as well as internationally. The stronger authority grows, the greater the State and its power, the less it can tolerate a similar authority or political power alongside of itself. The psychology of government demands that its influence and prestige constantly grow, at home and abroad, and it exploits every opportunity to increase it. This tendency is motivated by the financial and commercial interests back of the government, represented and served by it. The fundamental *raison d'être* of every government to which, incidentally, historians of former days wilfully shut their eyes, has become too obvious now even for professors to ignore.

The other factor which impels governments to become even more conservative and reactionary is their inherent distrust of the individual and fear of individuality. Our political and social scheme cannot afford to tolerate the individual and his constant quest for innovation. In "self-defense" the State therefore suppresses, persecutes, punishes and even deprives the individual of life. It is aided in this by every institution that stands for the preservation of the existing order. It resorts to every form of violence and force, and its efforts are supported by the "moral indignation" of the majority against the heretic, the social dissenter and the political rebel—the majority for centuries drilled in State worship, trained in discipline and obedience and subdued by the awe of authority in the home, the school, the church and the press.

The strongest bulwark of authority is uniformity; the least divergence from it is the greatest crime. The wholesale mechanisation of modern life has increased uniformity a thousandfold. It is everywhere present, in habits, tastes, dress, thoughts and ideas. Its most concentrated dullness is "public opinion." Few have the courage to stand out against it. He who refuses to submit is at once labelled "queer," "different," and decried as a disturbing element in the comfortable stagnancy of modern life.

Perhaps even more than constituted authority, it is social uniformity and sameness that harass the individual most. His very "uniqueness," "separateness" and "differentiation" make him an alien, not only in his native place, but even in his own home. Often more so than the foreign born who generally falls in with the established.

In the true sense one's native land, with its background

of tradition, early impressions, reminiscences and other
things dear to one, is not enough to make sensitive human
beings feel at home. A certain atmosphere of "belonging,"
the consciousness of being "at one" with the people and environment, is more essential to one's feeling of home. This
holds good in relation to one's family, the smaller local
circle, as well as the larger phase of the life and activities
commonly called one's country. The individual whose
vision encompasses the whole world often feels nowhere so
hedged in and out of touch with his surroundings than in his
native land.

In pre-war times the individual could at least escape
national and family boredom. The whole world was open to
his longings and his quests. Now the world has become a
prison, and life continual solitary confinement. Especially
is this true since the advent of dictatorship, right and left.

Friedrich Nietzsche called the State a cold monster.
What would he have called the hideous beast in the garb of
modern dictatorship? Not that government had ever allowed much scope to the individual; but the champions of
the new State ideology do not grant even that much. "The
individual is nothing," they declare, "it is the collectivity
which counts." Nothing less than the complete surrender of
the individual will satisfy the insatiable appetite of the new
deity.

Strangely enough, the loudest advocates of this new
gospel are to be found among the British and American
intelligentsia. Just now they are enamored with the "dictatorship of the proletariat." In theory only, to be sure. In
practice, they still prefer the few liberties in their own
respective countries. They go to Russia for a short visit or
as salesmen of the "revolution," but they feel safer and
more comfortable at home.

Perhaps it is not only lack of courage which keeps these
good Britishers and Americans in their native lands rather
than in the millennium to come. Subconsciously there may
lurk the feeling that individuality remains the most funda-

mental fact of all human association, suppressed and persecuted yet never defeated, and in the long run the victor.

The "genius of man," which is but another name for personality and individuality, bores its way through all the caverns of dogma, through the thick walls of tradition and custom, defying all taboos, setting authority at naught, facing contumely and the scaffold—ultimately to be blessed as prophet and martyr by succeeding generations. But for the "genuis of man," that inherent, persistent quality of individuality, we would be still roaming the primeval forests.

Peter Kropotkin has shown what wonderful results this unique force of man's individuality has achieved when strengthened by co-operation with other individualities. The one-sided and entirely inadequate Darwinian theory of the struggle for existence received its biological and sociological completion from the great Anarchist scientist and thinker. In his profound work, *Mutual Aid,* Kropotkin shows that in the animal kingdom, as well as in human society, co-operation—as opposed to internecine strife and struggle—has worked for the survival and evolution of the species. He demonstrated that only mutual aid and voluntary co-operation—not the omnipotent, all-devastating State—can create the basis for a free individual and associational life.

At present the individual is the pawn of the zealots of dictatorship and the equally obsessed zealots of "rugged individualism." The excuse of the former is its claim of a new objective. The latter does not even make a pretense of anything new. As a matter of fact "rugged individualism" has learned nothing and forgotten nothing. Under its guidance the brute struggle for physical existence is still kept up. Strange as it may seem, and utterly absurd as it is, the struggle for physical survival goes merrily on though the necessity for it has entirely disappeared. Indeed, the struggle is being continued apparently because there is no necessity for it. Does not so-called overproduction prove it? Is not the world-wide economic crisis an eloquent demon-

stration that the struggle for existence is being maintained
by the blindness of "rugged individualism" at the risk of its
own destruction?

One of the insane characteristics of this struggle is the
complete negation of the relation of the producer to the
things he produces. The average worker has no inner point
of contact with the industry he is employed in, and he is a
stranger to the process of production of which he is a
mechanical part. Like any other cog of the machine, he is
replaceable at any time by other similar depersonalized
human beings.

The intellectual proletarian, though he foolishly thinks
himself a free agent, is not much better off. He, too, has as
little choice or self-direction, in his particular métier, as his
brother who works with his hands. Material considerations
and desire for greater social prestige are usually the deciding factors in the vocation of the intellectual. Added to
these is the tendency to follow in the footsteps of family
tradition, and become doctors, lawyers, teachers, engineers,
etc. The groove requires less effort and personality. In
consequence nearly everybody is out of place in our
present scheme of things. The masses plod on, partly because their senses have been dulled by the deadly routine of
work and because they must eke out an existence. This
applies with even greater force to the political fabric of
today. There is no place in its texture for free choice of
independent thought and activity. There is a place only for
voting and tax-paying puppets.

The interests of the State and those of the individual
differ fundamentally and are antagonistic. The State and
the political and economic institutions it supports can exist
only by fashioning the individual to their particular purpose; training him to respect "law and order"; teaching him
obedience, submission and unquestioning faith in the wisdom and justice of government; above all, loyal service and
complete self-sacrifice when the State commands it, as in
war. The State puts itself and its interests even above the

claims of religion and of God. It punishes religious or conscientious scruples against individuality because there is no individuality without liberty, and liberty is the greatest menace to authority.

The struggle of the individual against these tremendous odds is the more difficult—too often dangerous to life and limb—because it is not truth or falsehood which serves as the criterion of the opposition he meets. It is not the validity or usefulness of his thought or activity which rouses against him the forces of the State and of "public opinion." The persecution of the innovator and protestant has always been inspired by fear on the part of constituted authority of having its infallibility questioned and its power undermined.

Man's true liberation, individual and collective, lies in his emancipation from authority and from the belief in it. All human evolution has been a struggle in that direction and for that object. It is not invention and mechanics which constitute development. The ability to travel at the rate of 100 miles an hour is no evidence of being civilized. True civilization is to be measured by the individual, the unit of all social life; by his individuality and the extent to which it is free to have its being, to grow and expand unhindered by invasive and coercive authority.

Socially speaking, the criterion of civilization and culture is the degree of liberty and economic opportunity which the individual enjoys; of social and international unity and co-operation unrestricted by man-made laws and other artificial obstacles; by the absence of privileged castes and by the reality of liberty and human dignity; in short, by the true emancipation of the individual.

Political absolutism has been abolished because men have realized in the course of time that absolute power is evil and destructive. But the same thing is true of all power, whether it be the power of privilege, of money, of the priest, of the politician or of so-called democracy. In its effect on individuality it matters little what the particular character of coercion is—whether it be as black as Fascism, as yellow as Nazism or as pretentiously red as Bolshevism. It is power that corrupts and degrades both master and slave and it makes no difference whether the power is wielded by an autocrat, by parliament or Soviets. More pernicious than the power of a dictator is that of a class; the most terrible— the tyranny of a majority.

The long process of history has taught man that division and strife mean death, and that unity and co-operation advance his cause, multiply his strength and further his welfare. The spirit of government has always worked against the social application of this vital lesson, except where it served the State and aided its own particular interests. It is this anti-progressive and anti-social spirit of the State and of the privileged castes back of it which has been responsible for the bitter struggle between man and man. The individual and ever larger groups of individuals are beginning to see beneath the surface of the established order of things. No longer are they so blinded as in the past by the glare and tinsel of the State idea, and of the "blessings" of "rugged individualism." Man is reaching out for the wider scope of human relations which liberty alone can give. For true liberty is not a mere scrap of paper called "constitution," "legal right" or "law." It is not an abstraction derived from the non-reality known as "the State." It is not the negative thing of being free from something, because with such freedom you may starve to death. Real freedom, true liberty is positive: it is freedom to something; it is the liberty to be, to do; in short, the liberty of actual and active opportunity.

That sort of liberty is not a gift: it is the natural right of man, of every human being. It cannot be given; it cannot be conferred by any law or government. The need of it, the longing for it, is inherent in the individual. Disobedience to every form of coercion is the instinctive expression of it. Rebellion and revolution are the more or less conscious attempt to achieve it. Those manifestations, individual and social, are fundamentally expressions of the values of man. That those values may be nurtured, the community must realize that its greatest and most lasting asset is the unit— the individual.

In religion, as in politics, people speak of abstractions and believe they are dealing with realities. But when it does come to the real and the concrete, most people seem to lose vital touch with it. It may well be because reality alone is too matter-of-fact, too cold to enthuse the human soul. It can be aroused to enthusiasm only by things out of the commonplace, out of the ordinary. In other words, the Ideal is the spark that fires the imagination and hearts of men. Some ideal is needed to rouse man out of the inertia and humdrum of his existence and turn the abject slave into an heroic figure.

Right here, of course, comes the Marxist objector who has outmarxed Marx himself. To such a one, man is a mere puppet in the hands of that metaphysical Almighty called economic determinism or, more vulgarly, the class struggle. Man's will, individual and collective, his psychic life and mental orientation count for almost nothing with our Marxist and do not affect his conception of human history.

No intelligent student will deny the importance of the economic factor in the social growth and development of mankind. But only narrow and wilful dogmatism can persist in remaining blind to the important role played by an idea as conceived by the imagination and aspirations of the individual.

It were vain and unprofitable to attempt to balance one factor as against another in human experience. No one single factor in the complex of individual or social behavior can be designated as the factor of decisive quality. We know too little, and may never know enough, of human psychology to weigh and measure the relative values of this or that factor in determining man's conduct. To form such dogmas in their social connotation is nothing short of bigotry; yet, perhaps, it has its uses, for the very attempt to do so proved the persistence of the human will and confutes the Marxists.

Fortunately even some Marxists are beginning to see that all is not well with the Marxian creed. After all, Marx was but human—all too human—hence by no means infallible. The practical application of economic determinism in Russia is helping to clear the minds of the more intelligent Marxists. This can be seen in the transvaluation of Marxian values going on in Socialist and even Communist ranks in some European countries. They are slowly realising that their theory has overlooked the human element, *den Menschen,* as a Socialist paper put it. Important as the economic factor is, it is not enough. The rejuvenation of mankind needs the inspiration and energising force of an ideal.

Such an ideal I see in Anarchism. To be sure, not in the popular misrepresentations of Anarchism spread by the worshippers of the State and authority. I mean the philosophy of a new social order based on the released energies of the individual and the free association of liberated individuals.

Of all social theories Anarchism alone steadfastly proclaims that society exists for man, not man for society. The sole legitimate purpose of society is to serve the needs and advance the aspiration of the individual. Only by doing so can it justify its existence and be an aid to progress and culture.

The political parties and men savagely scrambling for power will scorn me as hopelessly out of tune with our time. I cheerfully admit the charge. I find comfort in the assurance that their hysteria lacks enduring quality. Their hosanna is but of the hour.

Man's yearning for liberation from all authority and power will never be soothed by their cracked song. Man's quest for freedom from every shackle is eternal. It must and will go on.

PART TWO

SOCIAL INSTITUTIONS

PREFACE TO PART TWO

This section consists of a number of essays and speeches in which Goldman examines the extent to which society's major social institutions manipulate and control us. Supplementing the State's legal and military coercive paraphernalia, the schools, the family, the arts, the churches, moral attitudes—all reach into the corners of our lives to regulate our development and stifle our choices. Examining how each ties in with the system, Goldman proposes basic changes to bring about maximum freedom, even in such an ordinarily apolitical phenomenon as jealousy.

Of the ten lectures that follow, all but two were first published in *Mother Earth*. The pieces on "The Social Importance of the Modern School" (with the fragment on sex education that follows it) and "Jealousy," both undated, are from the Manuscript Division of the New York Public Library; they were probably written around 1912. "The Child and Its Enemies" appeared in April 1906, in the second issue of *Mother Earth*. "Victims of Morality" appeared in March and "The Failure of Christianity" in April of 1913; "The Philosophy of Atheism" in February of 1916; all three were subsequently circulated as pamphlets. "Intellectual Proletarians" was published in the February 1914 issue of *Mother Earth*. The remaining pieces ("The Tragedy of Women's Emancipation," "The Traffic in Women," and "Marriage and Love"), dealing with aspects of what was then called the Woman Question, were included by Goldman, along with two other essays on the subject, in her 1911 collection *Anarchism and Other Essays*.

The Woman Question was one to which Goldman was most sensitive and responsive. Her outspoken attitude toward sex and marriage accounted for much of her notoriety. Despite her romantic view of love, all her life she suffered and raged at being treated by the men she was involved with as a "mere woman," a sex object. At the same time, her libertarian soul was outraged by the deadly puritan hypocrisy and double standard which regulated all relations between the sexes. Unlike the suffragists, most of whom wanted to bring men under the same restrictions as women, she advocated free love and freedom of life-style for everyone. But unlike many bohemians who considered such matters strictly personal, she saw them as reflecting an authoritarian and thoroughly repressive system which used women as sex objects, breeders, and cheap labor. Neither getting the vote nor finding personal solutions was sufficient to change women's lot.[1] Prostitution seemed to Goldman the outstanding example and perfect model of the rampant social and economic exploitation of women, all of whom, she contended, were forced one way or another to sell their bodies or else become "compulsory vestals."

Though she sometimes referred to the "mother instinct," at other times she inveighed against the motherhood myth and actively fought the laws against birth control. Carrying her thought into action, she decided against motherhood for herself by refusing to have an operation which would have corrected her infertility, and, believing that every woman had a right to make the same choice, she challenged the birth-control laws until

---

[1] In this respect, she was closer to the radical feminists of the 1960's and 1970's than to the feminists of her own time. For a discussion of the feminist aspects of Emma Goldman's career, see Alix Shulman, "Emma Goldman, Anarchist and Feminist" in *Women: A Journal of Liberation* (Spring 1970), Vol. I, no. 3.

she was jailed. "In 1916 Emma Goldman was sent to prison for advocating that 'women need not always keep their mouths shut and their wombs open,' " wrote Margaret Anderson, editor of *The Little Review*.

Implementing her radical views of education, Goldman helped establish several Modern Schools, one in the anarchist community in Stelton, New Jersey, another in Manhattan. These were partly modeled on the European schools of Sebastian Faure and Francisco Ferrer, the latter a Spanish educator whose execution in Spain in 1909 for his educational and political activities became an anarchist *cause célèbre*. At the time of Goldman's deportation, the local Modern Schools were shut down, partly because of her connection with them. The following statement of the New York State Legislature's Seditious Activities Committee Report follows several pages of testimony, including that of Berkman and Goldman, on the principles of anarchism.

> Stripped of its verbiage the above examination indicates but one thing, and that is that in the Ferrer or Modern School, run by anarchists until a recent date in the City of New York, children at the most impressionable age were taught an utter disregard for our laws, and imbued with the idea that a state of anarchy was the true blissful state, and that this should be the aim and purpose of the little children who, in all their innocence, believe what their elders tell them. That such an institution should have been allowed to exist for almost ten years is not a very high compliment to the City of New York.[2]

Goldman's religious iconoclasm seems to have been only a little less shocking to public opinion than her views on sex; indeed, she could never pass up an opportunity for irreverence, participating in mock religious services and redefining the sacraments. She was temporarily shunned by all the women in her cellblock at Blackwell's Island Penitentiary because of her atheism; her name was anathema to orthodox Jewish communities; a

[2] New York State Legislative Committee, *Revolutionary Radicalism*, Part I, Vol. II, Albany, J. B. Lyon Co., 1920, p. 1447.

liberal Detroit minister who invited her to speak from his pulpit was forced to resign his post and move out of town in the ensuing scandal. But Goldman's atheism, like her view of sex, was grounded in her anti-institutional libertarianism, and her own social idealism was itself almost religious in character and intensity. As Margaret Anderson once said of her disparagingly "She believed in people." A rabbi who heard her lecture a large conference of clergymen on atheism probably came closer than the public to understanding her antireligious stand. "In spite of all Miss Goldman has said against religion," he announced, "she is the most religious person I know."

The Child and Its Enemies

Is the child to be considered as an individuality, or as an object to be moulded according to the whims and fancies of those about it? This seems to me to be the most important question to be answered by parents and educators. And whether the child is to grow from within, whether all that craves expression will be permitted to come forth toward the light of day; or whether it is to be kneaded like dough through external forces, depends upon the proper answer to this vital question.

The longing of the best and noblest of our times makes for the strongest individualities. Every sensitive being abhors the idea of being treated as a mere machine or as a mere parrot of conventionality and respectability; the human being craves recognition of his kind.

It must be borne in mind that it is through the channel of the child that the development of the mature man must go, and that the present ideas of the educating or training of the latter in the school and the family—even the family of the liberal or radical—are such as to stifle the natural growth of the child.

Every institution of our day, the family, the State, our

moral codes, sees in every strong, beautiful, uncompromising personality a deadly enemy; therefore every effort is
being made to cramp human emotion and originality of
thought in the individual into a strait-jacket from its
earliest infancy; or to shape every human being according
to one pattern; not into a well-rounded individuality, but
into a patient work slave, professional automaton, tax-
paying citizen, or righteous moralist. If one, nevertheless,
meets with real spontaneity (which, by the way, is a rare
treat), it is not due to our method of rearing or educating
the child: the personality often asserts itself, regardless of
official and family barriers. Such a discovery should be
celebrated as an unusual event, since the obstacles placed in
the way of growth and development of character are so
numerous that it must be considered a miracle if it retains
its strength and beauty and survives the various attempts at
crippling that which is most essential to it.

Indeed, he who has freed himself from the fetters of the
thoughtlessness and stupidity of the commonplace; he who
can stand without moral crutches, without the approval of
public opinion—private laziness, Friedrich Nietzsche called
it—may well intone a high and voluminous song of independence and freedom; he has gained the right to it through
fierce and fiery battles. These battles already begin at the
most delicate age.

The child shows its individual tendencies in its play, in its
questions, in its association with people and things. But it
has to struggle with everlasting external interference in its
world of thought and emotion. It must not express itself in
harmony with its nature, with its growing personality. It
must become a thing, an object. Its questions are met with
narrow, conventional, ridiculous replies, mostly based on
falsehoods; and, when, with large, wondering, innocent
eyes, it wishes to behold the wonders of the world, those
about it quickly lock the windows and doors, and keep the

delicate human plant in a hothouse atmosphere, where it can neither breathe nor grow freely.

Zola, in his novel *Fecundity*, maintains that large sections of people have declared death to the child, have conspired against the birth of the child—a very horrible picture indeed, yet the conspiracy entered into by civilization against the growth and making of character seems to me far more terrible and disastrous, because of the slow and gradual destruction of its latent qualities and traits and the stupefying and crippling effect thereof upon its social well-being.

Since every effort in our educational life seems to be directed toward making of the child a being foreign to itself, it must of necessity produce individuals foreign to one another, and in everlasting antagonism with each other.

The ideal of the average pedagogist is not a complete, well-rounded, original being; rather does he seek that the result of his art or pedagogy shall be automatons of flesh and blood, to best fit into the treadmill of society and the emptiness and dullness of our lives. Every home, school, college and university stands for dry, cold utilitarianism, over-flooding the brain of the pupil with a tremendous amount of ideas, handed down from generations past. "Facts and data," as they are called, constitute a lot of information, well enough perhaps to maintain every form of authority and to create much awe for the importance of possession, but only a great handicap to a true understanding of the human soul and its place in the world.

Truths dead and forgotten long ago, conceptions of the world and its people, covered with mould, even during the times of our grandmothers, are being hammered into the heads of our young generation. Eternal change, thousand-fold variations, continual innovation are the essence of life. Professional pedagogy knows nothing of it, the systems of education are being arranged into files, classified and numbered. They lack the strong fertile seed which, falling on rich soil, enables them to grow to great heights; they are worn and incapable of awakening spontaneity of character. Instructors and teachers, with dead souls, operate with dead values. Quantity is forced to take the place of quality. The consequences thereof are inevitable.

In whatever direction one turns, eagerly searching for human beings who do not measure ideas and emotions with the yardstick of expediency, one is confronted with the products, the herdlike drilling instead of the result of spontaneous and innate characteristics working themselves out in freedom.

> "No traces now I see
> Whatever of a spirit's agency.
> 'Tis drilling, nothing more."

These words of Faust fit our methods of pedagogy perfectly. Take, for instance, the way history is being taught in our schools. See how the events of the world become like a cheap puppet show, where a few wire-pullers are supposed to have directed the course of development of the entire human race.

And the history of *our own* nation! Was it not chosen by Providence to become the leading nation on earth? And does it not tower mountain high over other nations? Is it not the gem of the ocean? Is it not incomparably virtuous, ideal, and brave? The result of such ridiculous teaching is a dull, shallow patriotism, blind to its own limitations, with bull-like stubbornness, utterly incapable of judging of the capacities of other nations. This is the way the spirit of youth is emasculated, deadened through an over-estimation of one's own value. No wonder public opinion can be so easily manufactured.

"Predigested food" should be inscribed over every hall of learning as a warning to all who do not wish to lose their own personalities and their original sense of judgment, who, instead, would be content with a large amount of empty and shallow shells. This may suffice as a recognition of the manifold hindrances placed in the way of an independent mental development of the child.

Equally numerous, and not less important, are the difficulties that confront the emotional life of the young. Must not one suppose that parents should be united to children by the most tender and delicate chords? One should suppose it; yet, sad as it may be, it is, nevertheless, true, that parents are the first to destroy the inner riches of their children.

The Scriptures tell us that God created Man in His own image, which has by no means proven a success. Parents follow the bad example of their heavenly master; they use every effort to shape and mould the child according to their image. They tenaciously cling to the idea that the child is merely part of themselves—an idea as false as it is injurious, and which only increases the misunderstanding of the soul of the child, of the necessary consequences of enslavement and subordination thereof.

As soon as the first rays of consciousness illuminate the mind and heart of the child, it instinctively begins to compare its own personality with the personality of those about it. How many hard and cold stone cliffs meet its large wondering gaze? Soon enough it is confronted with the painful reality that it is here only to serve as inanimate matter for parents and guardians, whose authority alone gives it shape and form.

The terrible struggle of the thinking man and woman against political, social and moral conventions owes its origin to the family, where the child is ever compelled to battle against the internal and external use of force. The categorical imperatives: you shall! you must! this is right! that is wrong! this is true! that is false! shower like a violent rain upon the unsophisticated head of the young being and impress upon its sensibilities that it has to bow before the long-established and hard notions of thoughts and emotions. Yet the latent qualities and instincts seek to assert their own peculiar methods of seeking the foundation of things, of distinguishing between what is commonly called wrong, true or false. It is bent upon going its own way, since it is composed of the same nerves, muscles and blood, even as those who assume to direct its destiny. I fail to understand how parents hope that their children will ever grow up into independent, self-reliant spirits, when they strain every effort to abridge and curtail the various activities of their children, the plus in quality and character, which differentiates their offspring from themselves, and by the virtue of which they are eminently equipped carriers of new, invigorating ideas. A young delicate tree that is being clipped and cut by the gardener in order to give it an artificial form will never reach the majestic height and the beauty it would if allowed to grow in nature and freedom.

When the child reaches adolescence, it meets, added to the home and school restrictions, with a vast amount of hard traditions of social morality. The cravings of love and sex are met with absolute ignorance by the majority of parents, who consider it as something indecent and improper, something disgraceful, almost criminal, to be suppressed and fought like some terrible disease. The love and tender feelings in the young plant are turned into vulgarity and coarseness through the stupidity of those surrounding it, so that everything fine and beautiful is either crushed altogether or hidden in the innermost depths, as a great sin, that dares not face the light.

What is more astonishing is the fact that parents will strip themselves of everything, will sacrifice everything for the physical well-being of their child, will wake nights and stand in fear and agony before some physical ailment of their beloved one; but will remain cold and indifferent, without the slightest understanding, before the soul cravings and the yearnings of their child, neither hearing nor wishing to hear the loud knocking of the young spirit that demands recognition. On the contrary, they will stifle the beautiful voice of spring, of a new life of beauty and splendor of love; they will put the long lean finger of authority upon the tender throat and not allow vent to the silvery song of the individual growth, of the beauty of character, of the strength of love and human relation, which alone make life worth living.

And yet these parents imagine that they mean best for the child, and for aught I know, some really do; but their best means absolute death and decay to the bud in the making. After all, they are but imitating their own masters in State, commercial, social and moral affairs, by forcibly suppressing every independent attempt to analyze the ills of society and every sincere effort toward the abolition of these ills; never able to grasp the eternal truth that every method they employ serves as the greatest impetus to bring forth a greater longing for freedom and a deeper zeal to fight for it.

That compulsion is bound to awaken resistance, every parent and teacher ought to know. Great surprise is being expressed over the fact that the majority of children of radical parents are either altogether opposed to the ideas of the latter, many of them moving along the old antiquated paths, or that they are indifferent to the new thoughts and teachings of social regeneration. And yet there is nothing unusual in that. Radical parents, though emancipated from the belief of ownership in the human soul, still cling tenaciously to the notion that they own the child, and that they have the right to exercise their authority over it. So they set out to mould and form the child according to their own conception of what is right and wrong, forcing their ideas upon it with the same vehemence that the average Catholic parent uses. And, with the latter, they hold out the necessity before the young "to do as I tell you and not as I do." But

the impressionable mind of the child realizes early enough
that the lives of their parents are in contradiction to the
ideas they represent; that, like the good Christian who fervently prays on Sunday, yet continues to break the Lord's
commands the rest of the week, the radical parent arraigns
God, priesthood, church, government, domestic authority,
yet continues to adjust himself to the condition he abhors.
Just so, the Freethought parent can proudly boast that his
son of four will recognize the picture of Thomas Paine or
Ingersoll, or that he knows that the idea of God is stupid.
Or the Social Democratic father can point to his little
girl of six and say, "Who wrote *The Capital,* dearie?" "Karl
Marx, pa!" Or the Anarchistic mother can make it
known that her daughter's name is Louise Michel, Sophia
Perovskaya, or that she can recite the revolutionary poems
of Herwegh, Freiligrath or Shelley, and that she will point
out the faces of Spencer, Bakunin or Moses Harman almost
anywhere.

These are by no means exaggerations; they are sad facts
that I have met with in my experience with radical parents.
What are the results of such methods of biasing the mind?
The following is the consequence, and not very infrequent,
either. The child, being fed on one-sided, set and fixed
ideas, soon grows weary of rehashing the beliefs of its
parents, and it sets out in quest of new sensations; no matter
how inferior and shallow the new experience may be, the
human mind cannot endure sameness and monotony. So it
happens that that boy or girl, over-fed on Thomas Paine,
will land in the arms of the Church, or they will vote for
imperialism only to escape the drag of economic determinism and scientific socialism, or that they open a shirt-
waist factory and cling to their right of accumulating property only to find relief from the old-fashioned communism
of their father. Or that the girl will marry the next best man,
provided he can make a living, only to run away from the
everlasting talk on variety.

Such a condition of affairs may be very painful to the parents who wish their children to follow in their path, yet I look upon them as very refreshing and encouraging psychological forces. They are the greatest guarantee that the independent mind, at least, will always resist every external and foreign force exercised over the human heart and head.

Some will ask, what about weak natures, must they not be protected? Yes, but to be able to do that, it will be necessary to realize that education of children is not synonymous with herdlike drilling and training. If education should really mean anything at all, it must insist upon the free growth and development of the innate forces and tendencies of the child. In this way alone can we hope for the free individual and eventually also for a free community, which shall make interference and coercion of human growth impossible.

The Social Importance
of the Modern School

To fully grasp the social importance of the Modern School, we must understand first the school as it is being operated today, and secondly the idea underlying the modern educational movement.

What, then, is the school of today, no matter whether public, private, or parochial?

It is for the child what the prison is for the convict and the barracks for the soldier—a place where everything is being used to break the will of the child, and then to pound, knead, and shape it into a being utterly foreign to itself.

I do not mean to say that this process is carried on consciously; it is but a part of a system which can maintain itself only through absolute discipline and uniformity; therein, I think, lies the greatest crime of present-day society.

Naturally, the method of breaking man's will must begin at a very early age; that is, with the child, because at that time the human mind is most pliable; just as acrobats and contortionists, in order to achieve skill over their muscles, begin to drill and exercise when the muscles are still pliable.

The very notion that knowledge can be obtained only in school through systematic drilling, and that school time is the only period during which knowledge may be acquired, is in itself so preposterous as to completely condemn our system of education as arbitrary and useless.

Supposing anyone were to suggest that the best results for the individual and society could be derived through compulsory feeding. Would not the most ignorant rebel against such a stupid procedure? And yet the stomach has far greater adaptability to almost any situation than the brain. With all that, we find it quite natural to have compulsory mental feeding.

Indeed, we actually consider ourselves superior to other nations, because we have evolved a compulsory brain tube through which, for a certain number of hours every day, and for so many years, we can force into the child's mind a large quantity of mental nutrition.

Emerson said sixty years ago, "We are students of words; we are shut up in schools and colleges for ten or fifteen years and come out a bag of wind, a memory of words, and do not know a thing." Since these wise words were written, America has reached the very omnipotence of a school system, and yet we are face to face with the fact of complete impotence in results.

The great harm done by our system of education is not so much that it teaches nothing worth knowing, that it helps to perpetuate privileged classes, that it assists them in the criminal procedure of robbing and exploiting the masses; the harm of the system lies in its boastful proclamation that it stands for true education, thereby enslaving the masses a great deal more than could an absolute ruler.

Almost everyone in America, liberals and radicals included, believes that the Modern School for European countries is a great idea, but that it is unnecessary for us. "Look at our opportunities," they proclaim.

As a matter of fact, the modern methods of education are

needed in America much more than in Spain or in any other country, because nowhere is there such little regard for personal liberty and originality of thought. Uniformity and imitation is our motto. From the very moment of birth until life ceases this motto is imposed upon every child as the only possible path to success. There is not a teacher or educator in America who could keep his position if he dared show the least tendency to break through uniformity and imitation.

In New York a high school teacher, Henrietta Rodman, in her literature class, explained to her girls the relation of George Eliot to Lewes.* A little girl raised in a Catholic home, and the supreme result of discipline and uniformity, related the classroom incident to her mother. The latter reported it to the priest, and the priest saw fit to report Miss Rodman to the Board of Education. Remember, in America the State and Church are separate institutions, yet the Board of Education called Miss Rodman to account and made it very clear to her that if she were to permit herself any such liberties again she would be dismissed from her post.

In Newark, New Jersey, Mr. Stewart, a very efficient high school teacher, presided at the Ferrer Memorial meeting, thereby insulting the Catholics of that city, who promptly entered a protest with the Board of Education. Mr. Stewart was put on trial and was compelled to apologize in order to keep his position. In fact, our halls of learning, from the public school to the university, are but strait-jackets for teachers as well as pupils, simply because a strait-jacket of the mind is the greatest guarantee for a dull, colorless, inert mass moving like a pack of sheep between two high walls.

I think it is high time that all advanced people should be

* Editor's note: George Eliot lived for many years with George Henry Lewes, and was ostracized for this relationship.

clear on this point, that our present system of economic and political dependence is maintained not so much by wealth and courts as it is by an inert mass of humanity, drilled and pounded into absolute uniformity, and that the school today represents the most efficient medium to accomplish that end. I do not think that I am exaggerating, nor that I stand alone in this position; I quote from an article in *Mother Earth* of September 1910 by Dr. Hailman, a brilliant schoolteacher with nearly twenty-five years of experience, and this is what he has to say:

> Our schools have failed because they rest upon compulsion and restraint. Children are arbitrarily commanded what, when, and how to do things. Initiative and originality, self-expression, and individuality are tabooed. . . It is deemed possible and important that all should be interested in the same things, in the same sequence, and at the same time. The worship of the idol of uniformity continues openly and quietly. And to make doubly sure that there shall be no heterodox interference, school supervision dictates every step and even the manner and mode of it, so that disturbing initiative or originality and the rest may not enter by way of the teacher. We still hear overmuch of order, of methods, of system, of discipline, in the death dealing sense of long ago; and these aim at repression rather than at the liberation of life.
>
> Under the circumstances teachers are mere tools, automatons who perpetuate a machine that turns out automatons. They persist in forcing their knowledge upon the pupil, ignore or repress their instinctive yearning for use and beauty, and drag or drive them in an ill-named, logical course, into spiritless drill. They substitute for natural inner incentives that fear no difficulty and shrink from no effort, incentives of external compulsion and artificial bribes, which, usually based upon fear or upon anti-social greed or rivalry, arrest development of joy in the work for its own sake, are hostile to purposeful doing, quench the ardor of creative initiative and the fervor of social service, and sub-

stitute for these abiding motives, transient, perishable caprice.

It goes without saying that the child becomes stunted, that its mind is dulled, and that its very being becomes warped, thus making it unfit to take its place in the social struggle as an independent factor. Indeed, there is nothing hated so much in the world today as independent factors in whatever line.

The Modern School repudiates utterly this pernicious and truly criminal system of education. It maintains that there is no more harmony between compulsion and education than there is between tyranny and liberty; the two being as far apart as the poles. The underlying principle of the Modern School is this: education is a process of drawing out, not of driving in; it aims at the possibility that the child should be left free to develop spontaneously, directing his own efforts and choosing the branches of knowledge which he desires to study. That, therefore, the teacher, instead of opposing, or presenting as authoritative his own opinions, predilections, or beliefs should be a sensitive instrument responding to the needs of the child as they are at any time manifested; a channel through which the child may attain so much of the ordered knowledge of the world, as he shows himself ready to receive and assimilate. Scientific, demonstrable facts in the Modern School will be presented as facts, but no interpretation of theory—social, political, or religious—will be presented as having in itself such sanction, or intellectual sovereignty, as precludes the right to criticize or disbelieve.

The Modern School, then, must be *libertarian*. Each pupil must be left free to his true self. The main object of the school is the promotion of the harmonious development of all of the faculties latent in the child. There can be no coercion in the Modern School, nor any such rules or regulations. The teacher may well evoke, through his own enthusiasm and nobility of character, the latent enthusiasm and nobility of his pupils; but he will overstep the liberties of his function as soon as he attempts to force the child in any way whatsoever. To discipline a child is invariably to set up a false moral standard, since the child is thereby led to suppose that punishment is something to be imposed upon him from without, by a person more powerful, instead of being a natural and unavoidable reaction and result of his own acts.

The social purpose of the Modern School is to develop the individual through knowledge and the free play of characteristic traits, so that he may become a social being, because he has learned to know himself, to know his relation to his fellow-men, and to realize himself in a harmonious blending with society.

Naturally, the Modern School does not propose to throw aside all that educators have learned through the mistakes of the past. But though it will accept from past experience, it must at all times employ methods and materials that will tend to promote the self-expression of the child. To illustrate: the way composition is taught in our present-day school, the child is rarely allowed to use either judgment or free initiative. The Modern School aims to teach composition through original themes on topics chosen by the pupils from experience in their own lives; stories and sketches are suggested by the imaginative or actual experience of the pupils.

This new method immediately opens up a new vista of possibilities. Children are extremely impressionable, and very vivid; besides not yet having been pounded into uniformity, their experience will inevitably contain much more originality, as well as beauty, than that of the teacher; also it is reasonable to assume that the child is intensely interested in the things which concern its life. Must not, then, composition based upon the experience and imagination of the pupil furnish greater material for thought and development than can be derived from the clocklike method of today which is, at best, nothing but imitation?

Everyone at all conversant with the present method of education knows that in teaching history the child is being taught what Carlyle has called a "compilation of lies." A king here, a president there, and a few heroes who are to be worshipped after death make up the usual material which constitutes history. The Modern School, in teaching history, must bring before the child a panorama of dramatic periods and incidents, illustrative of the main movements and epochs of human development. It must, therefore, help to develop an appreciation in the child of the struggle of past generations for progress and liberty, and thereby develop a respect for every truth that aims to emancipate the human race. The underlying principle of the Modern School is to make impossible the mere instructionist: the instructionist blinded by his paltry specialty to the full life it is meant to serve; the narrow-minded worshipper of uniformity; the small-souled reactionary who cries for "more spelling and arithmetic and less life"; the self-sufficient apostle of consolation, who in his worship of what has been fails to see what is and what ought to be; the stupid adherent of a decaying age who makes war upon the fresh vigor that is sprouting from the soil—all these the Modern School aims to replace by life, the true interpreter of education.

A new day is dawning when the school will serve life in all its phases and reverently lift each human child to its appropriate place in a common life of beneficent social efficiency, whose motto will be not uniformity and discipline but freedom, expansion, good will, and joy for each and all.

Sex Education

An educational system which refuses to see in the young budding and sprouting personality independence of mind and wholesomeness of a freely developed body will certainly not admit the necessity of recognizing the phase of sex in the child. Children and adolescent people have their young dreams, their vague forebodings of the sexual urge. The senses open slowly like the petals of a bud, the approaching sex maturity enhances the sensibilities and intensifies the emotions. New vistas, fantastic pictures, colorful adventures follow one another in swift procession before the sex-awakened child. It is conceded by all sex psychologists that adolescence is the most sensitive and susceptible period for unusual fanciful and poetic impressions. The radiance of youth—alas, of so brief duration—is inseparably bound up with the awakening of eroticism. It is the period when ideas and ideals, aims and motives, begin to fashion themselves in the human breast; that which is ugly and mean in life still remains covered with a fantastic veil, because the age which marks the change from child to youth is indeed the most exquisitely poetic and magical phase in all human existence.

Puritans and moralists leave nothing undone to mar and besmirch this magic time. The child may not know his own personality, much less be conscious of its sex force. Puritans build a high wall around this great human fact; not a ray of light is permitted to penetrate through the conspiracy of silence. To keep the child in all matters of sex in dense ignorance is considered by educators as a sort of moral duty. Sexual manifestations are treated as if they were tendencies to crime, yet puritans and moralists more than anyone else know from personal experience that sex is a tremendous factor. Nevertheless, they continue to banish everything that might relieve the harassed mind and soul of the child, that might free him from fear and anxiety.

The same educators also know the evil and sinister results of ignorance in sex matters. Yet, they have neither understanding nor humanity enough to break down the wall which puritanism has built around sex. They are like parents who, having been maltreated in their childhood, now ill-treat and torture their children to avenge themselves upon their own childhood. In their youth the parents and educators had it dinned into their ears that sex is low, unclean, and loathsome. Therefore, they straightway proceed to din the same things into their children.

It certainly requires independent judgment and great courage to free oneself from such impressions. The two-legged animals called parents lack both. Hence, they make their children pay for the outrage perpetrated upon them by their parents—which only goes to prove that it takes centuries of enlightenment to undo the harm wrought by traditions and habits. According to these traditions, "innocence" has become synonymous with "ignorance"; ignorance is indeed considered the highest virtue, and represents the "triumph" of puritanism. But in reality, these traditions represent the crimes of puritanism, and have resulted in irreparable internal and external suffering to the child and youth.

It is essential that we realize once and for all that man is much more of a sex creature than a moral creature. The former is inherent, the other is grafted on. Whenever the dull moral demand conflicts with the sexual urge, the latter invariably conquers. But how? In secrecy, in lying and cheating, in fear and nerve-racking anxiety. Verily, not in the sexual tendency lies filth, but in the minds and hearts of the Pharisees: they pollute even the innocent, delicate manifestations in the life of the child. One often observes groups of children together, whispering, telling one another the legend of the stork. They have overheard something, they know it is a terrible thing, prohibited on pain of punishment to talk about in the open, and the moment the little ones spy one of their elders they fly apart like criminals caught in the act. How shamed they would feel if their conversation were overheard and how terrible it would be to be classed among the bad and the wicked.

These are the children who eventually are driven into the gutter because their parents and teachers consider every intelligent discussion of sex as utterly impossible and immoral. These little ones must seek for their enlightenment in other places, and though their store of natural science is only somewhat true, yet it is really wholesomer than the sham virtue of the grown-ups who stamp the natural sex symptoms in the child as a crime and a vice.

In their studies the young often come upon the glorification of love. They learn that love is the very foundation of religion, of duty, of virtue and other such wonderful things. On the other hand, love is made to appear as a loathsome caricature because of the element of sex. The rearing, then, of both sexes in truth and simplicity would help much to ameliorate this confusion. If in childhood both man and woman were taught a beautiful comradeship, it would neutralize the oversexed condition of both and would help woman's emancipation much more than all the laws upon the statute books and her right to vote.

Most moralists and many pedagogues still adhere to the antiquated notion that man and woman belong to two different species, moving in opposite directions, and hence, must be kept apart. Love, which should be the impetus for the harmonious blending of two beings, today drives the two apart as a result of the moral flagellation of the young into an overwrought, starved, unhealthy sexual embrace. This kind of satisfaction invariably leaves behind a bad taste and "bad conscience."

The advocates of puritanism, of morality, of the present system of education, only succeed in making life smaller, meaner, and more contemptible—and what fine personalities can tolerate such an outrage? It is therefore a human proposition to exterminate the system and all those who are engaged in so-called education. The best education of the child is to leave it alone and bring to it understanding and sympathy.

Victims of Morality

Not so very long ago I attended a meeting addressed by Anthony Comstock, who has for forty years been the guardian of American morals. A more incoherent, ignorant ramble I have never heard from any platform.

The question that presented itself to me, listening to the commonplace, bigoted talk of the man, was, How could anyone so limited and unintelligent wield the power of censor and dictator over a supposedly democratic nation? True, Comstock has the law to back him. Forty years ago, when puritanism was even more rampant than to-day, completely shutting out the light of reason and progress, Comstock succeeded, through shady machination and political wire pulling, to introduce a bill which gave him complete control over the Post Office Department—a control which has proved disastrous to the freedom of the press, as well as the right of privacy of the American citizen.

Since then, Comstock has broken into the private chambers of people, has confiscated personal correspondence, as well as works of art, and has established a system of espionage and graft which would put Russia to shame. Yet the law does not explain the power of Anthony Comstock. There is something else, more terrible than the law. It is the

narrow puritanic spirit, as represented in the sterile minds
of the Young-Men-and-Old-Maid's Christian Union, Tem-
perance Union, Sabbath Union, Purity League, etc. A spirit
which is absolutely blind to the simplest manifestations of
life; hence stands for stagnation and decay. As in ante-
bellum days, these old fossils lament the terrible immorality
of our time. Science, art, literature, the drama, are at the
mercy of bigoted censorship and legal procedure, with the
result that America, with all her boastful claims to progress
and liberty is still steeped in the densest provincialism.

The smallest dominion in Europe can boast of an art free
from the fetters of morality, an art that has the courage to
portray the great social problems of our time. With the
sharp edge of critical analysis, it cuts into every social ulcer,
every wrong, demanding fundamental changes and the
transvaluation of accepted values. Satire, wit, humor, as
well as the most intensely serious modes of expression, are
being employed to lay bare our conventional social and
moral lies. In America we would seek in vain for such a
medium, since even the attempt at it is made impossible by
the rigid régime, by the moral dictator and his clique.

The nearest approach, however, is our muckrakers, who
have no doubt rendered great service along economic and
social lines. Whether the muckrakers have or have not
helped to change conditions, at least they have torn the
mask from the lying face of our smug and self-satisfied
society.

Unfortunately, the Lie of Morality still stalks about in
fine feathers, since no one dares to come within hailing
distance of that holy of holies. Yet is is safe to say that no
other superstition is so detrimental to growth, so enervating
and paralyzing to the minds and hearts of the people, as the
superstition of Morality.

The most pathetic, and in a way discouraging, aspect of
the situation is a certain element of liberals, and even
of radicals, men and women apparently free from religious
and social spooks. But before the monster of Morality they

are as prostrate as the most pious of their kind—which is an additional proof to the extent to which the morality worm has eaten into the system of its victims and how far-going and thorough the measures must be which are to drive it out again.

Needless to say, society is obsessed by more than one morality. Indeed, every institution of to-day has its own moral standard. Nor could they ever have maintained themselves, were it not for religion, which acts as a shield, and for morality, which acts as the mask. This explains the interest of the exploiting rich in religion and morality. The rich preach, foster, and finance both, as an investment that pays good returns. Through the medium of religion they have paralyzed the mind of the people, just as morality has enslaved the spirit. In other words, religion and morality are a much better whip to keep people in submission than even the club and the gun.

To illustrate: The Property Morality declares that that institution is sacred. Woe to anyone that dares to question the sanctity of Property, or sins against it! Yet everyone knows that Property is robbery; that it represents the accumulated efforts of millions, who themselves are propertyless. And what is more terrible, the more poverty stricken the victim of Property Morality is, the greater his respect and awe for that master. Thus we hear advanced people, even so-called class-conscious workingmen, decry as immoral such methods as sabotage and direct action, because they aim at Property.

Verily, if the victims themselves are so blinded by the Property Morality, what need one expect from the masters? It therefore seems high time to bring home the fact that until the workers will lose respect for the instrument of their material enslavement, they need hope for no relief.

However, it is with the effect of Morality upon women that I am here mostly concerned. So disastrous, so paralyzing has this effect been, that some even of the most advanced among my sisters never thoroughly outgrow it.

It is Morality which condemns woman to the position of a celibate, a prostitute, or a reckless, incessant breeder of hapless children.

First, as to the celibate, the famished and withered human plant. When still a young, beautiful flower, she falls in love with a respectable young man. But Morality decrees that unless he can marry the girl, she must never know the raptures of love, the ecstasy of passion, which reaches its culminating expression in the sex embrace. The respectable young man is willing to marry, but the Property Morality, the Family and Social Moralities decree that he must first make his pile, must save up enough to establish a home and be able to provide for a family. The young people must wait, often many long, weary years.

Meanwhile the respectable young man, excited through the daily association and contact with his sweetheart, seeks an outlet for his nature in return for money. In ninety-nine cases out of a hundred, he will be infected, and when he is materially able to marry, he will infect his wife and possible offspring. And the young flower, with every fiber aglow with the fire of life, with all her being crying out for love and passion? She has no outlet. She develops headaches, insomnia, hysteria; grows embittered, quarrelsome, and soon becomes a faded, withered, joyless being, a nuisance to herself and everyone else. No wonder Stirner preferred the grisette to the maiden grown gray with virtue.

There is nothing more pathetic, nothing more terrible, than this gray-grown victim of a gray-grown Morality. This applies even with greater force to the masses of professional middle-class girls, than to those of the people. Through economic necessity the latter are thrust into life's jungle at an early age; they grow up with their male companions in the factory and shop, or at play and dance. The result is a more normal expression of their physical instincts. Then too, the young men and women of the people are not so hide-bound by externalities, and often follow the call of love and passion regardless of ceremony and tradition.

But the overwrought and oversexed middle-class girl, hedged in her narrow confines with family and social traditions, guarded by a thousand eyes, afraid of her own shadow—the yearning of her inmost being for the man or the child, must turn to cats, dogs, canary birds, or the Bible Class. Such is the cruel dictum of Morality, which is daily shutting out love, light, and joy from the lives of innumerable victims.

Now, as to the prostitute. In spite of laws, ordinances, persecution, and prisons; in spite of segregation, registration, vice crusades, and other similar devices, the prostitute is the real specter of our age. She sweeps across the plains like a fire burning into every nook of life, devastating, destroying.

After all, she is paying back, in a very small measure, the curse and horrors society has strewn in her path. She, weary with the tramp of ages, harassed and driven from pillar to post, at the mercy of all, is yet the Nemesis of modern times, the avenging angel, ruthlessly wielding the sword of fire. For has she not the man in her power? And, through him, the home, the child, the race. Thus she slays, and is herself the most brutally slain.

What has made her? Whence does she come? Morality, the Morality which is merciless in its attitude to women. Once she dared to be herself, to be true to her nature, to life, there is no return: the woman is thrust out from the pale and protection of society. The prostitute becomes the victim of Morality, even as the withered old maid is its victim. But the prostitute is victimized by still other forces, foremost among them the Property Morality, which compels woman to sell herself as a sex commodity for a dollar per, out of wedlock, or for fifteen dollars a week, in the sacred fold of matrimony. The latter is no doubt safer, more respected, more recognized, but of the two forms of prostitution the girl of the street is the least hypocritical, the least debased, since her trade lacks the pious mask of hypocrisy; and yet she is hounded, fleeced, outraged, and shunned, by the very powers that have made her: the financier, the priest, the moralist, the judge, the jailor, and the detective, not to forget her sheltered, respectably virtuous sister, who is the most relentless and brutal in her persecution of the prostitute.

Morality and its victim, the mother—what a terrible picture! Is there indeed anything more terrible, more criminal, than our glorified sacred function of motherhood? The woman, physically and mentally unfit to be a mother, yet condemned to breed; the woman, economically taxed to the very last spark of energy, yet forced to breed; the woman, tied to a man she loathes, whose very sight fills her with horror, yet made to breed; the woman, worn and used-up from the process of procreation, yet coerced to breed, more, ever more. What a hideous thing, this much-lauded motherhood! No wonder thousands of women risk mutilation, and prefer even death to this curse of the cruel imposition of the spook of Morality. Five thousand are yearly sacrificed upon the altar of this monster, that will not stand for prevention but would cure by abortion. Five thousand soldiers in the battle for their physical and spiritual freedom, and as many thousands more who are crippled and mutilated rather than bring forth life in a society based on decay and destruction.

Is it because the modern woman wants to shirk responsibility, or that she lacks love for her offspring, that she is driven to the most drastic and dangerous means to avoid bearing children? Only shallow, bigoted minds can bring such an accusation. Else they would know that the modern woman has become race-conscious, sensitive to the needs and rights of the child, as the unit of the race, and that therefore the modern woman has a sense of responsibility and humanity, which was quite foreign to her grandmother.

With the economic war raging all around her, with strife, misery, crime, disease, and insanity staring her in the face, with numberless little children ground into gold dust, how can the self- and race-conscious woman become a mother? Morality can not answer this question. It can only dictate, coerce, or condemn—and how many women are strong enough to face this condemnation, to defy the moral dicta? Few, indeed. Hence they fill the factories, the reformatories, the homes for feeble minded, the prisons, the insane asylums, or they die in the attempt to prevent child-birth. Oh, Motherhood, what crimes are committed in thy name! What hosts are laid at your feet, Morality, destroyer of life!

Fortunately, the Dawn is emerging from the chaos and darkness. Woman is awakening, she is throwing off the nightmare of Morality; she will no longer be bound. In her love for the man, she is not concerned in the contents of his pocketbook, but in the wealth of his nature, which alone is the fountain of life and joy. Nor does she need the sanction of the State. Her love is sanction enough for her. Thus she can abandon herself to the man of her choice, as the flowers abandon themselves to dew and light, in freedom, beauty, and ecstasy.

Through her re-born consciousness as a unit, a personality, a race builder, she will become a mother only if she desires the child, and if she can give to the child, even before its birth, all that her nature and intellect can yield: harmony, health, comfort, beauty, and, above all, understanding, reverence, and love, which is the only fertile soil for new life, a new being.

Morality has no terrors for her who has risen beyond good and evil. And though Morality may continue to devour its victims, it is utterly powerless in the face of the modern spirit, that shines in all its glory upon the brow of man and woman, liberated and unafraid.

The Tragedy of Woman's Emancipation

I begin with an admission: Regardless of all political and economic theories, treating of the fundamental differences between various groups within the human race, regardless of class and race distinctions, regardless of all artificial boundary lines between woman's rights and man's rights, I hold that there is a point where these differentiations may meet and grow into one perfect whole.

With this I do not mean to propose a peace treaty. The general social antagonism which has taken hold of our entire public life today, brought about through the force of opposing and contradictory interests, will crumble to pieces when the reorganization of our social life, based upon the principles of economic justice, shall have become a reality.

Peace or harmony between the sexes and individuals does not necessarily depend on a superficial equalization of human beings; nor does it call for the elimination of individual traits and peculiarities. The problem that confronts us today, and which the nearest future is to solve, is how to be one's self and yet in oneness with others, to feel deeply with all human beings and still retain one's own character-

istic qualities. This seems to me to be the basis upon which
the mass and the individual, the true democrat and the true
individuality, man and woman, can meet without antagonism and opposition. The motto should not be: Forgive one
another; rather, Understand one another. The oft-quoted
sentence of Madame de Staël: "To understand everything
means to forgive everything," has never particularly appealed to me; it has the odor of the confessional; to forgive
one's fellow-being conveys the idea of pharisaical superiority. To understand one's fellow-being suffices. The admission partly represents the fundamental aspect of my views
on the emancipation of woman and its effect upon the
entire sex.

Emancipation should make it possible for woman to be
human in the truest sense. Everything within her that craves
assertion and activity should reach its fullest expression; all
artificial barriers should be broken, and the road towards
greater freedom cleared of every trace of centuries of submission and slavery.

This was the original aim of the movement for woman's
emancipation. But the results so far achieved have isolated
woman and have robbed her of the fountain springs of that
happiness which is so essential to her. Merely external
emancipation has made of the modern woman an artificial
being, who reminds one of the products of French arbori-
culture with its arabesque trees and shrubs, pyramids,
wheels, and wreaths; anything, except the forms which
would be reached by the expression of her own inner
qualities. Such artificially grown plants of the female sex are
to be found in large numbers, especially in the so-called
intellectual sphere of our life.

Liberty and equality for woman! What hopes and aspirations these words awakened when they were first uttered by
some of the noblest and bravest souls of those days. The sun
in all his light and glory was to rise upon a new world; in
this world woman was to be free to direct her own destiny

—an aim certainly worthy of the great enthusiasm, courage, perseverance, and ceaseless effort of the tremendous host of pioneer men and women, who staked everything against a world of prejudice and ignorance.

My hopes also move towards that goal, but I hold that the emancipation of woman, as interpreted and practically applied today, has failed to reach that great end. Now, woman is confronted with the necessity of emancipating herself from emancipation, if she really desires to be free. This may sound paradoxical, but is, nevertheless, only too true.

What has she achieved through her emancipation? Equal suffrage in a few States. Has that purified our political life, as many well-meaning advocates predicted? Certainly not. Incidentally, it is really time that persons with plain, sound judgment should cease to talk about corruption in politics in a boarding-school tone. Corruption of politics has nothing to do with the morals, or the laxity of morals, of various political personalities. Its cause is altogether a material one. Politics is the reflex of the business and industrial world, the mottos of which are: "To take is more blessed than to give"; "buy cheap and sell dear"; "one soiled hand washes the other." There is no hope even that woman, with her right to vote, will ever purify politics.

Emancipation has brought woman economic equality with man; that is, she can choose her own profession and trade; but as her past and present physical training has not equipped her with the necessary strength to compete with man, she is often compelled to exhaust all her energy, use up her vitality, and strain every nerve in order to reach the market value. Very few ever succeed, for it is a fact that women teachers, doctors, lawyers, architects, and engineers are neither met with the same confidence as their male colleagues, nor receive equal remuneration. And those that do reach that enticing equality generally do so at the expense of their physical and psychical well-being. As to the great mass of working girls and women, how much independence is gained if the narrowness and lack of freedom of the home is exchanged for the narrowness and lack of freedom of the factory, sweat-shop, department store, or office? In addition is the burden which is laid on many women of looking after a "home, sweet home"—cold, dreary, disorderly, uninviting —after a day's hard work. Glorious independence! No wonder that hundreds of girls are so willing to accept the first offer of marriage, sick and tired of their "independence" behind the counter, at the sewing or typewriting machine. They are just as ready to marry as girls of the middle class, who long to throw off the yoke of parental supremacy. A so-called independence which leads only to earning the merest subsistence is not so enticing, not so ideal, that one could expect woman to sacrifice everything for it. Our highly praised independence is, after all, but a slow process of dulling and stifling woman's nature, her love instinct, and her mother instinct.

Nevertheless, the position of the working girl is far more natural and human than that of her seemingly more fortunate sister in the more cultured professional walks of life— teachers, physicians, lawyers, engineers, etc., who have to make a dignified, proper appearance, while the inner life is growing empty and dead.

The narrowness of the existing conception of woman's independence and emancipation; the dread of love for a man who is not her social equal; the fear that love will rob her of her freedom and independence; the horror that love or the joy of motherhood will only hinder her in the full exercise of her profession—all these together make of the emancipated modern woman a compulsory vestal, before whom life, with its great clarifying sorrows and its deep, entrancing joys, rolls on without touching or gripping her soul.

Emancipation, as understood by the majority of its adherents and exponents, is of too narrow a scope to permit the boundless love and ecstasy contained in the deep emotion of the true woman, sweetheart, mother, in freedom.

The tragedy of the self-supporting or economically free woman does not lie in too many, but in too few experiences. True, she surpasses her sister of past generations in knowledge of the world and human nature; it is just because of this that she feels deeply the lack of life's essence, which alone can enrich the human soul, and without which the majority of women have become mere professional automatons.

That such a state of affairs was bound to come was foreseen by those who realized that, in the domain of ethics, there still remained many decaying ruins of the time of the undisputed superiority of man; ruins that are still considered useful. And, what is more important, a goodly number of the emancipated are unable to get along without them. Every movement that aims at the destruction of existing institutions and the replacement thereof with something more advanced, more perfect, has followers who in theory stand for the most radical ideas, but who, nevertheless, in their every-day practice, are like the average Philistine, feigning respectability and clamoring for the good opinion of their opponents. There are, for example, Socialists, and even Anarchists, who stand for the idea that property is robbery, yet who will grow indignant if anyone owe them the value of a half-dozen pins.

The same Philistine can be found in the movement for woman's emancipation. Yellow journalists and milk-and-water littérateurs have painted pictures of the emancipated woman that make the hair of the good citizen and his dull companion stand up on end. Every member of the woman's rights movement was pictured as a George Sand in her absolute disregard of morality. Nothing was sacred to her. She had no respect for the ideal relation between man and woman. In short, emancipation stood only for a reckless life of lust and sin, regardless of society, religion, and morality.

The exponents of woman's rights were highly indignant at such misrepresentation, and, lacking humor, they exerted all their energy to prove that they were not at all as bad as they were painted, but the very reverse. Of course, as long as woman was the slave of man, she could not be good and pure, but now that she was free and independent she would prove how good she could be and that her influence would have a purifying effect on all institutions in society. True, the movement for woman's rights has broken many old fetters, but it has also forged new ones. The great movement of *true* emancipation has not met with a great race of women who could look liberty in the face. Their narrow, puritanical vision banished man, as a disturber and doubtful character, out of their emotional life. Man was not to be tolerated at any price, except perhaps as the father of a child, since a child could not very well come to life without a father. Fortunately, the most rigid Puritans never will be strong enough to kill the innate craving for motherhood. But woman's freedom is closely allied with man's freedom, and many of my so-called emancipated sisters seem to overlook the fact that a child born in freedom needs the love and devotion of each human being about him, man as well as woman. Unfortunately, it is this narrow conception of human relations that has brought about a great tragedy in the lives of the modern man and woman.

About fifteen years ago appeared a work from the pen of the brilliant Norwegian Laura Marholm, called *Woman, a Character Study*. She was one of the first to call attention to the emptiness and narrowness of the existing conception of woman's emancipation, and its tragic effect upon the inner life of woman. In her work Laura Marholm speaks of the fate of several gifted women of international fame: the genius Eleonora Duse; the great mathematician and writer Sonya Kovalevskaia; the artist and poet-nature Marie Bashkirtzeff, who died so young. Through each description of the lives of these women of such extraordinary mentality runs a marked trail of unsatisfied craving for a full, rounded, complete, and beautiful life, and the unrest and loneliness resulting from the lack of it. Through these masterly psychological sketches one cannot help but see that the higher the mental development of woman, the less possible it is for her to meet a congenial mate who will see in her, not only sex, but also the human being, the friend, the comrade and strong individuality, who cannot and ought not lose a single trait of her character.

The average man with his self-sufficiency, his ridiculously superior airs of patronage towards the female sex, is an impossibility for woman as depicted in the *Character Study* by Laura Marholm. Equally impossible for her is the man who can see in her nothing more than her mentality and her genius, and who fails to awaken her woman nature.

A rich intellect and a fine soul are usually considered necessary attributes of a deep and beautiful personality. In the case of the modern woman, these attributes serve as a hindrance to the complete assertion of her being. For over a hundred years the old form of marriage, based on the Bible, "Till death doth part," has been denounced as an institution that stands for the sovereignty of the man over the woman, of her complete submission to his whims and commands, and absolute dependence on his name and support. Time and again it has been conclusively proved that the old matrimonial relation restricted woman to the function of man's servant and the bearer of his children. And yet we find many emancipated women who prefer marriage, with all its deficiencies, to the narrowness of an unmarried life: narrow and unendurable because of the chains of moral and social prejudice that cramp and bind her nature.

The explanation of such inconsistency on the part of many advanced women is to be found in the fact that they never truly understood the meaning of emancipation. They thought that all that was needed was independence from external tyrannies; the internal tyrants, far more harmful to

life and growth—ethical and social conventions—were left
to take care of themselves; and they have taken care of
themselves. They seem to get along as beautifully in the
heads and hearts of the most active exponents of woman's
emancipation, as in the heads and hearts of our grandmothers.

These internal tyrants, whether they be in the form of
public opinion or what will mother say, or brother, father,
aunt, or relative of any sort; what will Mrs. Grundy, Mr.
Comstock, the employer, the Board of Education say? All
these busybodies, moral detectives, jailers of the human
spirit, what will they say? Until woman has learned to defy
them all, to stand firmly on her own ground and to insist
upon her own unrestricted freedom, to listen to the voice of
her nature, whether it call for life's greatest treasure, love
for a man, or her most glorious privilege, the right to give
birth to a child, she cannot call herself emancipated. How
many emancipated women are brave enough to acknowl-
edge that the voice of love is calling, wildly beating against
their breasts, demanding to be heard, to be satisfied.

The French writer Jean Reibrach, in one of his novels,
New Beauty, attempts to picture the ideal, beautiful, emancipated woman. This ideal is embodied in a young girl, a
physician. She talks very cleverly and wisely of how to feed
infants; she is kind, and administers medicines free to poor
mothers. She converses with a young man of her acquaint-
ance about the sanitary conditions of the future, and how
various bacilli and germs shall be exterminated by the use
of stone walls and floors, and by the doing away with rugs
and hangings. She is, of course, very plainly and practically
dressed, mostly in black. The young man, who, at their first
meeting, was overawed by the wisdom of his emancipated
friend, gradually learns to understand her, and recognizes
one fine day that he loves her. They are young, and she is
kind and beautiful, and though always in rigid attire, her

appearance is softened by a spotlessly clean white collar and cuffs. One would expect that he would tell her of his love, but he is not one to commit romantic absurdities. Poetry and the enthusiasm of love cover their blushing faces before the pure beauty of the lady. He silences the voice of his nature, and remains correct. She, too, is always exact, always rational, always well behaved. I fear if they had formed a union, the young man would have risked freezing to death. I must confess that I can see nothing beautiful in this new beauty, who is as cold as the stone walls and floors she dreams of. Rather would I have the love songs of romantic ages, rather Don Juan and Madame Venus, rather an elopement by ladder and rope on a moonlight night, followed by the father's curse, mother's moans, and the moral comments of neighbors, than correctness and propriety measured by yardsticks. If love does not know how to give and take without restrictions, it is not love, but a transaction that never fails to lay stress on a plus and a minus.

The greatest shortcoming of the emancipation of the present day lies in its artificial stiffness and its narrow respectabilities, which produce an emptiness in woman's soul that will not let her drink from the fountain of life. I once remarked that there seemed to be a deeper relationship between the old-fashioned mother and hostess, ever on the alert for the happiness of her little ones and the comfort of those she loves, and the truly new woman, than between the latter and her average emancipated sister. The disciples of emancipation pure and simple declared me a heathen, fit only for the stake. Their blind zeal did not let them see that my comparison between the old and the new was merely to prove that a goodly number of our grandmothers had more blood in their veins, far more humor and wit, and certainly a greater amount of naturalness, kind-heartedness, and simplicity, than the majority of our emancipated professional women who fill the colleges, halls of learning and various offices. This does not mean a wish to return to the past, nor does it condemn woman to her old sphere, the kitchen and the nursery.

Salvation lies in an energetic march onward towards a brighter and clearer future. We are in need of unhampered growth out of old traditions and habits. The movement for woman's emancipation has so far made but the first step in that direction. It is to be hoped that it will gather strength to make another. The right to vote, or equal civil rights, may be good demands, but true emancipation begins neither at the polls nor in courts. It begins in woman's soul. History tells us that every oppressed class gained true liberation from its masters through its own efforts. It is necessary that woman learn that lesson, that she realize that her freedom will reach as far as her power to achieve her freedom reaches. It is, therefore, far more important for her to begin with her inner regeneration, to cut loose from the weight of prejudices, traditions, and customs. The demand for equal rights in every vocation of life is just and fair; but, after all, the most vital right is the right to love and be loved. Indeed, if partial emancipation is to become a complete and true emancipation of woman, it will have to do away with the ridiculous notion that to be loved, to be sweetheart and mother, is synonymous with being slave or subordinate. It will have to do away with the absurd notion of the dualism of the sexes, or that man and woman represent two antagonistic worlds.

Pettiness separates; breadth unites. Let us be broad and big. Let us not overlook vital things because of the bulk of trifles confronting us. A true conception of the relation of the sexes will not admit of conqueror and conquered; it knows of but one great thing: to give of one's self boundlessly, in order to find one's self richer, deeper, better. That alone can fill the emptiness, and transform the tragedy of woman's emancipation into joy, limitless joy.

The Traffic in Women

Our reformers have suddenly made a great discovery—the white slave traffic. The papers are full of these "unheard-of conditions," and lawmakers are already planning a new set of laws to check the horror.

It is significant that whenever the public mind is to be diverted from a great social wrong, a crusade is inaugurated against indecency, gambling, saloons, etc. And what is the result of such crusades? Gambling is increasing, saloons are doing a lively business through back entrances, prostitution is at its height, and the system of pimps and cadets* is but aggravated.

How is it that an institution, known almost to every child, should have been discovered so suddenly? How is it that this evil, known to all sociologists, should now be made such an important issue?

To assume that the recent investigation of the white slave

* Editor's note: "Cadet" was slang for "a man who lives on the earnings of a prostitute with whom he cohabits; also, one who procures for brothels young women whom he first seduces." (*Webster's New International Dictionary, Second Edition, Unabridged.*)

traffic (and, by the way, a very superficial investigation)
has discovered anything new, is, to say the least, very
foolish. Prostitution has been, and is, a widespread evil, yet
mankind goes on its business, perfectly indifferent to the
sufferings and distress of the victims of prostitution. As
indifferent, indeed, as mankind has remained to our industrial system, or to economic prostitution.

Only when human sorrows are turned into a toy with
glaring colors will baby people become interested—for a
while at least. The people are a very fickle baby that must
have new toys every day. The "righteous" cry against the
white slave traffic is such a toy. It serves to amuse the
people for a little while, and it will help to create a few
more fat political jobs—parasites who stalk about the world
as inspectors, investigators, detectives, and so forth.

What is really the cause of the trade in women? Not
merely white women, but yellow and black women as well.
Exploitation, of course; the merciless Moloch of capitalism
that fattens on underpaid labor, thus driving thousands of
women and girls into prostitution. With Mrs. Warren* these
girls feel, "Why waste your life working for a few shillings a
week in a scullery, eighteen hours a day?"

Naturally our reformers say nothing about this cause.
They know it well enough, but it doesn't pay to say anything about it. It is much more profitable to play the
Pharisee, to pretend an outraged morality, than to go to the
bottom of things.

However, there is one commendable exception among
the young writers: Reginald Wright Kauffman, whose
work *The House of Bondage* is the first earnest attempt to
treat the social evil—not from a sentimental Philistine
viewpoint. A journalist of wide experience, Mr. Kauffman

---

* Editor's note: The title character, a prostitute, in George Bernard
Shaw's play *Mrs. Warren's Profession.*

proves that our industrial system leaves most women no alternative except prostitution. The women portrayed in *The House of Bondage* belong to the working class. Had the author portrayed the life of women in other spheres, he would have been confronted with the same state of affairs.

Nowhere is woman treated according to the merit of her work, but rather as a sex. It is therefore almost inevitable that she should pay for her right to exist, to keep a position in whatever line, with sex favors. Thus it is merely a question of degree whether she sells herself to one man, in or out of marriage, or to many men. Whether our reformers admit it or not, the economic and social inferiority of woman is responsible for prostitution.

Just at present our good people are shocked by the disclosures that in New York City alone one out of every ten women works in a factory, that the average wage received by women is six dollars per week for forty-eight to sixty hours of work, and that the majority of female wage workers face many months of idleness which leaves the average wage about $280 a year. In view of these economic horrors, is it to be wondered at that prostitution and the white slave trade have become such dominant factors?

Lest the preceding figures be considered an exaggeration, it is well to examine what some authorities on prostitution have to say:

"A prolific cause of female depravity can be found in the several tables, showing the description of the employment pursued, and the wages received, by the women previous to their fall, and it will be a question for the political economist to decide how far mere business consideration should be an apology on the part of employers for a reduction in their rates of remuneration, and whether the savings of a small percentage on wages is not more than counterbalanced by the enormous amount of taxation enforced on the public at large to defray the expenses incurred on account

of a system of vice, *which is the direct result, in many cases,
of insufficient compensation of honest labor.*"*

Our present-day reformers would do well to look into
Dr. Sanger's book. There they will find that out of 2,000
cases under his observation, but few came from the middle
classes, from well-ordered conditions, or pleasant homes.
By far the largest majority were working girls and working
women; some driven into prostitution through sheer want,
others because of a cruel, wretched life at home, others
again because of thwarted and crippled physical natures (of
which I shall speak later on). Also it will do the maintainers
of purity and morality good to learn that out of two thousand cases, 490 were married women, women who lived
with their husbands. Evidently there was not much of a
guaranty for their "safety and purity" in the sanctity of
marriage.†

Dr. Alfred Blaschko, in *Prostitution in the Nineteenth
Century,* is even more emphatic in characterizing economic
conditions as one of the most vital factors of prostitution:

"Although prostitution has existed in all ages, it was left
to the nineteenth century to develop it into a gigantic social
institution. The development of industry with vast masses of
people in the competitive market, the growth and congestion of large cities, the insecurity and uncertainty of employment, has given prostitution an impetus never dreamed
of at any period in human history."

And again Havelock Ellis, while not so absolute in dealing with the economic cause, is nevertheless compelled to
admit that it is indirectly and directly the main cause. Thus
he finds that a large percentage of prostitutes is recruited
from the servant class, although the latter have less care and
greater security. On the other hand, Mr. Ellis does not deny

---

* Dr. Sanger, *The History of Prostitution.*

† It is a significant fact that Dr. Sanger's book has been excluded from
the U.S. mails. Evidently the authorities are not anxious that the public
be informed as to the true cause of prostitution.

that the daily routine, the drudgery, the monotony of the servant girl's lot, and especially the fact that she may never partake of the companionship and joy of a home, are no mean factors in forcing her to seek recreation and forgetfulness in the gaiety and glimmer of prostitution. In other words, the servant girl, being treated as a drudge, never having the right to herself, and worn out by the caprices of her mistress, can find an outlet, like the factory or shopgirl, only in prostitution.

The most amusing side of the question now before the public is the indignation of our "good, respectable people," especially the various Christian gentlemen, who are always to be found in the front ranks of every crusade. Is it that they are absolutely ignorant of the history of religion, and especially of the Christian religion? Or is it that they hope to blind the present generation to the part played in the past by the Church in relation to prostitution? Whatever their reason, they should be the last to cry out against the unfortunate victims of today, since it is known to every intelligent student that prostitution is of religious origin, maintained and fostered for many centuries, not as a shame, but as a virtue, hailed as such by the Gods themselves.

"It would seem that the origin of prostitution is to be found primarily in a religious custom, religion, the great conserver of social tradition, preserving in a transformed shape a primitive freedom that was passing out of the general social life. The typical example is that recorded by Herodotus, in the fifth century before Christ, at the Temple of Mylitta, the Babylonian Venus, where every woman, once in her life, had to come and give herself to the first stranger, who threw a coin in her lap, to worship the goddess. Very similar customs existed in other parts of western Asia, in North Africa, in Cyprus, and other islands of the eastern Mediterranean, and also in Greece, where the temple of Aphrodite on the fort at Corinth possessed over a thousand hierodules, dedicated to the service of the goddess.

"The theory that religious prostitution developed, as a general rule, out of the belief that the generative activity of human beings possessed a mysterious and sacred influence in promoting the fertility of Nature is maintained by all authoritative writers on the subject. Gradually, however, and when prostitution became an organized institution under priestly influence, religious prostitution developed utilitarian sides, thus helping to increase public revenue.

"The rise of Christianity to political power produced little change in policy. The leading fathers of the Church tolerated prostitution. Brothels under municipal protection are found in the thirteenth century. They constituted a sort of public service, the directors of them being considered almost as public servants."*

To this must be added the following from Dr. Sanger's work:

"Pope Clement II issued a bull that prostitutes would be tolerated if they pay a certain amount of their earnings to the Church.

"Pope Sixtus IV was more practical; from one single brothel, which he himself had built, he received an income of 20,000 ducats."

In modern times the Church is a little more careful in that direction. At least she does not openly demand tribute from prostitutes. She finds it much more profitable to go in for real estate, like Trinity Church, for instance, to rent out death traps at an exorbitant price to those who live off and by prostitution.

Much as I should like to, my space will not admit speaking of prostitution in Egypt, Greece, Rome, and during the Middle Ages. The conditions in the latter period are particularly interesting, inasmuch as prostitution was organ-

---

* Havelock Ellis, *Sex and Society*.

ized into guilds, presided over by a brothel queen. These guilds employed strikes as a medium of improving their condition and keeping a standard price. Certainly that is more practical a method than the one used by the modern wage-slave in society.

It would be one-sided and extremely superficial to maintain that the economic factor is the only cause of prostitution. There are others no less important and vital. That, too, our reformers know, but dare discuss even less than the institution that saps the very life out of both men and women. I refer to the sex question, the very mention of which causes most people moral spasms.

It is a conceded fact that woman is being reared as a sex commodity, and yet she is kept in absolute ignorance of the meaning and importance of sex. Everything dealing with that subject is suppressed, and persons who attempt to bring light into this terrible darkness are persecuted and thrown into prison. Yet it is nevertheless true that so long as a girl is not to know how to take care of herself, not to know the function of the most important part of her life, we need not be surprised if she becomes an easy prey to prostitution, or to any other form of a relationship which degrades her to the position of an object for mere sex gratification.

It is due to this ignorance that the entire life and nature of the girl is thwarted and crippled. We have long ago taken it as a self-evident fact that the boy may follow the call of the wild; that is to say, that the boy may, as soon as his sex nature asserts itself, satisfy that nature; but our moralists are scandalized at the very thought that the nature of a girl should assert itself. To the moralist prostitution does not consist so much in the fact that the woman sells her body, but rather that she sells it out of wedlock. That this is no mere statement is proved by the fact that marriage for monetary considerations is perfectly legitimate, sanctified by law and public opinion, while any other union is condemned and repudiated. Yet a prostitute, if properly defined, means nothing else than "any person for whom sexual relationships are subordinated to gain."*

"Those women are prostitutes who sell their bodies for the exercise of the sexual act and make of this a profession."†

In fact, Banger goes further; he maintains that the act of prostitution is "intrinsically equal to that of a man or woman who contracts a marriage for economic reasons."

Of course, marriage is the goal of every girl, but as thousands of girls cannot marry, our stupid social customs condemn them either to a life of celibacy or prostitution. Human nature asserts itself regardless of all laws, nor is there any plausible reason why nature should adapt itself to a perverted conception of morality.

Society considers the sex experiences of a man as attributes of his general development, while similar experiences in the life of a woman are looked upon as a terrible calamity, a loss of honor and of all that is good and noble in a human being. This double standard of morality has played no little part in the creation and perpetuation of prostitution. It involves the keeping of the young in absolute ignorance on sex matters, which alleged "innocence," together with an overwrought and stifled sex nature, helps to bring about a state of affairs that our Puritans are so anxious to avoid or prevent.

Not that the gratification of sex must needs lead to prostitution; it is the cruel, heartless, criminal persecution of those who dare divert from the beaten track, which is responsible for it.

Girls, mere children, work in crowded, overheated rooms ten to twelve hours daily at a machine, which tends to keep them in a constant over-excited sex state. Many of these girls have no home or comforts of any kind; therefore the street or some place of cheap amusement is the only means

* Guyot, *La Prostitution.*
† Banger, *Criminalité et Condition Economique.*

of forgetting their daily routine. This naturally brings them into close proximity with the other sex. It is hard to say which of the two factors brings the girl's over-sexed condition to a climax, but it is certainly the most natural thing that a climax should result. That is the first step toward prostitution. Nor is the girl to be held responsible for it. On the contrary, it is altogether the fault of society, the fault of our lack of understanding, of our lack of appreciation of life in the making; especially is it the criminal fault of our moralists, who condemn a girl for all eternity, because she has gone from the "path of virtue"; that is, because her first sex experience has taken place without the sanction of the Church.

The girl feels herself a complete outcast, with the doors of home and society closed in her face. Her entire training and tradition is such that the girl herself feels depraved and fallen, and therefore has no ground to stand upon, or any hold that will lift her up, instead of dragging her down. Thus society creates the victims that it afterwards vainly attempts to get rid of. The meanest, most depraved and decrepit man still considers himself too good to take as his wife the woman whose grace he was quite willing to buy, even though he might thereby save her from a life of horror. Nor can she turn to her own sister for help. In her stupidity the latter deems herself too pure and chaste, not realizing that her own position is in many respects even more deplorable than her sister's of the streeet.

"The wife who married for money, compared with the prostitute," says Havelock Ellis, "is the true scab. She is paid less, gives much more in return in labor and care, and is absolutely bound to her master. The prostitute never signs away the right over her own person, she retains her freedom and personal rights, nor is she always compelled to submit to man's embrace."

Nor does the better-than-thou woman realize the apologist claim of Lecky that "though she may be the supreme

type of vice, she is also the most efficient guardian of virtue.
But for her, happy homes would be polluted, unnatural and
harmful practice would abound."

Moralists are ever ready to sacrifice one-half of the
human race for the sake of some miserable institution
which they can not outgrow. As a matter of fact, prostitution is no more a safeguard for the purity of the home than
rigid laws are a safeguard against prostitution. Fully fifty
per cent of married men are patrons of brothels. It is
through this virtuous element that the married women—
nay, even the children—are infected with venereal diseases.
Yet society has not a word of condemnation for the man,
while no law is too monstrous to be set in motion against
the helpless victim. She is not only preyed upon by those
who use her, but she is also absolutely at the mercy of every
policeman and miserable detective on the beat, the officials
at the station house, the authorities in every prison.

In a recent book by a woman who was for twelve years
the mistress of a "house," are to be found the following
figures: "The authorities compelled me to pay every month
fines between $14.70 to $29.70, the girls would pay from
$5.70 to $9.70 to the police." Considering that the writer
did her business in a small city, that the amounts she gives
do not include extra bribes and fines, one can readily see
the tremendous revenue the police department derives from
the blood money of its victims, whom it will not even protect. Woe to those who refuse to pay their toll; they would
be rounded up like cattle, "if only to make a favorable
impression upon the good citizens of the city, or if the
powers needed extra money on the side. For the warped
mind who believes that a fallen woman is incapable of
human emotion it would be impossible to realize the grief,
the disgrace, the tears, the wounded pride that was ours
every time we were pulled in."

Strange, isn't it, that a woman who has kept a "house"
should be able to feel that way? But stranger still that a

good Christian world should bleed and fleece such women, and give them nothing in return except obloquy and persecution. Oh, for the charity of a Christian world!

Much stress is laid on white slaves being imported into America. How would America ever retain her virtue if Europe did not help her out? I will not deny that this may be the case in some instances, any more than I will deny that there are emissaries of Germany and other countries luring economic slaves into America; but I absolutely deny that prostitution is recruited to any appreciable extent from Europe. It may be true that the majority of prostitutes of New York City are foreigners, but that is because the majority of the population is foreign. The moment we go to any other American city, to Chicago or the Middle West, we shall find that the number of foreign prostitutes is by far a minority.

Equally exaggerated is the belief that the majority of street girls in this city were engaged in this business before they came to America. Most of the girls speak excellent English, are Americanized in habits and appearance—a thing absolutely impossible unless they had lived in this country many years. That is, they were driven into prostitution by American conditions, by the thoroughly American custom for excessive display of finery and clothes, which, of course, necessitates money—money that cannot be earned in shops or factories.

In other words, there is no reason to believe that any set of men would go to the risk and expense of getting foreign products, when American conditions are overflooding the market with thousands of girls. On the other hand, there is sufficient evidence to prove that the export of American girls for the purpose of prostitution is by no means a small factor.

Thus Clifford G. Roe, ex-Assistant State Attorney of Cook County, Illinois, makes the open charge that New England girls are shipped to Panama for the express use of men in the employ of Uncle Sam. Mr. Roe adds that "there seems to be an underground railroad between Boston and Washington which many girls travel." Is it not significant that the railroad should lead to the very seat of Federal authority? That Mr. Roe said more than was desired in certain quarters is proved by the fact that he lost his position. It is not practical for men in office to tell tales from school.

The excuse given for the conditions in Panama is that there are no brothels in the Canal Zone. That is the usual avenue of escape for a hypocritical world that dares not face the truth. Not in the Canal Zone, not in the city limits—therefore prostitution does not exist.

Next to Mr. Roe, there is James Bronson Reynolds, who has made a thorough study of the white slave traffic in Asia. As a staunch American citizen and friend of the future Napoleon of America, Theodore Roosevelt, he is surely the last to discredit the virtue of his country. Yet we are informed by him that in Hong Kong, Shanghai, and Yokohama, the Augean stables of American vice are located. There American prostitutes have made themselves so conspicuous that in the Orient "American girl" is synonymous with prostitute. Mr. Reynolds reminds his countrymen that while Americans in China are under the protection of our consular representatives, the Chinese in America have no protection at all. Everyone who knows the brutal and barbarous persecution Chinese and Japanese endure on the Pacific Coast will agree with Mr. Reynolds.

In view of the above facts it is rather absurd to point to Europe as the swamp whence come all the social diseases of America. Just as absurd is it to proclaim the myth that the Jews furnish the largest contingent of willing prey. I am sure that no one will accuse me of nationalistic tendencies. I am glad to say that I have developed out of them, as out of many other prejudices. If, therefore, I resent the statement that Jewish prostitutes are imported, it is not because of any Judaistic sympathies, but because of the facts inherent in the lives of these people. No one but the most superficial will claim that Jewish girls migrate to strange lands, unless they have some tie or relation that brings them there. The Jewish girl is not adventurous. Until recent years she had never left home, not even so far as the next village or town, except it were to visit some relative. Is it then credible that Jewish girls would leave their parents or families, travel thousands of miles to strange lands, through the influence and promises of strange forces? Go to any of the large incoming steamers and see for yourself if these girls do not come either with their parents, brothers, aunts, or other kinsfolk. There may be exceptions, of course, but to state that large numbers of Jewish girls are imported for prostitution, or any other purpose, is simply not to know Jewish psychology.

Those who sit in a glass house do wrong to throw stones about them; besides, the American glass house is rather thin, it will break easily, and the interior is anything but a gainly sight.

To ascribe the increase of prostitution to alleged importation, to the growth of the cadet system, or similar causes, is highly superficial. I have already referred to the former. As to the cadet system, abhorrent as it is, we must not ignore the fact that it is essentially a phase of modern prostitution—a phase accentuated by suppression and graft, resulting from sporadic crusades against the social evil.

The procurer is no doubt a poor specimen of the human family, but in what manner is he more despicable than the policeman who takes the last cent from the street walker, and then locks her up in the station house? Why is the cadet more criminal, or a greater menace to society, than the owners of department stores and factories, who grow fat on the sweat of their victims, only to drive them to the streets? I make no plea for the cadet, but I fail to see why he should be mercilessly hounded, while the real perpetrators of all social iniquity enjoy immunity and respect. Then, too, it is well to remember that it is not the cadet who makes the prostitute. It is our sham and hypocrisy that create both the prostitute and the cadet.

Until 1894 very little was known in America of the procurer. Then we were attacked by an epidemic of virtue. Vice was to be abolished, the country purified at all cost. The social cancer was therefore driven out of sight, but deeper into the body. Keepers of brothels, as well as their unfortunate victims, were turned over to the tender mercies of the police. The inevitable consequence of exorbitant bribes, and the penitentiary, followed.

While comparatively protected in the brothels, where they represented a certain monetary value, the girls now found themselves on the street, absolutely at the mercy of the graft-greedy police. Desperate, needing protection and longing for affection, these girls naturally proved an easy prey for cadets, themselves the result of the spirit of our commercial age. Thus the cadet system was the direct outgrowth of police persecution, graft, and attempted suppression of prostitution. It were sheer folly to confound this modern phase of the social evil with the causes of the latter.

Mere suppression and barbaric enactments can serve but to embitter, and further degrade, the unfortunate victims of ignorance and stupidity. The latter has reached its highest expression in the proposed law to make humane treatment of prostitutes a crime, punishing any one sheltering a prostitute with five years' imprisonment and $10,000 fine. Such an attitude merely exposes the terrible lack of understanding of the true causes of prostitution, as a social factor, as well as manifesting the puritanic spirit of the Scarlet Letter days.

There is not a single modern writer on the subject who does not refer to the utter futility of legislative methods in coping with the issue. Thus Dr. Blaschko finds that governmental suppression and moral crusades accomplish nothing save driving the evil into secret channels, multiplying its dangers to society. Havelock Ellis, the most thorough and humane student of prostitution, proves by a wealth of data that the more stringent the methods of persecution the worse the condition becomes. Among other data we learn that in France, "in 1560, Charles IX abolished brothels through an edict, but the numbers of prostitutes were only increased, while many new brothels appeared in unsuspected shapes, and were more dangerous. In spite of all such legislation, *or because of it,* there has been no country in which prostitution has played a more conspicuous part."*

An educated public opinion, freed from the legal and moral hounding of the prostitute, can alone help to ameliorate present conditions. Wilful shutting of eyes and ignoring of the evil as a social factor of modern life can but aggravate matters. We must rise above our foolish notions of "better than thou," and learn to recognize in the prostitute a product of social conditions. Such a realization will sweep away the attitude of hypocrisy, and insure a great understanding and more humane treatment. As to a thorough eradication of prostitution, nothing can accomplish that save a complete transvaluation of all accepted values— especially the moral ones—coupled with the abolition of industrial slavery.

* *Sex and Society.*

Marriage and Love

The popular notion about marriage and love is that they are synonymous, that they spring from the same motives, and cover the same human needs. Like most popular notions this also rests not on actual facts, but on superstition.

Marriage and love have nothing in common; they are as far apart as the poles; are, in fact, antagonistic to each other. No doubt some marriages have been the result of love. Not, however, because love could assert itself only in marriage; much rather is it because few people can completely outgrow a convention. There are to-day large numbers of men and women to whom marriage is naught but a farce, but who submit to it for the sake of public opinion. At any rate, while it is true that some marriages are based on love, and while it is equally true that in some cases love continues in married life, I maintain that it does so regardless of marriage, and not because of it.

On the other hand, it is utterly false that love results from marriage. On rare occasions one does hear of a miraculous case of a married couple falling in love after marriage, but on close examination it will be found that it is a mere adjustment to the inevitable. Certainly the growing-used to each other is far away from the spontaneity, the intensity, and beauty of love, without which the intimacy of marriage must prove degrading to both the woman and the man.

Marriage is primarily an economic arrangement, an insurance pact. It differs from the ordinary life insurance agreement only in that it is more binding, more exacting. Its returns are insignificantly small compared with the investments. In taking out an insurance policy one pays for it in dollars and cents, always at liberty to discontinue payments. If, however, woman's premium is a husband, she pays for it with her name, her privacy, her self-respect, her very life, "until death doth part." Moreover, the marriage insurance condemns her to life-long dependency, to parasitism, to complete uselessness, individual as well as social. Man, too, pays his toll, but as his sphere is wider, marriage does not limit him as much as woman. He feels his chains more in an economic sense.

Thus Dante's motto over Inferno applies with equal force to marriage: "Ye who enter here leave all hope behind."

That marriage is a failure none but the very stupid will deny. One has but to glance over the statistics of divorce to realize how bitter a failure marriage really is. Nor will the stereotyped Philistine argument that the laxity of divorce laws and the growing looseness of woman account for the fact that: first, every twelfth marriage ends in divorce; second, that since 1870 divorces have increased from 28 to 73 for every hundred thousand population; third, that adultery, since 1867, as ground for divorce, has increased 270.8 per cent; fourth, that desertion increased 369.8 per cent.

Added to these startling figures is a vast amount of material, dramatic and literary, further elucidating this subject. Robert Herrick, in *Together;* Pinero, in *Mid-Channel;* Eugene Walter, in *Paid in Full,* and scores of other writers are discussing the barrenness, the monotony, the sordidness, the inadequacy of marriage as a factor for harmony and understanding.

The thoughtful social student will not content himself with the popular superficial excuse for this phenomenon. He will have to dig down deeper into the very life of the sexes to know why marriage proves so disastrous.

Edward Carpenter says that behind every marriage stands the life-long environment of the two sexes; an environment so different from each other that man and woman must remain strangers. Separated by an insurmountable wall of superstition, custom, and habit, marriage has not the potentiality of developing knowledge of, and respect for, each other, without which every union is doomed to failure.

Henrik Ibsen, the hater of all social shams, was probably the first to realize this great truth. Nora leaves her husband, not—as the stupid critic would have it—because she is tired of her responsibilities or feels the need of woman's rights, but because she has come to know that for eight years she had lived with a stranger and borne him children. Can there be anything more humiliating, more degrading than a life-long proximity between two strangers? No need for the woman to know anything of the man, save his income. As to the knowledge of the woman—what is there to know except that she has a pleasing appearance? We have not yet outgrown the theologic myth that woman has no soul, that she is a mere appendix to man, made out of his rib just for the convenience of the gentleman who was so strong that he was afraid of his own shadow.

Perchance the poor quality of the material whence woman comes is responsible for her inferiority. At any rate, woman has no soul—what is there to know about her? Besides, the less soul a woman has the greater her asset as a wife, the more readily will she absorb herself in her husband. It is this slavish acquiescence to man's superiority that has kept the marriage institution seemingly intact for so long a period. Now that woman is coming into her own, now that she is actually growing aware of herself as a being outside of the master's grace, the sacred institution of marriage is gradually being undermined, and no amount of sentimental lamentation can stay it.

From infancy, almost, the average girl is told that marriage is her ultimate goal; therefore her training and education must be directed towards that end. Like the mute beast fattened for slaughter, she is prepared for that. Yet, strange to say, she is allowed to know much less about her function as wife and mother than the ordinary artisan of his trade. It is indecent and filthy for a respectable girl to know anything of the marital relation. Oh, for the inconsistency of respectability, that needs the marriage vow to turn something which is filthy into the purest and most sacred arrangement that none dare question or criticize. Yet that is exactly the attitude of the average upholder of marriage. The prospective wife and mother is kept in complete ignorance of her only asset in the competitive field—sex. Thus she enters into life-long relations with a man only to find herself shocked, repelled, outraged beyond measure by the most natural and healthy instinct, sex. It is safe to say that a large percentage of the unhappiness, misery, distress, and physical suffering of matrimony is due to the criminal ignorance in sex matters that is being extolled as a great virtue. Nor is it at all an exaggeration when I say that more than one home has been broken up because of this deplorable fact.

If, however, woman is free and big enough to learn the mystery of sex without the sanction of State or Church, she will stand condemned as utterly unfit to become the wife of a "good" man, his goodness consisting of an empty head and plenty of money. Can there be anything more outrageous than the idea that a healthy, grown woman, full of life and passion, must deny nature's demand, must subdue her most intense craving, undermine her health and break her spirit, must stunt her vision, abstain from the depth and glory of sex experience until a "good" man comes along to take her unto himself as a wife? That is precisely what marriage means. How can such an arrangement end except in failure? This is one, though not the least important, factor of marriage, which differentiates it from love.

Ours is a practical age. The time when Romeo and Juliet risked the wrath of their fathers for love, when Gretchen exposed herself to the gossip of her neighbors for love, is no more. If, on rare occasions, young people allow themselves the luxury of romance, they are taken in care by the elders, drilled and pounded until they become "sensible."

The moral lesson instilled in the girl is not whether the man has aroused her love, but rather is it, "How much?" The important and only God of practical American life: Can the man make a living? Can he support a wife? That is the only thing that justifies marriage. Gradually this saturates every thought of the girl; her dreams are not of moonlight and kisses, of laughter and tears; she dreams of shopping tours and bargain counters. This soul-poverty and sordidness are the elements inherent in the marriage institution. The State and the Church approve of no other ideal, simply because it is the one that necessitates the State and Church control of men and women.

Doubtless there are people who continue to consider love above dollars and cents. Particularly is this true of that class whom economic necessity has forced to become self-supporting. The tremendous change in woman's position, wrought by that mighty factor, is indeed phenomenal when we reflect that it is but a short time since she has entered the industrial arena. Six million women wage-earners; six million women, who have the equal right with men to be exploited, to be robbed, to go on strike; aye, to starve even. Anything more, my lord? Yes, six million wage-workers in every walk of life, from the highest brain work to the most difficult menial labor in the mines and on the railroad tracks; yes, even detectives and policemen. Surely the emancipation is complete.

Yet with all that, but a very small number of the vast

army of women wage-workers look upon work as a permanent issue, in the same light as does man. No matter how decrepit the latter, he has been taught to be independent, self-supporting. Oh, I know that no one is really independent in our economic treadmill; still, the poorest specimen of a man hates to be a parasite; to be known as such, at any rate.

The woman considers her position as worker transitory, to be thrown aside for the first bidder. That is why it is infinitely harder to organize women than men. "Why should I join a union? I am going to get married, to have a home." Has she not been taught from infancy to look upon that as her ultimate calling? She learns soon enough that the home, though not so large a prison as the factory, has more solid doors and bars. It has a keeper so faithful that naught can escape him. The most tragic part, however, is that the home no longer frees her from wage-slavery; it only increases her task.

According to the latest statistics submitted before a Committee "on labor and wages, and congestion of population," ten per cent of the wage-workers in New York City alone are married, yet they must continue to work at the most poorly paid labor in the world. Add to this horrible aspect the drudgery of housework, and what remains of the protection and glory of the home? As a matter of fact, even the middle-class girl in marriage can not speak of her home, since it is the man who creates her sphere. It is not important whether the husband is a brute or a darling. What I wish to prove is that marriage guarantees woman a home only by the grace of her husband. There she moves about in *his* home, year after year, until her aspect of life and human affairs becomes as flat, narrow, and drab as her surroundings. Small wonder if she becomes a nag, petty, quarrelsome, gossipy, unbearable, thus driving the man from the house. She could not go, if she wanted to; there is no place to go. Besides, a short period of married life, of complete surrender of all faculties, absolutely incapacitates the average woman for the outside world. She becomes reckless in appearance, clumsy in her movements, dependent in her decisions, cowardly in her judgment, a weight and a bore, which most men grow to hate and despise. Wonderfully inspiring atmosphere for the bearing of life, is it not?

But the child, how is it to be protected, if not for marriage? After all, is not that the most important consideration? The sham, the hypocrisy of it! Marriage protecting the child, yet thousands of children destitute and homeless. Marriage protecting the child, yet orphan asylums and reformatories overcrowded, the Society for the Prevention of Cruelty to Children keeping busy in rescuing the little victims from "loving" parents, to place them under more loving care, the Gerry Society. Oh, the mockery of it!

Marriage may have the power to "bring the horse to water," but has it ever made him drink? The law will place the father under arrest, and put him in convict's clothes; but has that ever stilled the hunger of the child? If the parent has no work, or if he hides his identity, what does marriage do then? It invokes the law to bring the man to "justice," to put him safely behind closed doors; his labor, however, goes not to the child, but to the State. The child receives but a blighted memory of its father's stripes.

As to the protection of the woman—therein lies the curse of marriage. Not that it really protects her, but the very idea is so revolting, such an outrage and insult on life, so degrading to human dignity, as to forever condemn this parasitic institution.

It is like that other paternal arrangement—capitalism. It robs man of his birthright, stunts his growth, poisons his body, keeps him in ignorance, in poverty and dependence, and then institutes charities that thrive on the last vestige of man's self-respect.

The institution of marriage makes a parasite of woman, an absolute dependent. It incapacitates her for life's struggle, annihilates her social consciousness, paralyzes her imagination, and then imposes its gracious protection, which is in reality a snare, a travesty on human character.

If motherhood is the highest fulfillment of woman's nature, what other protection does it need save love and freedom? Marriage but defiles, outrages, and corrupts her fulfillment. Does it not say to woman, Only when you follow me shall you bring forth life? Does it not condemn her to the block, does it not degrade and shame her if she refuses to buy her right to motherhood by selling herself? Does not marriage only sanction motherhood, even though conceived in hatred, in compulsion? Yet, if motherhood be of free choice, of love, of ecstasy, of defiant passion, does it not place a crown of thorns upon an innocent head and carve in letters of blood the hideous epithet, Bastard? Were marriage to contain all the virtues claimed for it, its crimes against motherhood would exclude it forever from the realm of love.

Love, the strongest and deepest element in all life, the harbinger of hope, of joy, of ecstasy; love, the defier of all laws, of all conventions; love, the freest, the most powerful moulder of human destiny; how can such an all-compelling force be synonymous with that poor little State- and Church-begotten weed, marriage?

Free love? As if love is anything but free! Man has bought brains, but all the millions in the world have failed to buy love. Man has subdued bodies, but all the power on earth has been unable to subdue love. Man has conquered whole nations, but all his armies could not conquer love. Man has chained and fettered the spirit, but he has been utterly helpless before love. High on a throne, with all the splendor and pomp his gold can command, man is yet poor and desolate, if love passes him by. And if it stays, the poorest hovel is radiant with warmth, with life and color. Thus love has the magic power to make of a beggar a king. Yes, love is free; it can dwell in no other atmosphere. In freedom it gives itself unreservedly, abundantly, completely. All the laws on the statutes, all the courts in the universe, cannot tear it from the soil, once love has taken root. If, however, the soil is sterile, how can marriage make it bear fruit? It is like the last desperate struggle of fleeting life against death.

Love needs no protection; it is its own protection. So long as love begets life no child is deserted, or hungry, or famished for the want of affection. I know this to be true. I know women who became mothers in freedom by the men they loved. Few children in wedlock enjoy the care, the protection, the devotion free motherhood is capable of bestowing.

The defenders of authority dread the advent of a free motherhood, lest it will rob them of their prey. Who would fight wars? Who would create wealth? Who would make the policeman, the jailer, if woman were to refuse the indiscriminate breeding of children? The race, the race! shouts the king, the president, the capitalist, the priest. The race must be preserved, though woman be degraded to a mere machine—and the marriage institution is our only safety valve against the pernicious sex-awakening of woman. But in vain these frantic efforts to maintain a state of bondage. In vain, too, the edicts of the Church, the mad attacks of rulers, in vain even the arm of the law. Woman no longer wants to be a party to the production of a race of sickly, feeble, decrepit, wretched human beings, who have neither the strength nor moral courage to throw off the yoke of poverty and slavery. Instead she desires fewer and better children, begotten and reared in love and through free choice; not by compulsion, as marriage imposes. Our pseudo-moralists have yet to learn the deep sense of responsibility toward the child, that love in freedom has awakened in the breast of woman. Rather would she forego forever the glory of motherhood than bring forth life in an atmosphere that breathes only destruction and death. And if she

does become a mother, it is to give to the child the deepest
and best her being can yield. To grow with the child is her
motto; she knows that in that manner alone can she help
build true manhood and womanhood.

Ibsen must have had a vision of a free mother, when,
with a master stroke, he portrayed Mrs. Alving.* She was the
ideal mother because she had outgrown marriage and all its
horrors, because she had broken her chains, and set her
spirit free to soar until it returned a personality, regenerated and strong. Alas, it was too late to rescue her life's
joy, her Oswald; but not too late to realize that love in
freedom is the only condition of a beautiful life. Those who,
like Mrs. Alving, have paid with blood and tears for their
spiritual awakening, repudiate marriage as an imposition,
a shallow, empty mockery. They know, whether love last
but one brief span of time or for eternity, it is the only
creative, inspiring, elevating basis for a new race, a new
world.

In our present pygmy state love is indeed a stranger to
most people. Misunderstood and shunned, it rarely takes
root; or if it does, it soon withers and dies. Its delicate fiber
can not endure the stress and strain of the daily grind. Its
soul is too complex to adjust itself to the slimy woof of our
social fabric. It weeps and moans and suffers with those
who have need of it, yet lack the capacity to rise to love's
summit.

Some day, some day men and women will rise, they will
reach the mountain peak, they will meet big and strong and
free, ready to receive, to partake, and to bask in the golden
rays of love. What fancy, what imagination, what poetic
genius can foresee even approximately the potentialities of
such a force in the life of men and women. If the world is
ever to give birth to true companionship and oneness, not
marriage, but love will be the parent.

* Editor's note: A character in *Ghosts*.

Jealousy: Causes
and a Possible Cure

No one at all capable of an intense conscious inner life need ever hope to escape mental anguish and suffering. Sorrow and often despair over the so-called eternal fitness of things are the most persistent companions of our life. But they do not come upon us from the outside, through the evil deeds of particularly evil people. They are conditioned in our very being; indeed, they are interwoven through a thousand tender and coarse threads with our existence.

It is absolutely necessary that we realize this fact, because people who never get away from the notion that their misfortune is due to the wickedness of their fellows never can outgrow the petty hatred and malice which constantly blames, condemns, and hounds others for something that is inevitable as part of themselves. Such people will not rise to the lofty heights of the true humanitarian to whom good and evil, moral and immoral, are but limited terms for the inner play of human emotions upon the human sea of life.

The "beyond good and evil" philosopher, Nietzsche, is at present denounced as the perpetrator of national hatred and machine gun destruction; but only bad readers and bad pupils interpret him so. "Beyond good and evil" means beyond prosecution, beyond judging, beyond killing, etc. *Beyond Good and Evil* opens before our eyes a vista the background of which is individual assertion combined with the understanding of all others who are unlike ourselves, who are different.

By that I do not mean the clumsy attempt of democracy to regulate the complexities of human character by means of external equality. The vision of "beyond good and evil" points to the right to oneself, to one's personality. Such possibilities do not exclude pain over the chaos of life, but they do exclude the puritanic righteousness that sits in judgment on all others except oneself.

It is self-evident that the thoroughgoing radical—there are many half-baked ones, you know—must apply this deep, humane recognition to the sex and love relation. Sex emotions and love are among the most intimate, the most intense and sensitive, expressions of our being. They are so deeply related to individual physical and psychic traits as to stamp each love affair an independent affair, unlike any other love affair. In other words, each love is the result of the impressions and characteristics the two people involved give to it. Every love relation should by its very nature remain an absolutely private affair. Neither the State, the Church, morality, or people should meddle with it.

Unfortunately this is not the case. The most intimate relation is subject to proscriptions, regulations, and coercions, yet these external factors are absolutely alien to love, and as such lead to everlasting contradictions and conflict between love and law.

The result of it is that our love life is merged into corruption and degradation. "Pure love," so much hailed by the poets, is in the present matrimonial, divorce, and alienation wrangles, a rare specimen indeed. With money, social standing, and position as the criteria of love, prostitution is quite inevitable, even if it be covered with the mantle of legitimacy and morality.

The most prevalent evil of our mutilated love-life is

jealousy, often described as the "green-eyed monster" who lies, cheats, betrays, and kills. The popular notion is that jealousy is inborn and therefore can never be eradicated from the human heart. This idea is a convenient excuse for those who lack ability and willingness to delve into cause and effect.

Anguish over a lost love, over the broken thread of love's continuity, is indeed inherent in our very beings. Emotional sorrow has inspired many sublime lyrics, much profound insight and poetic exultation of a Byron, Shelley, Heine, and their kind. But will anyone compare this grief with what commonly passes as jealousy? They are as unlike as wisdom and stupidity. As refinement and coarseness. As dignity and brutal coercion. Jealousy is the very reverse of understanding, of sympathy, and of generous feeling. Never has jealousy added to character, never does it make the individual big and fine. What it really does is to make him blind with fury, petty with suspicion, and harsh with envy.

Jealousy, the contortions of which we see in the matrimonial tragedies and comedies, is invariably a one-sided, bigoted accuser, convinced of his own righteousness and the meanness, cruelty, and guilt of his victim. Jealousy does not even attempt to understand. Its one desire is to punish, and to punish as severely as possible. This notion is embodied in the code of honor, as represented in duelling or the unwritten law. A code which will have it that the seduction of a woman must be atoned with the death of the seducer. Even where seduction has not taken place, where both have voluntarily yielded to the innermost urge, honor is restored only when blood has been shed, either that of the man or the woman.

Jealousy is obsessed by the sense of possession and vengeance. It is quite in accord with all other punitive laws upon the statutes which still adhere to the barbarous notion that an offence, often merely the result of social wrongs, must be adequately punished or revenged.

A very strong argument against jealousy is to be found in

the data of historians like Morgan, Reclus, and others, as to the sex relations among primitive people. Anyone at all conversant with their works knows that monogamy is a much later sex form which came into being as a result of the domestication and ownership of women, and which created sex monopoly and the inevitable feeling of jealousy.

In the past, when men and women intermingled freely without interference of law and morality, there could be no jealousy, because the latter rests upon the assumption that a certain man has an exclusive sex monopoly over a certain woman and *vice-versa*. The moment anyone dares to trespass this sacred precept, jealousy is up in arms. Under such circumstances it is ridiculous to say that jealousy is perfectly natural. As a matter of fact, it is the artificial result of an artificial cause, nothing else.

Unfortunately, it is not only conservative marriages which are saturated with the notion of sex monopoly; the so-called free unions are also victims of it. The argument may be raised that this is one more proof that jealousy is an inborn trait. But it must be borne in mind that sex monopoly has been handed down from generation to generation as a sacred right and the basis of purity of the family and the home. And just as the Church and the State accepted sex monopoly as the only security to the marriage tie, so have both justified jealousy as the legitimate weapon of defense for the protection of the property right.

Now, while it is true that a great many people have outgrown the legality of sex monopoly, they have not outgrown its traditions and habits. Therefore they become as blinded by the "green-eyed monster" as their conservative neighbors the moment their possessions are at stake.

A man or woman free and big enough not to interfere or fuss over the outside attractions of the loved one is sure to be despised by his conservative, and ridiculed by his radical, friends. He will either be decried as a degenerate or a coward; often enough some petty material motives will be imputed to him. In any event, such men and women will be the target of coarse gossip or filthy jokes for no other reason than that they concede to wife, husband or lovers the right to their own bodies and their emotional expression, without making jealous scenes or wild threats to kill the intruder.

There are other factors in jealousy: the conceit of the male and the envy of the female. The male in matters sexual is an imposter, a braggart, who forever boasts of his exploits and success with women. He insists on playing the part of a conqueror, since he has been told that women want to be conquered, that they love to be seduced. Feeling himself the only cock in the barnyard, or the bull who must clash horns in order to win the cow, he feels mortally wounded in his conceit and arrogance the moment a rival appears on the scene—the scene, even among so-called refined men, continues to be woman's sex love, which must belong to only one master.

In other words, the endangered sex monopoly together with man's outraged vanity in ninety-nine cases out of a hundred are the antecedents of jealousy.

In the case of woman, economic fear for herself and children and her petty envy of every other woman who gains grace in the eyes of her supporter invariably create jealousy. In justice to woman be it said that for centuries past, physical attraction was her only stock in trade, therefore she must needs become envious of the charm and value of other women as threatening her hold upon her precious property.

The grotesque aspect of the whole matter is that men and women often grow violently jealous of those they really do not care much about. It is therefore not their outraged love, but their outraged conceit and envy which cry out against this "terrible wrong." Likely as not the woman never loved the man whom she now suspects and spies upon. Likely as not she never made an effort to keep his love. But the moment a competitor arrives, she begins to value her sex property for the defense of which no means are too despicable or cruel.

Obviously, then, jealousy is not the result of love. In fact, if it were possible to investigate most cases of jealousy, it would likely be found that the less people are imbued with a great love the more violent and contemptible is their jealousy. Two people bound by inner harmony and oneness are not afraid to impair their mutual confidence and security if one or the other has outside attractions, nor will their relations end in vile enmity, as is too often the case with many people. They may not be able, nor ought they to be expected, to receive the choice of the loved one into the intimacy of their lives, but that does not give either one the right to deny the necessity of the attraction.

As I shall discuss variety and monogamy two weeks from tonight, I will not dwell upon either here, except to say that to look upon people who can love more than one person as perverse or abnormal is to be very ignorant indeed. I have already discussed a number of causes for jealousy to which I must add the institution of marriage which the State and Church proclaim as "the bond until death doth part." This is accepted as the ethical mode of right living and right doing.

With love, in all its variability and changeability, fettered and cramped, it is small wonder if jealousy arises out of it. What else but pettiness, meanness, suspicion, and rancor can come when man and wife are officially held together with the formula "from now on you are one in body and spirit." Just take any couple tied in such a manner, dependent upon each other for every thought and feeling, without an outside interest or desire, and ask yourself whether such a relation must not become hateful and unbearable in time.

In some form or other the fetters are broken, and as the circumstances which bring this about are usually low and degrading, it is hardly surprising that they bring into play the shabbiest and meanest human traits and motives.

In other words, legal, religious, and moral interference are the parents of our present unnatural love and sex life, and out of it jealousy has grown. It is the lash which whips

and tortures poor mortals because of their stupidity, ignorance, and prejudice.

But no one need attempt to justify himself on the ground
of being a victim of these conditions. It is only too true that
we all smart under the burdens of iniquitous social arrangements, under coercion and moral blindness. But are we not
conscious individuals, whose aim it is to bring truth and
justice into human affairs? The theory that man is a product
of conditions has led only to indifference and to a sluggish
acquiescence in these conditions. Yet everyone knows that
adaptation to an unhealthy and unjust mode of life only
strengthens both, while man, the so-called crown of all
creation, equipped with a capacity to think and see and
above all to employ his powers of initiative, grows ever
weaker, more passive, more fatalistic.

In this sense I speak of a possible cure of jealousy, after I
have attempted to prove that its cause lies in our coerced,
crippled love-life. I hold that every man and woman can
help to cure jealousy. The first step towards this is a recognition that they are neither the owners nor controllers nor
dictators over the sex functions of the wife or the husband.
The second step is that they both grow too proud to accept
love or affection which is not gladly or voluntarily given.
Anything offered out of duty, because of the marriage
license, isn't the genuine thing. It is counterfeit. Whatever
we attempt to hold by force, by jealous threats or scenes,
through spying and snooping, through mean tricks and soul
tortures, is not worth keeping. It only leaves a bad taste
behind, and the mind and heart-destroying doubt whether
or not we have succeeded in bringing back the wayward
lamb.

There is nothing more terrible and fatal than to dig into
the vitals of one's loved ones and oneself. It can only help
to tear whatever slender threads of affection still inhere in
the relation and finally bring us to the last ditch, which

jealousy attempts to prevent, namely, the annihilation of love, friendship and respect.

Jealousy is indeed a poor medium to secure love, but it is a secure medium to destroy one's self-respect. For jealous people, like dope-fiends, stoop to the lowest level and in the end inspire only disgust and loathing.

Anguish over the loss of love or a nonreciprocated love among people who are capable of high and fine thoughts will never make a person coarse. Those who are sensitive and fine have only to ask themselves whether they can tolerate any obligatory relation, and an emphatic *no* would be the reply. But most people continue to live near each other although they have long ceased to live with each other —a life fertile enough for the operation of jealousy, whose methods go all the way from opening private correspondence to murder. Compared with such horrors, open adultery seems an act of courage and liberation.

A strong shield against the vulgarity of jealousy is that man and wife are not of one body and one spirit. They are two human beings, of different temperament, feelings, and emotions. Each is a small cosmos in himself, engrossed in his own thoughts and ideas. It is glorious and poetic if these two worlds meet in freedom and equality. Even if this lasts but a short time it is already worthwhile. But, the moment the two worlds are forced together all the beauty and fragrance ceases and nothing but dead leaves remain. Whoever grasps this truism will consider jealousy beneath him and will not permit it to hang as a sword of Damocles over him.

All lovers do well to leave the doors of their love wide open. When love can go and come without fear of meeting a watch-dog, jealousy will rarely take root because it will soon learn that where there are no locks and keys there is no place for suspicion and distrust, two elements upon which jealousy thrives and prospers.

Intellectual Proletarians

The proletarization of our time reaches far beyond the field of manual labor; indeed, in the larger sense all those who work for their living, whether with hand or brain, all those who must sell their skill, knowledge, experience and ability, are proletarians. From this point of view, our entire system, excepting a very limited class, has been proletarianized.

Our whole social fabric is maintained by the efforts of mental and physical labor. In return for that, the intellectual proletarians, even as the workers in shop and mine, eke out an insecure and pitiful existence, and are more dependent upon the masters than those who work with their hands.

No doubt there is a difference between the yearly income of a Brisbane* and a Pennsylvania mine worker. The former, with his colleagues in the newspaper office, in the theater, college and university, may enjoy material comfort and social position, but with it all they are proletarians, inasmuch as they are slavishly dependent upon the Hearsts, the Pulitzers, the Theater Trusts, the publishers and, above

* Editor's note: Arthur Brisbane was an influential editor and journalist for the Hearst newspapers.

all, upon a stupid and vulgar public opinion. This terrible
dependence upon those who can make the price and dictate
the terms of intellectual activities is more degrading than
the position of the worker in any trade. The pathos of it is
that those who are engaged in intellectual occupations, no
matter how sensitive they might have been in the beginning,
grow callous, cynical and indifferent to their degradation.
That has certainly happened to Brisbane, whose parents
were idealists working with Fourier in the early co-opera-
tive ventures. Brisbane, who himself began as a man of
ideals, but who has become so enmeshed by material success that he has forsworn and betrayed every principle of
his youth.

Naturally so. Success achieved by the most contemptible
means cannot but destroy the soul. Yet that is the goal of
our day. It helps to cover up the inner corruption and
gradually dulls one's scruples, so that those who begin with
some high ambition cannot, even if they would, create anything out of themselves.

In other words, those who are placed in positions which
demand the surrender of personality, which insist on strict
conformity to definite political policies and opinions, must
deteriorate, must become mechanical, must lose all capacity
to give anything really vital. The world is full of such unfortunate cripples. Their dream is to "arrive," no matter at
what cost. If only we would stop to consider what it means
to "arrive," we would pity the unfortunate victim. Instead
of that, we look to the artist, the poet, the writer, the
dramatist and thinker who have "arrived," as the final
authority on all matters, whereas in reality their "arrival" is
synonymous with mediocrity, with the denial and betrayal
of what might in the beginning have meant something real
and ideal.

The "arrived" artists are dead souls upon the intellectual
horizon. The uncompromising and daring spirits never "arrive." Their life represents an endless battle with the stupid-

ity and the dullness of their time. They must remain what Nietzsche calls "untimely," because everything that strives for new form, new expression or new values is always doomed to be untimely.

The real pioneers in ideas, in art and in literature have remained aliens to their time, misunderstood and repudiated. And if, as in the case of Zola, Ibsen and Tolstoy, they compelled their time to accept them, it was due to their extraordinary genius and even more so to the awakening and seeking of a small minority for new truths, to whom these men were the inspiration and intellectual support. Yet even to this day Ibsen is unpopular, while Poe, Whitman and Strindberg have never "arrived."

The logical conclusion is this: those who will not worship at the shrine of money need not not hope for recognition. On the other hand, they will also not have to think other people's thoughts or wear other people's political clothes. They will not have to proclaim as true that which is false, nor praise that as humanitarian which is brutal. I realize that those who have the courage to defy the economic and social whip are among the few, and we have to deal with the many.

Now, it is a fact that the majority of the intellectual proletarians are in the economic treadmill and have less freedom than those who work in the shops or mines. Unlike the latter, they cannot put on overalls and ride the bumpers to the next town in search of a job. In the first place, they have spent a lifetime on a profession, at the expense of all their other faculties. They are therefore unfitted for any other work except the one thing which, parrot-like, they have learned to repeat. We all know how cruelly difficult it is to find a job in any given trade. But to come to a new town without connections and find a position as teacher, writer, musician, bookkeeper, actress or nurse is almost impossible.

If, however, the intellectual proletarian has connections,

he must come to them in a presentable shape; he must keep up appearances. And that requires means, of which most professional people have as little as the workers, because even in their "good times" they rarely earn enough to make ends meet.

Then there are the traditions, the habits of the intellectual proletarians, the fact that they must live in a certain district, that they must have certain comforts, that they must buy clothes of a certain quality. All that has emasculated them, has made them unfit for the stress and strain of the life of the bohemian. If he and she drink coffee at night, they cannot sleep. If they stay up a little later than usual, they are unfitted for the next day's work. In short, they have no vitality and cannot, like the manual worker, meet the hardships of the road. Therefore they are tied in a thousand ways to the most galling, humiliating conditions. But so blind are they to their own lot that they consider themselves superior, better, and more fortunate than their fellow-comrades in the ranks of labor.

Then, too, there are the women who boast of their wonderful economic achievements, and that they can now be self-supporting. Every year our schools and colleges turn out thousands of competitors in the intellectual market, and everywhere the supply is greater than the demand. In order to exist, they must cringe and crawl and beg for a position. Professional women crowd the offices, sit around for hours, grow weary and faint with the search for employment, and yet deceive themselves with the delusion that they are superior to the working girl, or that they are economically independent.

The years of their youth are swallowed up in the acquisition of a profession, in the end to be dependent upon the board of education, the city editor, the publisher or the theatrical manager. The emancipated woman runs away from a stifling home atmosphere, only to rush from employment bureau to the literary broker, and back again. She points with moral disgust to the girl of the redlight district, and is not aware that she too must sing, dance, write or play, and otherwise sell herself a thousand times in return for her living. Indeed, the only difference between the working girl and the intellectual female or male proletarian is a matter of four hours. At 5 A.M. the former stands in line waiting to be called to the job and often face to face with a sign, "No hands wanted." At 9 A.M. the professional woman must face the sign, "No brains wanted."

Under such a state of affairs, what becomes of the high mission of the intellectuals, the poets, the writers, the composers and what not? What are they doing to cut loose from their chains, and how dare they boast that they are helping the masses? Yet you know that they are engaged in uplift work. What a farce! They, so pitiful and low in their slavery themselves, so dependent and helpless! The truth is, the people have nothing to learn from this class of intellectuals, while they have everything to give to them. If only the intellectuals would come down from their lofty pedestal and realize how closely related they are to the people! But they will not do that, not even the radical and liberal intellectuals.

Within the last ten years the intellectual proletarians of advanced tendencies have entered every radical movement. They could, if they would, be of tremendous importance to the workers. But so far they have remained without clarity of vision, without depth of conviction, and without real daring to face the world. It is not because they do not feel deeply the mind- and soul-destroying effects of compromise, or that they do not know the corruption, the degradation in our social, political, business, and family life. Talk to them in private gatherings, or when you get them alone, and they will admit that there isn't a single institution worth preserving. But only privately. Publicly they continue in the same rut as their conservative colleagues. They write the stuff that will sell, and do not go an inch farther than public taste will permit. They speak their thoughts, careful not to offend anyone, and live according to the most stupid conventions of the day. Thus we find men in the legal profession, intellectually emancipated from the belief in government, yet looking to the fleshpots of a judgeship; men who know the corruption of politics, yet belonging to political parties and championing Mr. Roosevelt. Men who realize the prostitution of mind in the newspaper profession, yet holding responsible positions therein. Women who deeply feel the fetters of the marital institution and the indignity of our moral precepts, who yet submit to both; who either stifle their nature or have clandestine relations—but God forbid they should face the world and say, "Mind your own damned business!"

Even in their sympathies for labor—and some of them have genuine sympathies—the intellectual proletarians do not cease to be middle-class, respectable and aloof. This may seem sweeping and unfair, but those who know the various groups will understand that I am not exaggerating. Women of every profession have flocked to Lawrence, to Little Falls, to Paterson, and to the strike districts in this city. Partly out of curiosity, often out of interest. But always they have remained rooted to their middle-class traditions. Always they have deceived themselves and the workers with the notion that they must give the strike respectable prestige, to help the cause.

In the shirtwaistmakers' strike professional women were told to rig themselves out in their best furs and most expensive jewelry, if they wanted to help the girls. Is it necessary to say that while scores of girls were manhandled and brutally hustled into the patrol wagons, the well-dressed pickets were treated with deference and allowed to go home? Thus they had their excitement, and only hurt the cause of labor.

The police are indeed stupid, but not so stupid as not to know the difference in the danger to themselves and their masters from those who are driven to strike by necessity, and those who go into the strike for pastime or "copy." This difference doesn't come from the degree of feeling, nor even the cut of clothes, but from the degree of incentive and courage; and those who still compromise with appearances have no courage.

The police, the courts, the prison authorities and the newspaper owners know perfectly well that the liberal intellectuals, even as the conservatives, are slaves to appearances. That is why their muckraking, their investigations, their sympathies with the workers are never taken seriously. Indeed, they are welcomed by the press, because the reading public loves sensation, hence the muckraker represents a good investment for the concern and for himself. But as far as danger to the ruling class is concerned, it is like the babbling of an infant.

Mr. Sinclair would have died in obscurity but for *The Jungle,* which didn't move a hair upon the heads of the Armours, but netted the author a large sum and a reputation. He may now write the most stupid stuff, sure of finding a market. Yet there is not a workingman anywhere so cringing before respectability as Mr. Sinclair.

Mr. Kibbe Turner* would have remained a penny-a-liner but for our political mudslingers, who used him to make capital against Tammany Hall. Yet the poorest-paid laborer is more independent than Mr. Turner, and certainly more honest than he.

Mr. Hillquit† would have remained the struggling revolutionist I knew him twenty-four years ago, but for the workers who helped him to his legal success. Yet there is not a single Russian worker on the East Side so thoroughly

---

* Editor's note: George Kibbe Turner was a muckraking journalist who wrote exposés of white slavery and Chicago corruption for *McClure's* magazine.

† Editor's note: Morris Hillquit, Socialist party leader; candidate for mayor of New York City in 1917.

bound to respectability and public opinion as Mr. Hillquit.

I could go on indefinitely proving that, though the intellectuals are really proletarians, they are so steeped in middle-class traditions and conventions, so tied and gagged by them, that they dare not move a step.

The cause of it is, I believe, to be sought in the fact that the intellectuals of America have not yet discovered their relation to the workers, to the revolutionary elements which at all times and in every country have been the inspiration of men and women who worked with their brains. They seem to think that they and not the workers represent the creators of culture. But that is a disastrous mistake, as proved in all countries. Only when the intellectual forces of Europe had made common cause with the struggling masses, when they came close to the depths of society, did they give to the world a real culture.

With us, this depth in the minds of our intellectuals is only a place for slumming, for newspaper copy, or on a very rare occasion for a little theoretic sympathy. Never was the latter strong or deep enough to pull them out of themselves, or make them break with their traditions and surroundings. Strikes, conflicts, the use of dynamite, or the efforts of the I.W.W. are exciting to our intellectual proletarians, but after all very foolish when considered in the light of the logical, cool-headed observer. Of course they feel with the I.W.W. man when he is beaten and brutally treated, or with the McNamaras,* who cleared the horizon from the foggy belief that in America no one needed use violence. The intellectuals gall too much under their own dependence not to sympathize in such a case. But the sympathy is never strong enough to establish a bond, a

* Editor's note: The McNamara brothers, J. J. and J. B., were conservative trade-unionists who pleaded guilty to dynamiting the *Los Angeles Times* in 1910. Goldman was among the few radicals who refused to condemn them, holding that labor violence resulted from employer violence.

solidarity between him and the disinherited. It is the sympathy of aloofness, of experiment.

In other words, it is a theoretic sympathy which all those have who still enjoy a certain amount of comfort and therefore do not see why anyone should break into a fashionable restaurant. It is the kind of sympathy Mrs. Belmont has when she goes to night courts. Or the sympathy of the Osbornes, Dottys and Watsons when they had themselves locked up in prison for a few days. The sympathy of the millionaire Socialist who speaks of "economic determinism."

The intellectual proletarians who are radical and liberal are still so much of the bourgeois régime that their sympathy with the workers is dilettante and does not go farther than the parlor, the so-called salon, or Greenwich Village. It may in a measure be compared to the early period of the awakening of the Russian intellectuals described by Turgenev in *Fathers and Sons*.

The intellectuals of that time, while never so superficial as those I am talking about, indulged in revolutionary ideas, split hairs through the early morning hours, philosophized about all sorts of questions and carried their superior wisdom to the people with their feet deeply rooted in the old. Of course they failed. They were indignant with Turgenev and considered him a traitor to Russia. But he was right. Only when the Russian intellectuals completely broke with their traditions; only when they fully realized that society rests upon a lie, and that they must give themselves to the new completely and unreservedly, did they become a forceful factor in the life of the people. The Kropotkins, the Perovskayas, the Breshkovskayas, and hosts of others repudiated wealth and station and refused to serve King Mammon. They went among the people, not to lift them up but themselves to be lifted up, to be instructed, and in return to give themselves wholly to the people. That accounts for the heroism, the art, the literature of Russia, the unity between the people, the mujik and the intellectual. That to some extent explains the literature of all European countries, the fact that the Strindbergs, the Hauptmanns, the Wedekinds, the Brieux, the Mirbeaus, the Steinlins and Rodins have never dissociated themselves from the people.

Will that ever come to pass in America? Will the American intellectual proletarians ever love the ideal more than their comforts, ever be willing to give up external success for the sake of the vital issues of life? I think so, and that for two reasons. First, the proletarization of the intellectuals will compel them to come closer to labor. Secondly, because of the rigid régime of puritanism, which is causing a tremendous reaction against conventions and narrow moral ties. Struggling artists, writers and dramatists who strive to create something worth while aid in breaking down dominant conventions; scores of women who wish to live their lives are helping to undermine our morality of to-day in their proud defiance of the rules of Mrs. Grundy. Alone they cannot accomplish much. They need the bold indifference and courage of the revolutionary workers, who have broken with all the old rubbish. It is therefore through the co-operation of the intellectual proletarians, who try to find expression, and the revolutionary proletarians who seek to remould life, that we in America will establish a real unity and by means of it wage a successful war against present society.

The Failure of Christianity

The counterfeiters and poisoners of ideas, in their attempt to obscure the line between truth and falsehood, find a valuable ally in the conservatism of language.

Conceptions and words that have long ago lost their original meaning continue through centuries to dominate mankind. Especially is this true if these conceptions have become a common-place, if they have been instilled in our beings from our infancy as great and irrefutable verities. The average mind is easily content with inherited and acquired things, or with the dicta of parents and teachers, because it is much easier to imitate than to create.

Our age has given birth to two intellectual giants, who have undertaken to transvalue the dead social and moral values of the past, especially those contained in Christianity. Friedrich Nietzsche and Max Stirner have hurled blow upon blow against the portals of Christianity, because they saw in it a pernicious slave morality, the denial of life, the destroyer of all the elements that make for strength and character. True, Nietzsche has opposed the slave-morality idea inherent in Christianity in behalf of a master morality for the privileged few. But I venture to suggest that his master idea had nothing to do with the vulgarity of station, caste, or wealth. Rather did it mean the masterful in human possibilities, the masterful in man that would help him to overcome old traditions and worn-out values, so that he may learn to become the creator of new and beautiful things.

Both Nietzsche and Stirner saw in Christianity the leveler of the human race, the breaker of man's will to dare and to do. They saw in every movement built on Christian morality and ethics attempts not at the emancipation from slavery, but for the perpetuation thereof. Hence they opposed these movements with might and main.

Whether I do or do not entirely agree with these iconoclasts, I believe, with them, that Christianity is most admirably adapted to the training of slaves, to the perpetuation of a slave society; in short, to the very conditions confronting us to-day. Indeed, never could society have degenerated to its present appalling stage, if not for the assistance of Christianity. The rulers of the earth have realized long ago what potent poison inheres in the Christian religion. That is the reason they foster it; that is why they leave nothing undone to instill it into the blood of the people. They know only too well that the subtleness of the Christian teachings is a more powerful protection against rebellion and discontent than the club or the gun.

No doubt I will be told that, though religion is a poison and institutionalized Christianity the greatest enemy of progress and freedom, there is some good in Christianity "itself." What about the teachings of Christ and early Christianity, I may be asked; do they not stand for the spirit of humanity, for right and justice?

It is precisely this oft-repeated contention that induced me to choose this subject, to enable me to demonstrate that the abuses of Christianity, like the abuses of government, are conditioned in the thing itself, and are not to be charged to the representatives of the creed. Christ and his teachings are the embodiment of submission, of inertia, of the denial of life; hence responsible for the things done in their name.

I am not interested in the theological Christ. Brilliant minds like Bauer, Strauss, Renan, Thomas Paine, and others refuted that myth long ago. I am even ready to admit that the theological Christ is not half so dangerous as the ethical and social Christ. In proportion as science takes the place of blind faith, theology loses its hold. But the ethical and poetical Christ-myth has so thoroughly saturated our lives that even some of the most advanced minds find it difficult to emancipate themselves from its yoke. They have rid themselves of the letter, but have retained the spirit; yet it is the spirit which is back of all the crimes and horrors committed by orthodox Christianity. The Fathers of the Church can well afford to preach the gospel of Christ. It contains nothing dangerous to the régime of authority and wealth; it stands for self-denial and self-abnegation, for penance and regret, and is absolutely inert in the face of every [in]dignity, every outrage imposed upon mankind.

Here I must revert to the counterfeiters of ideas and words. So many otherwise earnest haters of slavery and injustice confuse, in a most distressing manner, the teachings of Christ with the great struggles for social and economic emancipation. The two are irrevocably and forever opposed to each other. The one necessitates courage, daring, defiance, and strength. The other preaches the gospel of non-resistance, of slavish acquiescence in the will of others; it is the complete disregard of character and self-reliance, and therefore destructive of liberty and well-being.

Whoever sincerely aims at a radical change in society, whoever strives to free humanity from the scourge of dependence and misery, must turn his back on Christianity, on the old as well as the present form of the same.

Everywhere and always, since its very inception, Christianity has turned the earth into a vale of tears; always it has made of life a weak, diseased thing, always it has instilled fear in man, turning him into a dual being, whose life energies are spent in the struggle between body and soul. In decrying the body as something evil, the flesh as the tempter to everything that is sinful, man has mutilated his being in the vain attempt to keep his soul pure, while his body rotted away from the injuries and tortures inflicted upon it.

The Christian religion and morality extols the glory of the Hereafter, and therefore remains indifferent to the horrors of the earth. Indeed, the idea of self-denial and of all that makes for pain and sorrow is its test of human worth, its passport to the entry into heaven.

The poor are to own heaven, and the rich will go to hell. That may account for the desperate efforts of the rich to make hay while the sun shines, to get as much out of the earth as they can: to wallow in wealth and superfluity, to tighten their iron hold on the blessed slaves, to rob them of their birthright, to degrade and outrage them every minute of the day. Who can blame the rich if they revenge them-selves on the poor, for now is their time, and the merciful Christian God alone knows how ably and completely the rich are doing it.

And the poor? They cling to the promise of the Christian heaven, as the home for old age, the sanitarium for crippled bodies and weak minds. They endure and submit, they suffer and wait, until every bit of self-respect has been knocked out of them, until their bodies become emaciated and withered, and their spirit broken from the wait, the weary endless wait for the Christian heaven.

Christ made his appearance as the leader of the people, the redeemer of the Jews from Roman dominion; but the moment he began his work, he proved that he had no interest in the earth, in the pressing immediate needs of the poor and the disinherited of his time. What he preached was a sentimental mysticism, obscure and confused ideas lack-ing originality and vigor.

When the Jews, according to the gospels, withdrew from Jesus, when they turned him over to the cross, they may have been bitterly disappointed in him who promised them so much and gave them so little. He promised joy and bliss in another world, while the people were starving, suffering, and enduring before his very eyes.

It may also be that the sympathy of the Romans, especially of Pilate, was given Christ because they regarded him as perfectly harmless to their power and sway. The philosopher Pilate may have considered Christ's "eternal truths" as pretty anaemic and lifeless, compared with the array of strength and force they attempted to combat. The Romans, strong and unflinching as they were, must have laughed in their sleeves over the man who talked repentance and patience, instead of calling to arms against the despoilers and oppressors of his people.

The public career of Christ begins with the edict, "Repent, for the Kingdom of Heaven is at hand."

Why repent, why regret, in the face of something that was supposed to bring deliverance? Had not the people suffered and endured enough; had they not earned their right to deliverance by their suffering? Take the Sermon on the Mount, for instance. What is it but a eulogy on submission to fate, to the inevitability of things?

"Blessed are the poor in spirit, for theirs is the Kingdom of Heaven."

Heaven must be an awfully dull place if the poor in spirit live there. How can anything creative, anything vital, useful and beautiful come from the poor in spirit? The idea conveyed in the Sermon on the Mount is the greatest indictment against the teachings of Christ, because it sees in the poverty of mind and body a virtue, and because it seeks to maintain this virtue by reward and punishment. Every intelligent being realizes that our worst curse is the poverty of the spirit; that it is productive of all evil and misery, of all the injustice and crimes in the world. Every one knows that nothing good ever came or can come of the poor in spirit; surely never liberty, justice, or equality.

"Blessed are the meek, for they shall inherit the earth."

What a preposterous notion! What incentive to slavery, inactivity, and parasitism! Besides, it is not true that the meek can inherit anything. Just because humanity has been meek, the earth has been stolen from it.

Meekness has been the whip, which capitalism and governments have used to force man into dependency, into his slave position. The most faithful servants of the State, of wealth, of special privilege, could not preach a more convenient gospel than did Christ, the "redeemer" of the people.

"Blessed are they that hunger and thirst for righteousness, for they shall be filled."

But did not Christ exclude the possibility of righteousness when he said, "The poor ye have always with you"? But, then, Christ was great on dicta, no matter if they were utterly opposed to each other. This is nowhere demonstrated so strikingly as in his command, "Render to Caesar the things that are Caesar's, and to God the things that are God's."

The interpreters claim that Christ had to make these concessions to the powers of his time. If that be true, this single compromise was sufficient to prove, down to this very day, a most ruthless weapon in the hands of the oppressor, a fearful lash and relentless tax-gatherer, to the impoverishment, the enslavement, and degradation of the very people for whom Christ is supposed to have died. And when we are assured that "Blessed are they that hunger and thirst for righteousness, for they shall be filled," are we told the how? How? Christ never takes the trouble to explain that. Righteousness does not come from the stars, nor because Christ willed it so. Righteousness grows out of liberty, of social and economic opportunity and equality. But how can the meek, the poor in spirit, ever establish such a state of affairs?

"Blessed are ye when men shall revile you and persecute you, and say all manner of evil against you falsely, for my sake. Rejoice, and be exceeding glad: for great is your reward in heaven."

The reward in heaven is the perpetual bait, a bait that has caught man in an iron net, a strait-jacket which does not let him expand or grow. All pioneers of truth have been, and still are, reviled; they have been, and still are, persecuted. But did they ask humanity to pay the price? Did they seek to bribe mankind to accept their ideas? They knew too well that he who accepts a truth because of the bribe, will soon barter it away to a higher bidder.

Good and bad, punishment and reward, sin and penance, heaven and hell, as the moving spirit of the Christ-gospel have been the stumbling-block in the world's work. It contains everything in the way of orders and commands, but entirely lacks the very things we need most.

The worker who knows the cause of his misery, who understands the make-up of our iniquitous social and industrial system can do more for himself and his kind than Christ and the followers of Christ have ever done for humanity; certainly more than meek patience, ignorance, and submission have done.

How much more ennobling, how much more beneficial is the extreme individualism of Stirner and Nietzsche than the sick-room atmosphere of the Christian faith. If they repudiate altruism as an evil, it is because of the example contained in Christianity, which set a premium on parasitism and inertia, gave birth to all manner of social disorders that are to be cured with the preachment of love and sympathy.

Proud and self-reliant characters prefer hatred to such sickening artificial love. Not because of any reward does a free spirit take his stand for a great truth, nor has such a one ever been deterred because of fear of punishment.

"Think not that I come to destroy the law or the prophets. I am not come to destroy, but to fulfill."

Precisely. Christ was a reformer, ever ready to patch up, to fulfill, to carry on the old order of things; never to destroy and rebuild. That may account for the fellow-feeling all reformers have for him.

Indeed, the whole history of the State, Capitalism, and the Church proves that they have perpetuated themselves because of the idea "I come not to destroy the law." This is the key to authority and oppression. Naturally so, for did not Christ praise poverty as a virtue; did he not propagate non-resistance to evil? Why should not poverty and evil continue to rule the world?

Much as I am opposed to every religion, much as I think them an imposition upon, and crime against, reason and progress, I yet feel that no other religion has done so much harm or has helped so much in the enslavement of man as the religion of Christ.

Witness Christ before his accusers. What lack of dignity, what lack of faith in himself and in his own ideas! So weak and helpless was this "Saviour of Men" that he must needs the whole human family to pay for him, unto all eternity, because he "hath died for them." Redemption through the Cross is worse than damnation, because of the terrible burden it imposes upon humanity, because of the effect it has on the human soul, fettering and paralyzing it with the weight of the burden exacted through the death of Christ.

Thousands of martyrs have perished, yet few, if any, of them have proved so helpless as the great Christian God. Thousands have gone to their death with greater fortitude, with more courage, with deeper faith in their ideas than the Nazarene. Nor did they expect eternal gratitude from their fellow-men because of what they endured for them.

Compared with Socrates and Bruno, with the great martyrs of Russia, with the Chicago Anarchists, Francisco Ferrer, and unnumbered others, Christ cuts a poor figure indeed. Compared with the delicate, frail Spiridonova who underwent the most terrible tortures, the most horrible indignities, without losing faith in herself or her cause, Jesus is a veritable nonentity. They stood their ground and faced their executioners with unflinching determination, and though they, too, died for the people, they asked nothing in return for their great sacrifice.

Verily, we need redemption from the slavery, the deadening weakness, and humiliating dependency of Christian morality.

The teachings of Christ and of his followers have failed because they lacked the vitality to lift the burdens from the shoulders of the race; they have failed because the very essence of that doctrine is contrary to the spirit of life, exposed to the manifestations of nature, to the strength and beauty of passion.

Never can Christianity, under whatever mask it may appear—be it New Liberalism, Spiritualism, Christian Science, New Thought, or a thousand and one other forms of hysteria and neurasthenia—bring us relief from the terrible pressure of conditions, the weight of poverty, the horrors of our iniquitous system. Christianity is the conspiracy of ignorance against reason, of darkness against light, of submission and slavery against independence and freedom; of the denial of strength and beauty, against the affirmation of the joy and glory of life.

The Philosophy of Atheism

To give an adequate exposition of the Philosophy of Atheism, it would be necessary to go into the historical changes of the belief in a Deity, from its earliest beginning to the present day. But that is not within the scope of the present paper. However, it is not out of place to mention, in passing, that the concept God, Supernatural Power, Spirit, Deity, or in whatever other term the essence of Theism may have found expression, has become more indefinite and obscure in the course of time and progress. In other words, the God idea is growing more impersonal and nebulous in proportion as the human mind is learning to understand natural phenomena and in the degree that science progressively correlates human and social events.

God, today, no longer represents the same forces as in the beginning of His existence; neither does He direct human destiny with the same iron hand as of yore. Rather does the God idea express a sort of spiritualistic stimulus to satisfy the fads and fancies of every shade of human weakness. In the course of human development the God idea has been forced to adapt itself to every phase of human affairs, which is perfectly consistent with the origin of the idea itself.

The conception of gods originated in fear and curiosity. Primitive man, unable to understand the phenomena of nature and harassed by them, saw in every terrifying manifestation some sinister force expressly directed against him; and as ignorance and fear are the parents of all superstition, the troubled fancy of primitive man wove the God idea.

Very aptly, the world-renowned atheist and anarchist, Michael Bakunin, says in his great work *God and the State:* "All religions, with their gods, their demi-gods, and their prophets, their messiahs and their saints, were created by the prejudiced fancy of men who had not attained the full development and full possession of their faculties. Consequently, the religious heaven is nothing but the mirage in which man, exalted by ignorance and faith, discovered his own image, but enlarged and reversed—that is divinised. The history of religions, of the birth, grandeur, and the decline of the gods who had succeeded one another in human belief, is nothing, therefore, but the development of the collective intelligence and conscience of mankind. As fast as they discovered, in the course of their historically-progressive advance, either in themselves or in external nature, a quality, or even any great defect whatever, they attributed it to their gods, after having exaggerated and enlarged it beyond measure, after the manner of children, by an act of their religious fancy. . . . With all due respect, then, to the metaphysicians and religious idealists, philosophers, politicians or poets: the idea of God implies the abdication of human reason and justice; it is the most decisive negation of human liberty, and necessarily ends in the enslavement of mankind, both in theory and practice."

Thus the God idea, revived, readjusted, and enlarged or narrowed, according to the necessity of the time, has dominated humanity and will continue to do so until man will raise his head to the sunlit day, unafraid and with an awakened will to himself. In proportion as man learns to realize himself and mold his own destiny theism becomes superfluous. How far man will be able to find his relation to his fellows will depend entirely upon how much he can outgrow his dependence upon God.

Already there are indications that theism, which is the theory of speculation, is being replaced by Atheism, the science of demonstration; the one hangs in the metaphysical clouds of the Beyond, while the other has its roots firmly in the soil. It is the earth, not heaven, which man must rescue if he is truly to be saved.

The decline of theism is a most interesting spectacle, especially as manifested in the anxiety of the theists, whatever their particular brand. They realize, much to their distress, that the masses are growing daily more atheistic, more anti-religious; that they are quite willing to leave the Great Beyond and its heavenly domain to the angels and sparrows; because more and more the masses are becoming engrossed in the problems of their immediate existence.

How to bring the masses back to the God idea, the spirit, the First Cause, etc.—that is the most pressing question to all theists. Metaphysical as all these questions seem to be, they yet have a very marked physical background. Inasmuch as religion, "Divine Truth," rewards and punishments are the trade-marks of the largest, the most corrupt and pernicious, the most powerful and lucrative industry in the world, not excepting the industry of manufacturing guns and munitions. It is the industry of befogging the human mind and stifling the human heart. Necessity knows no law; hence the majority of theists are compelled to take up every subject, even if it has no bearing upon a deity or revelation or the Great Beyond. Perhaps they sense the fact that humanity is growing weary of the hundred and one brands of God.

How to raise this dead level of theistic belief is really a

matter of life and death for all denominations. Therefore their tolerance; but it is a tolerance not of understanding, but of weakness. Perhaps that explains the efforts fostered in all religious publications to combine variegated religious philosophies and conflicting theistic theories into one denominational trust. More and more, the various concepts "of the only true God, the only pure spirit, the only true religion" are tolerantly glossed over in the frantic effort to establish a common ground to rescue the modern mass from the "pernicious" influence of atheistic ideas.

It is characteristic of theistic "tolerance" that no one really cares what the people believe in, just so they believe or pretend to believe. To accomplish this end, the crudest and vulgarest methods are being used. Religious endeavor meetings and revivals with Billy Sunday as their champion —methods which must outrage every refined sense, and which in their effect upon the ignorant and curious often tend to create a mild state of insanity not infrequently coupled with eroto-mania. All these frantic efforts find approval and support from the earthly powers; from the Russian despot to the American President; from Rockefeller and Wanamaker down to the pettiest business man. They know that capital invested in Billy Sunday, the Y.M.C.A., Christian Science, and various other religious institutions will return enormous profits from the subdued, tamed, and dull masses.

Consciously or unconsciously, most theists see in gods and devils, heaven and hell, reward and punishment, a whip to lash the people into obedience, meekness and contentment. The truth is that theism would have lost its footing long before this but for the combined support of Mammon and power. How thoroughly bankrupt it really is, is being demonstrated in the trenches and battlefields of Europe today.

Have not all theists painted their Deity as the god of love and goodness? Yet after thousands of years of such preach-ments the gods remain deaf to the agony of the human race. Confucius cares not for the poverty, squalor and misery of the people of China. Buddha remains undisturbed in his philosophical indifference to the famine and starvation of the outraged Hindoos; Jahve continues deaf to the bitter cry of Israel; while Jesus refuses to rise from the dead against his Christians who are butchering each other.

The burden of all song and praise "unto the Highest" has been that God stands for justice and mercy. Yet injustice among men is ever on the increase; the outrages committed against the masses in this country alone would seem enough to overflow the very heavens. But where are the gods to make an end to all these horrors, these wrongs, this inhumanity to man? No, not the gods, but MAN must rise in his mighty wrath. He, deceived by all the deities, betrayed by their emissaries, he, himself, must undertake to usher in justice upon the earth.

The philosophy of Atheism expresses the expansion and growth of the human mind. The philosophy of theism, if we can call it philosophy, is static and fixed. Even the mere attempt to pierce these mysteries represents, from the theistic point of view, non-belief in the all-embracing omnipotence, and even a denial of the wisdom of the divine powers outside of man. Fortunately, however, the human mind never was, and never can be, bound by fixities. Hence it is forging ahead in its restless march towards knowledge and life. The human mind is realizing "that the universe is not the result of a creative fiat by some divine intelligence, out of nothing, producing a masterpiece chaotic in perfect operation," but that it is the product of chaotic forces operating through aeons of time, of clashes and cataclysms, of repulsion and attraction crystalizing through the principle of selection into what the theists call, "the universe guided into order and beauty." As Joseph McCabe well points out in his *Existence of God:* "a law of nature is not a formula drawn up by a legislator, but a mere summary of the observed facts—a 'bundle of facts.' Things do not act in a particular way because there is a law, but we state the 'law' because they act in that way."

The philosophy of Atheism represents a concept of life without any metaphysical Beyond or Divine Regulator. It is the concept of an actual, real world with its liberating, expanding and beautifying possibilities, as against an unreal world, which, with its spirits, oracles, and mean contentment has kept humanity in helpless degradation.

It may seem a wild paradox, and yet it is pathetically true, that this real, visible world and our life should have been so long under the influence of metaphysical speculation, rather than of physical demonstrable forces. Under the lash of the theistic idea, this earth has served no other purpose than as a temporary station to test man's capacity for immolation to the will of God. But the moment man attempted to ascertain the nature of that will, he was told that it was utterly futile for "finite human intelligence" to get beyond the all-powerful infinite will. Under the terrific weight of this omnipotence, man has been bowed into the dust—a will-less creature, broken and sweating in the dark. The triumph of the philosophy of Atheism is to free man from the nightmare of gods; it means the dissolution of the phantoms of the beyond. Again and again the light of reason has dispelled the theistic nightmare, but poverty, misery and fear have recreated the phantoms—though whether old or new, whatever their external form, they differed little in their essence. Atheism, on the other hand, in its philosophic aspect refuses allegiance not merely to a definite concept of God, but it refuses all servitude to the God idea, and opposes the theistic principle as such. Gods in their individual function are not half as pernicious as the principle of theism which represents the belief in a supernatural, or even omnipotent, power to rule the earth and man upon it. It is the absolutism of theism, its pernicious

influence upon humanity, its paralyzing effect upon thought
and action, which Atheism is fighting with all its power.

The philosophy of Atheism has its root in the earth, in
this life; its aim is the emancipation of the human race from
all God-heads, be they Judaic, Christian, Mohammedan,
Buddhistic, Brahministic, or what not. Mankind has been
punished long and heavily for having created its gods;
nothing but pain and persecution have been man's lot since
gods began. There is but one way out of this blunder: Man
must break his fetters which have chained him to the gates
of heaven and hell, so that he can begin to fashion out of his
reawakened and illumined consciousness a new world upon
earth.

Only after the triumph of the Atheistic philosophy in the
minds and hearts of man will freedom and beauty be realized. Beauty as a gift from heaven has proved useless. It
will, however, become the essence and impetus of life when
man learns to see in the earth the only heaven fit for man.
Atheism is already helping to free man from his dependence
upon punishment and reward as the heavenly bargain-
counter for the poor in spirit.

Do not all theists insist that there can be no morality, no
justice, honesty or fidelity without the belief in a Divine
Power? Based upon fear and hope, such morality has
always been a vile product, imbued partly with self-
righteousness, partly with hypocrisy. As to truth, justice,
and fidelity, who have been their brave exponents and
daring proclaimers? Nearly always the godless ones: the
Atheists; they lived, fought, and died for them. They knew
that justice, truth, and fidelity are not conditioned in
heaven, but that they are related to and interwoven with the
tremendous changes going on in the social and material life
of the human race; not fixed and eternal, but fluctuating,
even as life itself. To what heights the philosophy of Atheism may yet attain, no one can prophesy. But this much can

already be predicted: only by its regenerating fire will human relations be purged from the horrors of the past.

Thoughtful people are beginning to realize that moral precepts, imposed upon humanity through religious terror, have become stereotyped and have therefore lost all vitality. A glance at life today, at its disintegrating character, its conflicting interests with their hatreds, crimes, and greed, suffices to prove the sterility of theistic morality.

Man must get back to himself before he can learn his relation to his fellows. Prometheus chained to the Rock of Ages is doomed to remain the prey of the vultures of darkness. Unbind Prometheus, and you dispel the night and its horrors.

Atheism in its negation of gods is at the same time the strongest affirmation of man, and through man, the eternal yea to life, purpose, and beauty.

PART THREE

VIOLENCE

PREFACE TO PART THREE

One subject on which Emma Goldman's views underwent considerable change in her life was that of political violence. Early in her revolutionary career she believed not only in the necessity of collective revolutionary violence against the ruling class, but in the efficacy of individual acts of violence. By the end of her life, she had reexamined and agonized over both beliefs.

As a young girl, admiring such political martyrs as the assassins of Russia's Czar Alexander II, she was eager to participate personally in any apocalyptic act that might hasten the revolution, embracing, quite simply, the doctrine that "the end justifies the means." As early as her first prison term in 1893, she reports, she began to see things differently. It was with horror that she recalled in the middle of her life an earlier time when she had been perfectly willing to experiment with explosives in a crowded tenement, endangering the lives of "the innocent" for the sake of "the Cause," or to contemplate blowing up a newspaper office. After the total failure of Berkman's *attentat*—the failure to kill Frick, the failure to help the Homestead strikers, and the failure to be understood—Goldman began to reexamine the efficacy of individual acts of political violence against the not-so-innocent. Eventually she came to see Berkman, like Frick, as a victim—just as Czolgosz and other "successful" assassins seemed to her victims. Although she understood and continued to sympathize with political criminals, she came to consider their acts "deeds of misplaced protest," which she could no longer condone. But she would not condemn them either, preferring instead to explain them as reactions to the much greater and more brutal institutionalized violence in society at large. It was for her refusal to condemn, for her explanation of terrorist activity as a result rather than as a cause—a view that has gained considerable acceptance nowadays[1]—that Goldman was most widely feared and hated.

But though Goldman grew skeptical about the value of individual acts of violence, in her remaining years in America she never doubted the necessity for collective revolutionary violence against capitalism and State. At the same time, she stepped up her denunciation of the State's own institutionalized forms of violence, of which she was a frequent victim, steadily urging resistance and even sabotage.

After her experience of Bolshevik terror in Russia in 1920 to 1921, she began to reexamine her feelings about sustained collective revolutionary violence as well. "The argument that destruction and terror are part of the revolution I do not dispute," she wrote in her preface to *My Disillusionment in Russia*. She continued:

> I know that in the past every great political and social change necessitated violence. . . . Yet it is one thing to employ

[1] One after another of the recent examinations of violence in America undertaken since the increase in political violence in the 1960's has acknowledged Goldman's basic point. Richard Hofstadter: "The primary precedent and the primary rationale for violence comes from the established order itself." (From his introductory essay, "Reflections on Violence in the United States," in *American Violence: A Documentary History*, New York, Knopf, 1970, p. 30.) Howard Zinn: "Those outbreaks of either civil disobedience or disorder we have had in the United States have been not the *cause* of our troubles, but the result of them." Thomas Rose: "The cause of much violence in America lies within the process of allowing and keeping one third of a nation poor. This is obviously linked to the institutionalization of social, economic, and political inequality." (Both the Zinn and the Rose quotations are from Rose's introduction to *Violence in America: A Contemporary Reader*, New York, Random House, 1969, the pages of which are peppered with similar statements.)

violence in combat as a means of defence. It is quite another
thing to make a principle of terrorism, to institutionalize it, to
assign it the most vital place in the social struggle. Such
terrorism begets counter-revolution and in turn itself becomes
counter-revolutionary.

Her hesitation was not about the violence necessary to bring
about a new order, but rather about the violence institutionalized
when the new order is imposed on the people by some outside
authority. Attributing the Russian terror to statism rather than
revolution, in the afterword of her book on Russia (reprinted
in Part Four of this collection) she wrote:

> There is no greater fallacy than the belief that aims and pur-
> poses are one thing, while methods and tactics are another. This
> conception is a potent menace to social regeneration. All human
> experience teaches that methods and means cannot be separated
> from the ultimate aim. . . . To divest one's methods of ethical
> concepts means to sink into the depths of utter demoralization.

The methods she was referring to are the methods of imposing
order once the revolution is achieved; the amount of violence
necessary to achieve it is a question of expediency. In 1923 she
wrote her friend Bayard Boyseren:[2] "The one thing I am convinced of as I have never been in my life is that the gun decides
nothing at all. Even if it accomplishes what it sets out to do—
which it rarely does—it brings so many evils in its wake as to
defeat its original aim." And in a letter to Berkman in 1928,[3]
when she was still closer to despairing of ever seeing the
anarchist revolution in her lifetime, she went even further:

> Unless we set our face against the old attitude to revolution as
> a violent eruption destroying everything of what had been

[2] Letter to Bayard Boyersen dated Feb. 20, 1923, on microfilm in the
New York Public Library.

[3] Quoted by Richard Drinnon in "Emma Goldman, Alexander Berkman,
and the Dream We Hark Back To," in *Anarchy 114* (Aug. 1970), Vol.
10, no. 8, p. 237.

built up over the centuries of painful and painstaking effort not by the bourgeoisie but by the combined effort of humanity, we must become Bolsheviks, accept terror and all it implys [sic] or become Tolstoyans. There is no other way. . . . I insist [that] if we can undergo changes in every other method of dealing with the social issues we will also have to learn to change in the methods of revolution. I think it can be done. If not, I shall relinquish my belief in revolution.

She did not, however, come to that. At the end of her life, when the possibility of a revolution on anarchist lines arose in Spain, she rushed to join it, doing her utmost to raise money and arms. If the doubts about violence she had expressed in her letters were serious, they were nevertheless dispensable in the face of the Spanish revolution. They were doubts, after all, about the methods of but not the need for revolution. In the midst of the war, as more and more volunteers underwent military training, she struggled with the dilemma of how to fight violence with violence for any length of time, but she never faltered in her support of the anarchists.

This section includes seven selections from Emma Goldman's writings about violence, the first three on individual violence, the last four on institutionalized violence. The attitudes toward revolutionary violence she ultimately held will be presented in Part Four.

The first essay, "The Psychology of Political Violence," was included in the 1911 collection, *Anarchism and Other Essays,* as Goldman's statement on the genesis of individual terrorism.

Her early enthusiasm for deeds-of-propaganda is recalled in "What We Did About the Slaughter at Homestead," her reminiscence of the events leading to Berkman's attempt on Frick's life. The section is taken from pp. 85–95 of the one-volume edition of *Living My Life.*

The government's attempt to implicate her in the McKinley assassination is described in the portion of *Living My Life* (pp. 295–317 of the one-volume edition) that appeared in the *Amer-*

ican Mercury, Vol. XXIV, in September 1931, pp. 53–67, under
the title "The Assassination of McKinley."

Of American institutionalized violence, Goldman had considerable experience. "Lynching and vigilantism have so few
parallels or equivalents elsewhere that they can be regarded as
distinctively American institutions," noted Richard Hofstadter.
Goldman's encounter with the vigilantes of San Diego, California, circa 1912, is recounted in the excerpt from *Living My
Life* (pp. 495–501 of the one-volume edition) here entitled
"Outrage at San Diego."

In "Prisons: A Social Crime and Failure," published in
Anarchism and Other Essays in 1911, Goldman condemns the
brutality and uselessness of the institution of prison by examining the nature of crime and "the conditions that breed both the
prisoner and the jailer."

In "Preparedness: The Road to Universal Slaughter," Goldman attacks the violence institutionalized as militarism, distinguishing it from the class war, which she considered legitimate.
Widely circulated as a pamphlet, this particular antiwar speech
appeared originally in the December 1915 issue of *Mother
Earth.*

The final selection in Part Three is Goldman's "Address to the
Jury." Though eloquent, it did not prevent her conviction and
that of her codefendant Alexander Berkman, in July 1917, of
"conspiracy to induce persons not to register" for conscription
into the armed forces. It appeared in a booklet issued in 1917 by
the Mother Earth Publishing Association entitled "Trial
and Speeches of Alexander Berkman and Emma Goldman in the
U.S. District Court in the City of New York, July 1917." Her
conviction at this trial virtually ended her American career.

The Psychology of
Political Violence

To analyze the psychology of political violence is not only extremely difficult, but also very dangerous. If such acts are treated with understanding, one is immediately accused of eulogizing them. If, on the other hand, human sympathy is expressed with the *Attentäter,** one risks being considered a possible accomplice. Yet it is only intelligence and sympathy that can bring us closer to the source of human suffering, and teach us the ultimate way out of it.

The primitive man, ignorant of natural forces, dreaded their approach, hiding from the perils they threatened. As man learned to understand Nature's phenomena, he realized that though these may destroy life and cause great loss, they also bring relief. To the earnest student it must be apparent that the accumulated forces in our social and economic life, culminating in a political act of violence, are similar to the terrors of the atmosphere, manifested in storm and lightning.

To thoroughly appreciate the truth of this view, one must

* A revolutionist committing an act of political violence.

feel intensely the indignity of our social wrongs; one's very being must throb with the pain, the sorrow, the despair millions of people are daily made to endure. Indeed, unless we have become a part of humanity, we cannot even faintly understand the just indignation that accumulates in a human soul, the burning, surging passion that makes the storm inevitable.

The ignorant mass looks upon the man who makes a violent protest against our social and economic iniquities as upon a wild beast, a cruel, heartless monster, whose joy it is to destroy life and bathe in blood; or at best, as upon an irresponsible lunatic. Yet nothing is further from the truth. As a matter of fact, those who have studied the character and personality of these men, or who have come in close contact with them, are agreed that it is their supersensitiveness to the wrong and injustice surrounding them which compels them to pay the toll of our social crimes. The most noted writers and poets, discussing the psychology of political offenders, have paid them the highest tribute. Could anyone assume that these men had advised violence, or even approved of the acts? Certainly not. Theirs was the attitude of the social student, of the man who knows that beyond every violent act there is a vital cause.

Björnstjerne Björnson, in the second part of *Beyond Human Power,* emphasizes the fact that it is among the Anarchists that we must look for the modern martyrs who pay for their faith with their blood, and who welcome death with a smile, because they believe, as truly as Christ did, that their martyrdom will redeem humanity.

François Coppé, the French novelist, thus expresses himself regarding the psychology of the *Attentäter:*

"The reading of the details of Vaillant's execution left me in a thoughtful mood. I imagined him expanding his chest under the ropes, marching with firm step, stiffening his will, concentrating all his energy, and, with eyes fixed upon the knife, hurling finally at society his cry of malediction. And, in spite of me, another spectacle rose suddenly before my mind. I saw a group of men and women pressing against each other in the middle of the oblong arena of the circus, under the gaze of thousands of eyes, while from all the steps of the immense amphitheatre went up the terrible cry, *Ad leones!* and, below, the opening cages of the wild beasts.

"I did not believe the execution would take place. In the first place, no victim had been struck with death, and it had long been the custom not to punish an abortive crime with the last degree of severity. Then, this crime, however terrible in intention, was disinterested, born of an abstract idea. The man's past, his abandoned childhood, his life of hardship, pleaded also in his favor. In the independent press generous voices were raised in his behalf, very loud and eloquent. 'A purely literary current of opinion' some have said, with no little scorn. *It is, on the contrary, an honor to the men of art and thought to have expressed once more their disgust at the scaffold.*"

Again Zola, in *Germinal* and *Paris*, describes the tenderness and kindness, the deep sympathy with human suffering, of these men who close the chapter of their lives with a violent outbreak against our system.

Last, but not least, the man who probably better than anyone else understands the psychology of the *Attentäter* is M. Hamon, the author of the brilliant work *Une Psychologie du Militaire Professionnel*, who has arrived at these suggestive conclusions:

"The positive method confirmed by the rational method enables us to establish an ideal type of Anarchist, whose mentality is the aggregate of common psychic characteristics. Every Anarchist partakes sufficiently of this ideal type to make it possible to differentiate him from other men. The typical Anarchist, then, may be defined as follows: A man perceptible by the spirit of revolt under one or more of its forms—opposition, investigation, criticism, innovation—endowed with a strong love of liberty, egoistic or individualistic, and possessed of great curiosity, a keen desire to know. These traits are supplemented by an ardent love of others, a highly developed moral sensitiveness, a profound sentiment of justice, and imbued with missionary zeal."

To the above characteristics, says Alvin F. Sanborn, must be added these sterling qualities: a rare love of animals, surpassing sweetness in all the ordinary relations of life, exceptional sobriety of demeanor, frugality and regularity, austerity, even, of living, and courage beyond compare.*

"There is a truism that the man in the street seems always to forget, when he is abusing the Anarchists, or whatever party happens to be his *bête noire* for the moment, as the cause of some outrage just perpetrated. This indisputable fact is that homicidal outrages have, from time immemorial, been the reply of goaded and desperate classes, and goaded and desperate individuals, to wrongs from their fellowmen, which they felt to be intolerable. Such acts are the violent recoil from violence, whether aggressive or repressive; they are the last desperate struggle of outraged and exasperated human nature for breathing space and life. And their cause lies not in any special conviction, but in the depths of that human nature itself. The whole course of history, political and social, is strewn with evidence of this fact. To go no further, take the three most notorious examples of political parties goaded into violence during the last fifty years: the Mazzinians in Italy, the Fenians in Ireland, and the Terrorists in Russia. Were these people Anarchists? No. Did they all three even hold the same political opinions? No. The Mazzinians were Republicans, the Fenians political separatists, the Russians Social Democrats or Constitutionalists. But all were driven by desperate circumstances into this terrible form of revolt. And when we turn from parties to

* *Paris and the Social Revolution.*

individuals who have acted in like manner, we stand appalled by the number of human beings goaded and driven by sheer desperation into conduct obviously violently opposed to their social instincts.

"Now that Anarchism has become a living force in society, such deeds have been sometimes committed by Anarchists, as well as by others. For no new faith, even the most essentially peaceable and humane the mind of man has yet accepted, but at its first coming has brought upon earth not peace, but a sword; not because of anything violent or anti-social in the doctrine itself; simply because of the ferment any new and creative idea excites in men's minds, whether they accept or reject it. And a conception of Anarchism, which, on one hand, threatens every vested interest, and, on the other, holds out a vision of a free and noble life to be won by a struggle against existing wrongs, is certain to rouse the fiercest opposition, and bring the whole repressive force of ancient evil into violent contact with the tumultuous outburst of a new hope.

"Under miserable conditions of life, any vision of the possibility of better things makes the present misery more intolerable, and spurs those who suffer to the most energetic struggles to improve their lot, and if these struggles only immediately result in sharper misery, the outcome is sheer desperation. In our present society, for instance, an exploited wage worker, who catches a glimpse of what work and life might and ought to be, finds the toilsome routine and the squalor of his existence almost intolerable; and even when he has the resolution and courage to continue steadily working his best, and waiting until new ideas have so permeated society as to pave the way for better times, the mere fact that he has such ideas and tries to spread them brings him into difficulties with his employers. How many thousands of Socialists, and above all Anarchists, have lost work and even the chance of work, solely on the ground of their opinions. It is only the specially gifted craftsman, who, if he be a zealous propagandist, can hope to retain permanent employment. And what happens to a man with his brain working actively with a ferment of new ideas, with a vision before his eyes of a new hope dawning for toiling and agonizing men, with the knowledge that his suffering and that of his fellows in misery is not caused by the cruelty of fate, but by the injustice of other human beings—what happens to such a man when he sees those dear to him starving, when he himself is starved? Some natures in such a plight, and those by no means the least social or the least sensitive, will become violent, and will even feel that their violence is social and not anti-social, that in striking when and how they can, they are striking, not for themselves, but for human nature, outraged and despoiled in their persons and in those of their fellow sufferers. And are we, who ourselves are not in this horrible predicament, to stand by and coldly condemn these piteous victims of the Furies and Fates? Are we to decry as miscreants these human beings who act with heroic self-devotion, sacrificing their lives in protest, where less social and less energetic natures would lie down and grovel in abject submission to injustice and wrong? Are we to join the ignorant and brutal outcry which stigmatizes such men as monsters of wickedness, gratuitously running amuck in a harmonious and innocently peaceful society? No! We hate murder with a hatred that may seem absurdly exaggerated to apologists for Matabele massacres,* to callous acquiescers in hangings and bombardments, but we decline in such cases of homicide, or attempted homicide, as those of which we are treating, to be guilty of the cruel injustice of flinging the whole responsibility of the deed upon the immediate perpetrator. The guilt of these homicides lies upon every man and woman who,

---

* Editor's note: The Matabele were a Bantu-speaking South African people whose land was occupied and armies massacred by the forces of the British South African Company in the 1890's, resulting in the establishment of north and south Rhodesia under British rule.

intentionally or by cold indifference, helps to keep up social conditions that drive human beings to despair. The man who flings his whole life into the attempt, at the cost of his own life, to protest against the wrongs of his fellow men, is a saint compared to the active and passive upholders of cruelty and injustice, even if his protest destroy other lives besides his own. Let him who is without sin in society cast the first stone at such an one."*

That every act of political violence should nowadays be attributed to Anarchists is not at all surprising. Yet it is a fact known to almost everyone familiar with the Anarchist movement that a great number of acts, for which Anarchists had to suffer, either originated with the capitalist press or were instigated, if not directly perpetrated, by the police.

For a number of years acts of violence had been committed in Spain, for which the Anarchists were held responsible, hounded like wild beasts, and thrown into prison. Later it was disclosed that the perpetrators of these acts were not Anarchists, but members of the police department. The scandal became so widespread that the conservative Spanish papers demanded the apprehension and punishment of the gang-leader, Juan Rull, who was subsequently condemned to death and executed. The sensational evidence, brought to light during the trial, forced Police Inspector Momento to exonerate completely the Anarchists from any connection with the acts committed during a long period. This resulted in the dismissal of a number of police officials, among them Inspector Tressols, who, in revenge, disclosed the fact that behind the gang of police bomb throwers were others of far higher position, who provided them with funds and protected them.

This is one of the many striking examples of how Anarchist conspiracies are manufactured.

* From a pamphlet issued by the Freedom Group of London.

That the American police can perjure themselves with the same ease, that they are just as merciless, just as brutal and cunning as their European colleagues, has been proven on more than one occasion. We need only recall the tragedy of the eleventh of November, 1887, known as the Haymarket Riot.

No one who is at all familiar with the case can possibly doubt that the Anarchists, judicially murdered in Chicago, died as victims of a lying, bloodthirsty press and of a cruel police conspiracy. Has not Judge Gary himself said: "Not because you have caused the Haymarket bomb, but because you are Anarchists, you are on trial."

The impartial and thorough analysis by Governor Altgeld of that blotch on the American escutcheon verified the brutal frankness of Judge Gary. It was this that induced Altgeld to pardon the three Anarchists, thereby earning the lasting esteem of every liberty-loving man and woman in the world.

When we approach the tragedy of September sixth, 1901,* we are confronted by one of the most striking examples of how little social theories are responsible for an act of political violence. "Leon Czolgosz, an Anarchist, incited to commit the act by Emma Goldman." To be sure, has she not incited violence even before her birth, and will she not continue to do so beyond death? Everything is possible with the Anarchists.

Today, even, nine years after the tragedy, after it was proven a hundred times that Emma Goldman had nothing to do with the event, that no evidence whatsoever exists to indicate that Czolgosz ever called himself an Anarchist, we are confronted with the same lie, fabricated by the police and perpetuated by the press. No living soul ever heard Czolgosz make that statement, nor is there a single written word to prove that the boy ever breathed the accusation.

* Editor's note: The day President McKinley was shot.

Nothing but ignorance and insane hysteria, which have never yet been able to solve the simplest problem of cause and effect.

The President of a free Republic killed! What else can be the cause, except that the *Attentäter* must have been insane, or that he was incited to the act.

A free Republic! How a myth will maintain itself, how it will continue to deceive, to dupe, and blind even the comparatively intelligent to its monstrous absurdities. A free Republic! And yet within a little over thirty years a small band of parasites have successfully robbed the American people, and trampled upon the fundamental principles, laid down by the fathers of this country, guaranteeing to every man, woman, and child "life, liberty, and the pursuit of happiness." For thirty years they have been increasing their wealth and power at the expense of the vast mass of workers, thereby enlarging the army of the unemployed, the hungry, homeless, and friendless portion of humanity, who are tramping the country from east to west, from north to south, in a vain search for work. For many years the home has been left to the care of the little ones, while the parents are exhausting their life and strength for a mere pittance. For thirty years the sturdy sons of America have been sacrificed on the battlefield of industrial war, and the daughters outraged in corrupt factory surroundings. For long and weary years this process of undermining the nation's health, vigor, and pride, without much protest from the disinherited and oppressed, has been going on. Maddened by success and victory, the money powers of this "free land of ours" became more and more audacious in their heartless, cruel efforts to compete with the rotten and decayed European tyrannies for supremacy of power.

In vain did a lying press repudiate Leon Czolgosz as a foreigner. The boy was a product of our own free American soil, that lulled him to sleep with,

> My country, 'tis of thee,
> Sweet land of liberty.

Who can tell how many times this American child had gloried in the celebration of the Fourth of July, or of Decoration Day, when he faithfully honored the Nation's dead? Who knows but that he, too, was willing to "fight for his country and die for her liberty," until it dawned upon him that those he belonged to have no country, because they have been robbed of all that they have produced; until he realized that the liberty and independence of his youthful dreams were but a farce. Poor Leon Czolgosz, your crime consisted of too sensitive a social consciousness. Unlike your idealless and brainless American brothers, your ideals soared above the belly and the bank account. No wonder you impressed the one human being among all the infuriated mob at your trial—a newspaper woman—as a visionary, totally oblivious to your surroundings. Your large, dreamy eyes must have beheld a new and glorious dawn.

Now, to a recent instance of police-manufactured Anarchist plots. In that bloodstained city Chicago, the life of Chief of Police Shippy was attempted by a young man named Averbuch. Immediately the cry was sent to the four corners of the world that Averbuch was an Anarchist, and that the Anarchists were responsible for the act. Everyone who was at all known to entertain Anarchist ideas was closely watched, a number of people arrested, the library of an Anarchist group confiscated, and all meetings made impossible. It goes without saying that, as on various previous occasions, I must needs be held responsible for the act. Evidently the American police credit me with occult powers. I did not know Averbuch; in fact, had never before heard his name, and the only way I could have possibly "conspired" with him was in my astral body. But, then, the police are not concerned with logic or justice. What they seek is a target, to mask their absolute ignorance of the cause, of the psychology of a political act. Was Averbuch an Anarchist? There is no positive proof of it. He had been but three months in the country, did not know the language, and, as far as I could ascertain, was quite unknown to the Anarchists of Chicago.

What led to his act? Averbuch, like most young Russian immigrants, undoubtedly believed in the mythical liberty of America. He received his first baptism by the policeman's club during the brutal dispersement of the unemployed parade. He further experienced American equality and opportunity in the vain efforts to find an economic master. In short, a three months' sojourn in the glorious land brought him face to face with the fact that the disinherited are in the same position the world over. In his native land he probably learned that necessity knows no law—there was no difference between a Russian and an American policeman.

The question to the intelligent social student is not whether the acts of Czolgosz or Averbuch were practical, any more than whether the thunderstorm is practical. The thing that will inevitably impress itself on the thinking and feeling man and woman is that the sight of brutal clubbing of innocent victims in a so-called free Republic, and the degrading, soul-destroying economic struggle, furnish the spark that kindles the dynamic force in the overwrought, outraged souls of men like Czolgosz or Averbuch. No amount of persecution, of hounding, of repression, can stay this social phenomenon.

But, it is often asked, have not acknowledged Anarchists committed acts of violence? Certainly they have, always, however, ready to shoulder the responsibility. My contention is that they were impelled, not by the teachings of Anarchism, but by the tremendous pressure of conditions making life unbearable to their sensitive natures. Obviously, Anarchism, or any other social theory, making man a conscious social unit, will act as a leaven for rebellion. This is not a mere assertion, but a fact verified by all experience. A close examination of the circumstances bearing upon this question will further clarify my position.

Let us consider some of the most important Anarchist acts within the last two decades. Strange as it may seem, one of the most significant deeds of political violence occurred here in America, in connection with the Homestead strike of 1892.

During that memorable time the Carnegie Steel Company organized a conspiracy to crush the Amalgamated Association of Iron and Steel Workers. Henry Clay Frick, then Chairman of the Company, was intrusted with that democratic task. He lost no time in carrying out the policy of breaking the Union, the policy which he had so successfully practiced during his reign of terror in the coke regions. Secretly, and while peace negotiations were being purposely prolonged, Frick supervised the military preparations, the fortification of the Homestead Steel Works, the erection of a high board fence, capped with barbed wire and provided with loopholes for sharpshooters. And then, in the dead of night, he attempted to smuggle his army of hired Pinkerton thugs into Homestead, which act precipitated the terrible carnage of the steel workers. Not content with the death of eleven victims, killed in the Pinkerton skirmish, Henry Clay Frick, good Christian and free American, straightway began the hounding down of the helpless wives and orphans, by ordering them out of the wretched Company houses.

The whole country was aroused over these inhuman outrages. Hundreds of voices were raised in protest, calling on Frick to desist, not to go too far. Yes, hundreds of people protested—as one objects to annoying flies. Only one there was who actively responded to the outrage at Homestead—Alexander Berkman. Yes, he was an Anarchist. He gloried in the fact, because it was the only force that made the discord between his spiritual longing and the world without at all bearable. Yet not Anarchism, as such, but the brutal slaughter of the eleven steel workers was the urge for Alexander Berkman's act, his attempt on the life of Henry Clay Frick.

The record of European acts of political violence affords numerous and striking instances of the influence of environment upon sensitive human beings.

The court speech of Vaillant, who, in 1894, exploded a bomb in the Paris Chamber of Deputies, strikes the true keynote of the psychology of such acts:

"Gentlemen, in a few minutes you are to deal your blow, but in receiving your verdict I shall have at least the satisfaction of having wounded the existing society, that cursed society in which one may see a single man spending, uselessly, enough to feed thousands of families; an infamous society which permits a few individuals to monopolize all the social wealth, while there are hundreds of thousands of unfortunates who have not even the bread that is not refused to dogs, and while entire families are committing suicide for want of the necessities of life.

"Ah, gentlemen, if the governing classes could go down among the unfortunates! But no, they prefer to remain deaf to their appeals. It seems that a fatality impels them, like the royalty of the eighteenth century, toward the precipice which will engulf them, for woe be to those who, believing themselves of superior essence, assume the right to exploit those beneath them! There comes a time when the people no longer reason; they rise like a hurricane, and pass away like a torrent. Then we see bleeding heads impaled on pikes.

"Among the exploited, gentlemen, there are two classes of individuals. Those of one class, not realizing what they are and what they might be, take life as it comes, believe that they are born to be slaves, and content themselves with the little that is given them in exchange for their labor. But there are others, on the contrary, who think, who study, and who, looking about them, discover social iniquities. Is it their fault if they see clearly and suffer at seeing others suffer? Then they throw themselves into the struggle, and make themselves the bearers of the popular claims.

"Gentlemen, I am one of these last. Wherever I have gone, I have seen unfortunates bent beneath the yoke of capital. Everywhere I have seen the same wounds causing tears of blood to flow, even in the remoter parts of the inhabited districts of South America, where I had the right to believe that he who was weary of the pains of civilization might rest in the shade of the palm trees and there study nature. Well, there even, more than elsewhere, I have seen capital come, like a vampire, to suck the last drop of blood of the unfortunate pariahs.

"Then I came back to France, where it was reserved for me to see my family suffer atrociously. This was the last drop in the cup of my sorrow. Tired of leading this life of suffering and cowardice, I carried this bomb to those who are primarily responsible for social misery.

"I am reproached with the wounds of those who were hit by my projectiles. Permit me to point out in passing that, if the bourgeois had not massacred or caused massacres during the Revolution, it is probable that they would still be under the yoke of the nobility. On the other hand, figure up the dead and wounded of Tonquin, Madagascar, Dahomey, adding thereto the thousands, yes, millions of unfortunates who die in the factories, the mines, and wherever the grinding power of capital is felt. Add also those who die of hunger, and all this with the assent of our Deputies. Beside all this, of how little weight are the reproaches now brought against me!

"It is true that one does not efface the other; but, after all, are we not acting on the defensive when we respond to the blows which we receive from above? I know very well that I shall be told that I ought to have confined myself to speech for the vindication of the people's claims. But what can you expect! It takes a loud voice to make the deaf hear. Too long have they answered our voices by imprisonment, the rope, rifle volleys. Make no mistake; the explosion of my bomb is not only the cry of the rebel Vaillant, but the cry of an entire class which vindicates its rights, and which will soon add acts to words. For, be sure of it, in vain will they pass laws. The ideas of the thinkers will not halt; just as, in the last century, all the governmental forces could not prevent the Diderots and the Voltaires from spreading emancipating ideas among the people, so all the existing governmental forces will not prevent the Reclus, the Darwins, the Spencers, the Ibsens, the Mirbeaus, from spreading the ideas of justice and liberty which will annihilate the prejudices that hold the mass in ignorance. And these ideas, welcomed by the unfortunate, will flower in acts of revolt as they have done in me, until the day when the disappearance of authority shall permit all men to organize freely according to their choice, when everyone shall be able to enjoy the product of his labor, and when those moral maladies called prejudices shall vanish, permitting human beings to live in harmony, having no other desire than to study the sciences and love their fellows.

"I conclude, gentlemen, by saying that a society in which one sees such social inequalities as we see all about us, in which we see every day suicides caused by poverty, prostitution flaring at every street corner—a society whose principal monuments are barracks and prisons—such a society must be transformed as soon as possible, on pain of being eliminated, and that speedily, from the human race. Hail to him who labors, by no matter what means, for this transformation! It is this idea that has guided me in my duel with authority, but as in this duel I have only wounded my adversary, it is now its turn to strike me.

"Now, gentlemen, to me it matters little what penalty you may inflict, for, looking at this assembly with the eyes of reason, I can not help smiling to see you, atoms lost in matter, and reasoning only because you possess a prolongation of the spinal marrow, assume the right to judge one of your fellows.

"Ah! gentlemen, how little a thing is your assembly and your verdict in the history of humanity; and human history, in its turn, is likewise a very little thing in the whirlwind which bears it through immensity, and which is destined to disappear, or at least to be transformed, in order to begin again the same history and the same facts, a veritably perpetual play of cosmic forces renewing and transferring themselves forever."

Will anyone say that Vaillant was an ignorant, vicious man, or a lunatic? Was not his mind singularly clear and analytic? No wonder that the best intellectual forces of France spoke in his behalf, and signed the petition to President Carnot, asking him to commute Vaillant's death sentence.

Carnot would listen to no entreaty; he insisted on more than a pound of flesh, he wanted Vaillant's life, and then— the inevitable happened: President Carnot was killed. On the handle of the stiletto used by the *Attentäter* was engraved, significantly,

VAILLANT!

Santo Caserio was an Anarchist. He could have gotten away, saved himself; but he remained, he stood the consequences.

His reasons for the act are set forth in so simple, dignified, and childlike a manner that one is reminded of the touching tribute paid Caserio by his teacher of the little village school, Ada Negri, the Italian poet, who spoke of him as a sweet, tender plant, of too fine and sensitive texture to stand the cruel strain of the world.

"Gentlemen of the Jury! I do not propose to make a defense, but only an explanation of my deed.

"Since my early youth I began to learn that present society is badly organized, so badly that every day many wretched men commit suicide, leaving women and children in the most terrible distress. Workers, by thousands, seek for work and can not find it. Poor families beg for food and shiver with cold; they suffer the greatest misery; the little ones ask their miserable mothers for food, and the mothers cannot give it to them, because they have nothing. The few things which the home contained have already been sold or pawned. All they can do is beg alms; often they are arrested as vagabonds.

"I went away from my native place because I was frequently moved to tears at seeing little girls of eight or ten years obliged to work fifteen hours a day for the paltry pay of twenty centimes. Young women of eighteen or twenty also work fifteen hours daily, for a mockery of remuneration. And that happens not only to my fellow countrymen, but to all the workers, who sweat the whole day long for a crust of bread, while their labor produces wealth in abundance. The workers are obliged to live under the most wretched conditions, and their food consists of a little bread, a few spoonfuls of rice, and water; so by the time they are thirty or forty years old, they are exhausted, and go to die in the hospitals. Besides, in consequence of bad food and overwork, these unhappy creatures are, by hundreds, devoured by pellagra—a disease that, in my country, attacks, as the physicians say, those who are badly fed and lead a life of toil and privation.

"I have observed that there are a great many people who are hungry, and many children who suffer, whilst bread and clothes abound in the towns. I saw many and large shops full of clothing and woolen stuffs, and I also saw warehouses full of wheat and Indian corn, suitable for those who are in want. And, on the other hand, I saw thousands of people who do not work, who produce nothing and live on the labor of others; who spend every day thousands of francs for their amusement; who debauch the daughters of the workers; who own dwellings of forty or fifty rooms; twenty or thirty horses, many servants; in a word, all the pleasures of life.

"I believed in God; but when I saw so great an inequality between men, I acknowledged that it was not God who created man, but man who created God. And I discovered that those who want their property to be respected have an interest in preaching the existence of paradise and hell, and in keeping the people in ignorance.

"Not long ago, Vaillant threw a bomb in the Chamber of Deputies, to protest against the present system of society. He killed no one, only wounded some persons; yet bourgeois justice sentenced him to death. And not satisfied with the condemnation of the guilty man, they began to pursue the Anarchists, and arrest not only those who had known Vaillant, but even those who had merely been present at any Anarchist lecture.

"The government did not think of their wives and children. It did not consider that the men kept in prison were not the only ones who suffered, and that their little ones cried for bread. Bourgeois justice did not trouble itself about these innocent ones, who did not yet know what society is. It is no fault of theirs that their fathers are in prison; they only want to eat.

"The government went on searching private houses, opening private letters, forbidding lectures and meetings, and practicing the most infamous oppressions against us. Even now, hundreds of Anarchists are arrested for having

written an article in a newspaper, or for having expressed
an opinion in public.

"Gentlemen of the Jury, you are representatives of bourgeois society. If you want my head, take it; but do not
believe that in so doing you will stop the Anarchist propaganda. Take care, for men reap what they have sown."

During a religious procession in 1896, at Barcelona, a
bomb was thrown. Immediately three hundred men and
women were arrested. Some were Anarchists, but the
majority were trade-unionists and Socialists. They were
thrown into that terrible bastille Montjuich, and subjected
to most horrible tortures. After a number had been killed,
or had gone insane, their cases were taken up by the liberal
press of Europe, resulting in the release of a few survivors.

The man primarily responsible for this revival of the
Inquisition was Canovas del Castillo, Prime Minister of
Spain. It was he who ordered the torturing of the victims,
their flesh burned, their bones crushed, their tongues cut
out. Practiced in the art of brutality during his régime in
Cuba, Canovas remained absolutely deaf to the appeals and
protests of the awakened civilized conscience.

In 1897 Canovas del Castillo was shot to death by a
young Italian, Angiolillo. The latter was an editor in his
native land, and his bold utterances soon attracted the
attention of the authorities. Persecution began, and Angiolillo fled from Italy to Spain, thence to France and Belgium,
finally settling in England. While there he found employment as a compositor, and immediately became the friend
of all his colleagues. One of the latter thus described Angiolillo: "His appearance suggested the journalist rather than
the disciple of Gutenberg. His delicate hands, moreover,
betrayed the fact that he had not grown up at the 'case.'
With his handsome frank face, his soft dark hair, his alert
expression, he looked the very type of the vivacious South-
erner. Angiolillo spoke Italian, Spanish, and French, but no

English; the little French I knew was not sufficient to carry on a prolonged conversation. However, Angiolillo soon began to acquire the English idiom; he learned rapidly, playfully, and it was not long until he became very popular with his fellow compositors. His distinguished and yet modest manner, and his consideration towards his colleagues, won him the heart of all the boys."

Angiolillo soon became familiar with the detailed accounts in the press. He read of the great wave of human sympathy with the helpless victims at Montjuich. On Trafalgar Square he saw with his own eyes the results of those atrocities, when the few Spaniards, who escaped Castillo's clutches, came to seek asylum in England. There, at the great meeting, these men opened their shirts and showed the horrible scars of burned flesh. Angiolillo saw, and the effect surpassed a thousand theories; the impetus was beyond words, beyond arguments, beyond himself even.

Señor Antonio Canovas del Castillo, Prime Minister of Spain, sojourned at Santa Agueda. As usual in such cases, all strangers were kept away from his exalted presence. One exception was made, however, in the case of a distinguished looking, elegantly dressed Italian—the representative, it was understood, of an important journal. The distinguished gentleman was—Angiolillo.

Señor Canovas, about to leave his house, stepped on the veranda. Suddenly Angiolillo confronted him. A shot rang out, and Canovas was a corpse.

The wife of the Prime Minister rushed upon the scene. "Murderer! Murderer!" she cried, pointing at Angiolillo. The latter bowed. "Pardon, Madame," he said, "I respect you as a lady, but I regret that you were the wife of that man."

Calmly Angiolillo faced death. Death in its most terrible form—for the man whose soul was as a child's.

He was garroted. His body lay, sun-kissed, till the day hid

in twilight. And the people came, and pointing the finger of terror and fear, they said: "There—the criminal—the cruel murderer."

How stupid, how cruel is ignorance! It misunderstands always, condemns always.

A remarkable parallel to the case of Angiolillo is to be found in the act of Gaetano Bresci, whose *Attentat* upon King Umberto made an American city famous.

Bresci came to this country, this land of opportunity, where one has but to try to meet with golden success. Yes, he too would try to succeed. He would work hard and faithfully. Work had no terrors for him, if it would only help him to independence, manhood, self-respect.

Thus full of hope and enthusiasm he settled in Paterson, New Jersey, and there found a lucrative job at six dollars per week in one of the weaving mills of the town. Six whole dollars per week was, no doubt, a fortune for Italy, but not enough to breathe on in the new country. He loved his little home. He was a good husband and devoted father to his *bambina* Bianca, whom he adored. He worked and worked for a number of years. He actually managed to save one hundred dollars out of his six dollars per week.

Bresci had an ideal. Foolish, I know, for a workingman to have an ideal—the Anarchist paper published in Paterson, *La Questione Sociale*.

Every week, though tired from work, he would help to set up the paper. Until late hours he would assist, and when the little pioneer had exhausted all resources and his comrades were in despair, Bresci brought cheer and hope, one hundred dollars, the entire savings of years. That would keep the paper afloat.

In his native land people were starving. The crops had been poor, and the peasants saw themselves face to face with famine. They appealed to their good King Umberto; he would help. And he did.The wives of the peasants who had gone to the palace of the King held up in mute silence their emaciated infants. Surely that would move him. And then the soldiers fired and killed those poor fools.

Bresci, at work in the weaving mill at Paterson, read of horrible massacre. His mental eye beheld the defenceless women and innocent infants of his native land, slaughtered right before the good King. His soul recoiled in horror. At night he heard the groans of the wounded. Some may have been his comrades, his own flesh. Why, why these foul murders?

The little meeting of the Italian Anarchist group in Paterson ended almost in a fight. Bresci had demanded his hundred dollars. His comrades begged, implored him to give them a respite. The paper would go down if they were to return him his loan. But Bresci insisted on its return.

How cruel and stupid is ignorance. Bresci got the money, but lost the good will, the confidence of his comrades. They would have nothing more to do with one whose greed was greater than his ideals.

On the twenty-ninth of July, 1900, King Umberto was shot at Monzo. The young Italian weaver of Paterson, Gaetano Bresci, had taken the life of the good King.

Paterson was placed under police surveillance, everyone known as an Anarchist hounded and persecuted, and the act of Bresci ascribed to the teachings of Anarchism. As if the teachings of Anarchism in its extremest form could equal the force of those slain women and infants, who had pilgrimed to the King for aid. As if any spoken word, ever so eloquent, could burn into a human soul with such white heat as the lifeblood trickling drop by drop from those dying forms. The ordinary man is rarely moved either by word or deed; and those whose social kinship is the greatest living force need no appeal to respond—even as does steel to the magnet—to the wrongs and horrors of society.

If a social theory is a strong factor inducing acts of political violence, how are we to account for the recent violent outbreaks in India, where Anarchism has hardly been born.

More than any other old philosophy, Hindu teachings have exalted passive resistance, the drifting of life, the Nirvana, as the highest spiritual ideal. Yet the social unrest in India is daily growing, and has only recently resulted in an act of political violence, the killing of Sir Curzon Wyllie by the Hindu Madar Sol Dhingra.

If such a phenomenon can occur in a country socially and individually permeated for centuries with the spirit of passivity, can one question the tremendous, revolutionizing effect on human character exerted by great social iniquities? Can one doubt the logic, the justice of these words:

"Repression, tyranny, and indiscriminate punishment of innocent men have been the watchwords of the government of the alien domination in India ever since we began the commercial boycott of English goods. The tiger qualities of the British are much in evidence now in India. They think that by the strength of the sword they will keep down India! It is this arrogance that has brought about the bomb, and the more they tyrannize over a helpless and unarmed people, the more terrorism will grow. We may deprecate terrorism as outlandish and foreign to our culture, but it is inevitable as long as this tyranny continues, for it is not the terrorists that are to be blamed, but the tyrants who are responsible for it. It is the only resource for a helpless and unarmed people when brought to the verge of despair. It is never criminal on their part. The crime lies with the tyrant."*

Even conservative scientists are beginning to realize that heredity is not the sole factor moulding human character. Climate, food, occupation; nay, color, light, and sound must be considered in the study of human psychology.

If that be true, how much more correct is the contention that great social abuses will and must influence different minds and temperaments in a different way. And how

* *The Free Hindustan.*

utterly fallacious the stereotyped notion that the teachings of Anarchism, or certain exponents of these teachings, are responsible for the acts of political violence.

Anarchism, more than any other social theory, values human life above things. All Anarchists agree with Tolstoy in this fundamental truth: if the production of any commodity necessitates the sacrifice of human life, society should do without that commodity, but it can not do without that life. That, however, nowise indicates that Anarchism teaches submission. How can it, when it knows that all suffering, all misery, all ills, result from the evil of submission?

Has not some American ancestor said, many years ago, that resistance to tyranny is obedience to God? And he was not an Anarchist even. I would say that resistance to tyranny is man's highest ideal. So long as tyranny exists, in whatever form, man's deepest aspiration must resist it as inevitably as man must breathe.

Compared with the wholesale violence of capital and government, political acts of violence are but a drop in the ocean. That so few resist is the strongest proof how terrible must be the conflict between their souls and unbearable social iniquities.

High strung, like a violin string, they weep and moan for life, so relentless, so cruel, so terribly inhuman. In a desperate moment the string breaks. Untuned ears hear nothing but discord. But those who feel the agonized cry understand its harmony; they hear in it the fulfillment of the most compelling moment of human nature.

Such is the psychology of political violence.

What We Did About
the Slaughter at Homestead

In May 1892, labor trouble erupted at the Homestead, Pennsylvania, plant of the Carnegie Steel Corporation between the Amalgamated Association of Iron and Steel Workers and the company, then under the direction of Henry Clay Frick. Determined to crush the union, Frick proposed a 22-percent wage cut, an offer the union immediately rejected. In response, Frick closed down the plant and prepared to reopen with non-union workers.

At the time, the three comrades, Goldman, Berkman (Sasha), and Fedya, were in Worcester, Massachusetts, running an ice-cream parlor. Their intention was to amass enough money to get them all back to their native Russia, where they felt they could most effectively advance the revolution. Once they became absorbed in the events in Homestead, however, they had to revise their plans.

Editor's note

. . . Our hearts were fired with admiration for the men of Homestead.

We continued our daily work, waiting on customers, frying pancakes, serving tea and ice-cream; but our thoughts were in Homestead, with the brave steel-workers. We became so absorbed in the news that we would not permit ourselves enough time even for sleep. At daybreak one of the boys would be off to get the first editions of the papers. We saturated ourselves with the events in Homestead to the exclusion of everything else. Entire nights we would sit up discussing the various phases of the situation, almost engulfed by the possibilities of the gigantic struggle.

One afternoon a customer came in for an ice-cream, while I was alone in the store. As I set the dish down before him, I caught the large headlines of his paper: "LATEST DEVELOPMENTS IN HOMESTEAD—FAMILIES OF STRIKERS EVICTED FROM THE COMPANY HOUSES—WOMAN IN CONFINEMENT CARRIED OUT INTO STREET BY SHERIFFS." I read over the man's shoulder Frick's dictum to the workers: he would rather see them dead than concede to their demands, and he threatened to import Pinkerton detectives. The brutal bluntness of the account, the inhumanity of Frick towards the evicted mother, inflamed my mind. Indignation swept my whole being. I heard the man at the table ask: "Are you sick, young lady? Can I do anything for you?" "Yes, you can let me have your paper," I blurted out. "You won't have to pay me for the ice-cream. But I must ask you to leave. I must close the store." The man looked at me as if I had gone crazy.

I locked up the store and ran full speed the three blocks to our little flat. It was Homestead, not Russia; I knew it now. We belonged in Homestead. The boys, resting for the evening shift, sat up as I rushed into the room, newspaper clutched in my hand. "What has happened, Emma? You look terrible!" I could not speak. I handed them the paper.

Sasha was the first on his feet. "Homestead!" he exclaimed. "I must go to Homestead!" I flung my arms around him, crying out his name. I, too, would go. "We must go tonight," he said; "the great moment has come at last!" Being internationalists, he added, it mattered not to us where the blow was struck by the workers; we must be with them. We must bring them our great message and help them see that it was not only for the moment that they must strike, but for all time, for a free life, for anarchism. Russia had many heroic men and women, but who was there in America? Yes, we must go to Homestead, tonight!

I had never heard Sasha so eloquent. He seemed to have grown in stature. He looked strong and defiant, an inner light on his face making him beautiful, as he had never appeared to me before.

We immediately went to our landlord and informed him of our decision to leave. He replied that we were mad; we were doing so well, we were on the way to fortune. If we would hold out to the end of the summer, we would be able to clear at least a thousand dollars. But he argued in vain— we were not to be moved. We invented the story that a very dear relative was in a dying condition, and that therefore we must depart. We would turn the store over to him; all we wanted was the evening's receipts. We would remain until closing-hours, leave everything in order, and give him the keys.

That evening we were especially busy. We had never before had so many customers. By one o'clock we had sold out everything. Our receipts were seventy-five dollars. We left on an early morning train.

On the way we discussed our immediate plans. First of all, we would print a manifesto to the steel-workers. We would have to find somebody to translate it into English, as we were still unable to express our thoughts correctly in that tongue. We would have the German and English texts printed in New York and take them with us to Pittsburgh. With the help of the German comrades there, meetings could be organized for me to address. Fedya was to remain in New York till further developments.

From the station we went straight to the flat of Mollock, an Austrian comrade we had met in the *Autonomie* group. He was a baker who worked at night; but Peppie, his wife, with her two children, was at home. We were sure she could put us up.

She was surprised to see the three of us march in, bag and baggage, but she made us welcome, fed us, and suggested that we go to bed. But we had other things to do.

Sasha and I went in search of Claus Timmermann, an ardent German anarchist we knew. He had considerable poetic talent and wrote forceful propaganda. In fact, he had been the editor of an anarchist paper in St. Louis before coming to New York. He was a likable fellow and entirely trustworthy, though a considerable drinker. We felt that Claus was the only person we could safely draw into our plan. He caught our spirit at once. The manifesto was written that afternoon. It was a flaming call to the men of Homestead to throw off the yoke of capitalism, to use their present struggle as a stepping-stone to the destruction of the wage system, and to continue towards social revolution and anarchism.

A few days after our return to New York the news was flashed across the country of the slaughter of steel-workers by Pinkertons. Frick had fortified the Homestead mills, built a high fence around them. Then, in the dead of night, a barge packed with strike-breakers, under protection of heavily armed Pinkerton thugs, quietly stole up the Monongahela River. The steel-men had learned of Frick's move. They stationed themselves along the shore, determined to drive back Frick's hirelings. When the barge got within range, the Pinkertons had opened fire, without warning, killing a number of Homestead men on the shore, among them a little boy, and wounding scores of others.

The wanton murders aroused even the daily papers. Several came out in strong editorials, severely criticizing Frick. He had gone too far; he had added fuel to the fire in

the labour ranks and would have himself to blame for any
desperate acts that might come.

We were stunned. We saw at once that the time for our
manifesto had passed. Words had lost their meaning in the
face of the innocent blood spilled on the banks of the
Monongahela. Intuitively each felt what was surging in
the heart of the others. Sasha broke the silence. "Frick is the
responsible factor in this crime," he said; "he must be made
to stand the consequences." It was the psychological moment for an *Attentat;* the whole country was aroused,
everybody was considering Frick the perpetrator of a cold-
blooded murder. A blow aimed at Frick would re-echo in
the poorest hovel, would call the attention of the whole
world to the real cause behind the Homestead struggle. It
would also strike terror in the enemy's ranks and make
them realize that the proletariat of America had its
avengers.

Sasha had never made bombs before, but Most's *Science
of Revolutionary Warfare* was a good text-book. He would
procure dynamite from a comrade he knew on Staten
Island. He had waited for this sublime moment to serve the
Cause, to give his life for the people. He would go to
Pittsburgh.

"We will go with you!" Fedya and I cried together. But
Sasha would not listen to it. He insisted that it was unnecessary and criminal to waste three lives on one man.

We sat down, Sasha between us, holding our hands. In a
quiet and even tone he began to unfold to us his plan. He
would perfect a time regulator for the bomb that would
enable him to kill Frick, yet save himself. Not because he
wanted to escape. No; he wanted to live long enough to
justify his act in court, so that the American people might
know that he was not a criminal, but an idealist.

"I will kill Frick," Sasha said, "and of course I shall be
condemned to death. I will die proudly in the assurance that
I gave my life for the people. But I will die by my own

hand, like Lingg. Never will I permit our enemies to kill me."

I hung on his lips. His clarity, his calmness and force, the sacred fire of his ideal, enthralled me, held me spellbound. Turning to me, he continued in his deep voice. I was the born speaker, the propagandist, he said. I could do a great deal for his act. I could articulate its meaning to the workers. I could explain that he had had no personal grievance against Frick, that as a human being Frick was no less to him than anyone else. Frick was the symbol of wealth and power, of the injustice and wrong of the capitalistic class, as well as personally responsible for the shedding of the workers' blood. Sasha's act would be directed against Frick, not as a man, but as the enemy of labour. Surely I must see how important it was that I remain behind to plead the meaning of his deed and its message throughout the country.

Every word he said beat upon my brain like a sledge-hammer. The longer he talked, the more conscious I became of the terrible fact that he had no need of me in his last great hour. The realization swept away everything else—message, Cause, duty, propaganda. What meaning could these things have compared with the force that had made Sasha flesh of my flesh and blood of my blood from the moment that I had heard his voice and felt the grip of his hand at our first meeting? Had our three years together shown him so little of my soul that he could tell me calmly to go on living after he had been blown to pieces or strangled to death? Is not true love—not ordinary love, but the love that longs to share to the uttermost with the beloved—is it not more compelling than aught else? Those Russians had known it, Jessie Helfmann and Sophia Perovskaya; they had gone with their men in life and in death. I could do no less.

"I will go with you, Sasha," I cried; "I must go with you! I know that as a woman I can be of help. I could gain access to Frick easier than you. I could pave the way for your act. Besides, I simply must go with you. Do you understand, Sasha?"

We had a feverish week. Sasha's experiments took place at night when everybody was asleep. While Sasha worked, I kept watch. I lived in dread every moment for Sasha, for our friends in the flat, the children, and the rest of the tenants. What if anything should go wrong—but, then, did not the end justify the means? Our end was the sacred cause of the oppressed and exploited people. It was for them that we were going to give our lives. What if a few should have to perish?—the many would be made free and could live in beauty and in comfort. Yes, the end in this case justified the means.

After we had paid our fare from Worcester to New York, we had about sixty dollars left. Twenty had already been used up since our arrival. The material Sasha bought for the bomb had cost a good deal and we still had another week in New York. Besides, I needed a dress and shoes, which, together with the fare to Pittsburgh, would amount to fifty dollars. I realized with a start that we required a large sum of money. I knew no one who could give us so much; besides, I could never tell him the purpose. After days of canvassing in the scorching July heat I succeeded in collecting twenty-five dollars. Sasha finished his preparatory work and went to Staten Island to test the bomb. When he returned, I could tell by his expression that something terrible had happened. I learned soon enough; the bomb had not gone off.

Sasha said it was due either to the wrong chemical directions or to the dampness of the dynamite. The second bomb, having been made from the same material, would most likely also fail. A week's work and anxiety and forty precious dollars wasted! What now? We had no time for lamentations or regrets; we had to act quickly.

. . . Sasha said that the act must be carried out, no

matter how we got the money. It was now clear that the two of us would not be able to go. I would have to listen to his plea and let him go alone. He reiterated his faith in me and in my strength and assured me of the great joy I had given him when I insisted upon going with him to Pittsburgh. "But," he said, "we are too poor. Poverty is always a deciding factor in our actions. Besides, we are merely dividing our labours, each doing what he is best fitted for." He was not an agitator; that was my field, and it would be my task to interpret his act to the people. I cried out against his arguments, though I felt their force. We had no money. I knew that he would go in any event; nothing would stop him, of that I was certain.

Our whole fortune consisted of fifteen dollars. That would take Sasha to Pittsburgh, buy some necessaries, and still leave him a dollar for the first day's food and lodging. Our Allegheny comrades Nold and Bauer, whom Sasha meant to look up, would give him hospitality for a few days until I could raise more money. Sasha had decided not to confide his mission to them; there was no need for it, he felt, and it was never advisable for too many people to be taken into conspiratorial plans. He would require at least another twenty dollars for a gun and a suit of clothes. He might be able to buy the weapon cheap at some pawnshop. I had no idea where I could get the money, but I knew that I would find it somehow.

Those with whom we were staying were told that Sasha would leave that evening, but the motive for his departure was not revealed. There was a simple farewell supper, everyone joked and laughed, and I joined in the gaiety. I strove to be jolly to cheer Sasha, but it was laughter that masked suppressed sobs. Later we accompanied Sasha to the Baltimore and Ohio Station. Our friends kept in the distance, while Sasha and I paced the platform, our hearts too full for speech.

The conductor drawled out: "All aboard!" I clung to

Sasha. He was on the train, while I stood on the lower step. His face bent low to mine, his hand holding me, he whispered: "My sailor girl," (his pet name for me), "comrade, you will be with me to the last. You will proclaim that I gave what was dearest to me for an ideal, for the great suffering people."

The train moved. Sasha loosened my hold, gently helping me to jump off the step. I ran after the vanishing train, waving and calling to him: "Sasha, Sashenka!" The steaming monster disappeared round the bend and I stood glued, straining after it, my arms outstretched for the precious life that was being snatched away from me.

I woke up with a very clear idea of how I could raise the money for Sasha. I would go on the street. I lay wondering how such a notion could have come to me. I recollected Dostoyevsky's *Crime and Punishment,* which had made a profound impression on me, especially the character of Sonya, Marmeladov's daughter. She had become a prostitute in order to support her little brothers and sisters and to relieve her consumptive stepmother of worry. I visioned Sonya as she lay on her cot, face to the wall, her shoulders twitching. I could almost feel the same way. Sensitive Sonya could sell her body; why not I? My cause was greater than hers. It was Sasha—his great deed—the people. But should I be able to do it, to go with strange men—for money? The thought revolted me. I buried my face in the pillow to shut out the light. "Weakling, coward," an inner voice said. "Sasha is giving his life, and you shrink from giving your body, miserable coward!" It took me several hours to gain control of myself. When I got out of bed my mind was made up.

My main concern now was whether I could make myself attractive enough to men who seek out girls on the street. I stepped over to the mirror to inspect my body. I looked tired, but my complexion was good. I should need no make-up. My curly blond hair showed off well with my blue eyes. Too large in the hips for my age, I thought; I was just twenty-three. Well, I came from Jewish stock. Besides, I would wear a corset and I should look taller in high heels (I had never worn either before).

Corsets, slippers with high heels, dainty underwear— where should I get money for it all? I had a white linen dress, trimmed with Caucasian embroidery. I could get some soft flesh-coloured material and sew the underwear myself. I knew the stores on Grand Street carried cheap goods.

I dressed hurriedly and went in search of the servant in the apartment who had shown a liking for me, and she lent me five dollars without any question. I started off to make my purchases. When I returned, I locked myself in my room. I would see no one. I was busy preparing my outfit and thinking of Sasha. What would he say? Would he approve? Yes, I was sure he would. He had always insisted that the end justified the means, that the true revolutionist will not shrink from anything to serve the Cause.

Saturday evening, July 16, 1892, I walked up and down Fourteenth Street, one of the long procession of girls I had so often seen plying their trade. I felt no nervousness at first, but when I looked at the passing men and saw their vulgar glances and their manner of approaching the women, my heart sank. I wanted to take flight, run back to my room, tear off my cheap finery, and scrub myself clean. But a voice kept on ringing in my ears: "You must hold out; Sasha—his act—everything will be lost if you fail."

I continued my tramp, but something stronger than my reason would compel me to increase my pace the moment a man came near me. One of them was rather insistent, and I fled. By eleven o'clock I was utterly exhausted. My feet hurt from the high heels, my head throbbed. I was close to tears from fatigue and disgust with my inability to carry out what I had come to do.

I made another effort. I stood on the corner of Fourteenth Street and Fourth Avenue, near the bank building.
The first man that invited me—I would go with him, I had
decided. A tall, distinguished-looking person, well dressed,
came close. "Let's have a drink, little girl," he said. His hair
was white, he appeared to be about sixty, but his face was
ruddy. "All right," I replied. He took my arm and led me to
a wine house on Union Square which Most had often fre-
quented with me. "Not here!" I almost screamed; "please,
not here." I led him to the back entrance of a saloon on
Thirteenth Street and Third Avenue. I had once been there
in the afternoon for a glass of beer. It had been clean and
quiet then.

That night it was crowded, and with difficulty we secured
a table. The man ordered drinks. My throat felt parched and
I asked for a large glass of beer. Neither of us spoke. I was
conscious of the man's scrutiny of my face and body. I felt
myself growing resentful. Presently he asked: "You're a
novice in the business, aren't you?" "Yes, this is my first
time—but how did you know?" "I watched you as you
passed me," he replied. He told me that he had noticed my
haunted expression and my increased pace the moment a
man came near me. He understood then that I was inexperienced; whatever might have been the reason that
brought me to the street, he knew it was not mere looseness
or love of excitement. "But thousands of girls are driven by
economic necessity," I blurted out. He looked at me in
surprise. "Where did you get that stuff?" I wanted to tell
him all about the social question, about my idea, who and
what I was, but I checked myself. I must not disclose my
identity: it would be too dreadful if he should learn that
Emma Goldman, the anarchist, had been found soliciting
on Fourteenth Street. What a juicy story it would make for
the press!

He said he was not interested in economic problems and

did not care what the reason was for my actions. He only wanted to tell me that there was nothing in prostitution unless one had the knack for it. "You haven't got it, that's all there is to it," he assured me. He took out a ten-dollar bill and put it down before me. "Take this and go home," he said. "But why should you give me money if you don't want me to go with you?" I asked. "Well, just to cover the expenses you must have had to rig yourself out like that," he replied; "your dress is awfully nice, even if it does not go with those cheap shoes and stockings." I was too astounded for speech.

I had met two categories of men: vulgarians and idealists. The former would never have let an opportunity pass to possess a woman and they would give her no other thought save sexual desire. The idealists stoutly defended the equality of the sexes, at least in theory, but the only men among them who practised what they preached were the Russian and Jewish radicals. This man, who had picked me up on the street and who was now with me in the back of a saloon, seemed an entirely new type. He interested me. He must be rich. But would a rich man give something for nothing? The manufacturer Garson came to my mind; he would not even give me a small raise in wages.

Perhaps this man was one of those soul-savers I had read about—people who were always cleansing New York City of vice. I asked him. He laughed and said he was not a professional busybody. If he had thought that I really wanted to be on the street, he would not have cared. "Of course, I may be entirely mistaken," he added, "but I don't mind. Just now I am convinced that you are not intended to be a streetwalker, and that even if you do succeed, you will hate it afterwards." If he were not convinced of it, he would take me for his mistress. "For always?" I cried. "There you are!" he replied; "you are scared by the mere suggestion and yet you hope to succeed on the street. You're an

awfully nice kid, but you're silly, inexperienced, childish."
"I was twenty-three last month," I protested, resentful of
being treated like a child. "You are an old lady," he said
with a grin, "but even old folks can be babes in the woods.
Look at me; I'm sixty-one and I often do foolish things."
"Like believing in my innocence, for instance," I retorted.
The simplicity of his manner pleased me. I asked for his
name and address so as to be able to return his ten dollars
some day. But he refused to give them to me. He loved
mysteries, he said. On the street he held my hand for a
moment, and then we turned in opposite directions.

That night I tossed about for hours. My sleep was restless; my dreams were of Sasha, Frick, Homestead, Fourteenth
Street, and the affable stranger. Long after waking the next
morning the dream pictures persisted. Then my eye caught
my little purse on the table. I jumped up, opened it with
trembling hands—it did contain the ten dollars! It had
actually happened, then!

On Monday a short note arrived from Sasha. He had met
Carl Nold and Henry Bauer, he wrote. He had set the
following Saturday for his act, provided I could send some
money he needed at once. He was sure I would not fail him.
I was a little disappointed by the letter. Its tone was cold
and perfunctory, and I wonder how the stranger would
write to the woman he loved. With a start I shook myself
free. It was crazy to have such thoughts when Sasha was
preparing to take a life and lose his own in the attempt.
How could I think of that stranger and Sasha in the same
breath? I must get more money for my boy.

I would wire Helena for fifteen dollars. I had not written
my dear sister for many weeks, and I hated to ask her for
money, knowing how poor she was. It seemed criminal.
Finally I wired her that I had been taken ill and needed
fifteen dollars. I knew that nothing would prevent her from
getting the money if she thought that I was ill. But a sense

of shame oppressed me, as once before, in St. Petersburg, when I had deceived her.

I received the money from Helena by wire. I sent twenty dollars to Sasha and returned the five I had borrowed for my finery.

The Assassination of McKinley

On September 5, 1901, I came to St. Louis for the purpose of selling a new kind of album, which my friend Ed Brady had invented in collaboration with another man, his partner in the venture. The following day, September 6, I canvassed every important stationery and novelty store in the city for orders for Ed's firm, but I failed to interest anyone in my samples. Only in one store was I told to call the next day to see the boss. As I stood at a street-corner wearily waiting for a car, I heard a newsboy cry: "Extra! Extra! President McKinley shot!" I bought a paper, but the car was so jammed that it was impossible to read. Around me people were talking about the shooting of the President.

Carl Nold, who had done so much for my dear Sasha (Alexander Berkman), had arrived at my house before me. He had already read the account. The President had been shot at the Exposition grounds in Buffalo by a young man by the name of Leon Czolgosz. "I never heard the name," Carl said, "have you?"

"No, never," I replied.

"It is fortunate that you are here and not in Buffalo," he

continued. "As usual, the papers will connect you with this act."

"Nonsense." I said. "The American press is fantastic enough, but it would hardly concoct such a crazy story."

The next morning I went to the stationery store to see the owner. After considerable persuasion I succeeded in getting an order amounting to a thousand dollars, the largest I had ever secured. Naturally I was very happy over it. While I was waiting for the man to fill out his order, I caught the headline of the newspaper lying on his desk: "ASSASSIN OF PRESIDENT MCKINLEY AN ANARCHIST. CONFESSES TO HAVING BEEN INCITED BY EMMA GOLDMAN. WOMAN ANARCHIST WANTED."

By great effort I strove to preserve my composure, completed the business, and walked out of the store. At the next corner I bought several papers and went to a restaurant to read them. They were filled with the details of the tragedy, reporting also the police raid of the Isaak house in Chicago and the arrest of everyone found there. Isaak was then editor of the anarchistic *Free Society*. The authorities were going to hold the prisoners until Emma Goldman was found, the papers stated. Already two hundred detectives had been sent out throughout the country to track down Emma Goldman.

On the inside page of one of the papers was a picture of McKinley's slayer. "Why, that's Nieman!" I gasped. The same Nieman who had asked me for anarchistic literature some time ago at one of my lectures in Cleveland!

When I was through with the papers, it became clear to me that I must immediately go to Chicago. The Isaak family, Hippolyte Havel, our old comrade Jay Fox, a most active man in the labor movement, and a number of others were being held without bail until I should be found. It was plainly my duty to surrender myself. I knew there was neither reason nor the least proof to connect me with the shooting. I would go to Chicago.

Stepping into the street, I bumped into V., the "rich man from New Mexico" who had managed my lecture in Los Angeles some years before. The moment he saw me he turned white with fear.

"For God's sake, Emma, what are you doing here?" he cried in a quavering voice. "Don't you know the police of the whole country are looking for you?"

While he was speaking, his eyes roved uneasily over the street. It was evident he was panicky. I had to make sure that he would not disclose my presence in the city. Familiarly I took his arm and whispered: "Let's go to some quiet place."

Sitting in a corner, away from possible eavesdroppers, I said to him: "Once you assured me of your undying love. You even made me an offer of marriage. It was only four years ago. Is anything left of that affection? If so, will you give me your word of honor that you will not breathe to anybody that you have seen me here? I do not want to be arrested in St. Louis—I intend to give Chicago that honor. Tell me quickly if I can depend on you to keep silent." He promised solemnly.

When we reached the street, he walked away in great haste. I was sure he would keep his word, but I knew that my former devotee was no hero.

When I told Carl I was going to Chicago, he said that I must be out of my senses. He pleaded with me to give up the idea, but I remained adamant. He left me to gather up a few trusted friends, whose opinion he knew I valued, hoping they would be able to persuade me not to surrender myself. They argued with me for hours, but they failed to change my decision. I told them jokingly that they had better give me a good send-off, as we probably should never again have an opportunity for a jolly evening together. They engaged a private dining-room at a restaurant, where we were treated to a Lucullan meal, and then they accompanied me to the Wabash Station, Carl having secured a sleeper for me.

In the morning the car was agog with the Buffalo tragedy, Czolgosz and Emma Goldman. "A beast, a bloodthirsty monster!" I heard someone say. "She should have been locked up long ago." "Locked up nothing!" another retorted. "She should be strung up to the first lamppost."

I listened to the good Christians while resting in my berth. I chuckled to myself at the thought of how they would look if I were to step out and announce: "Here, ladies and gentlemen, true followers of the gentle Jesus, here is Emma Goldman!" But I did not have the heart to cause them such a shock and I remained behind my curtain.

Half an hour before the train pulled into the station I got dressed. I wore a small sailor hat with a bright blue veil, much in style then. I left my glasses off and pulled the veil over my face. The platform was jammed with people, among them several men who looked like detectives. I asked a fellow passenger to be kind enough to keep an eye on my two suitcases while I went in search of a porter. I finally got one, walking the whole length of the platform to my luggage, then back again with the porter to the checkroom. Securing my receipt, I left the station.

The only person in Chicago who knew of my coming was my good friend Max Baginski, to whom I had sent a cautious wire. I caught sight of him before he saw me. Passing him slowly, I whispered: "Walk toward the next street. I'll do the same." No one seemed to follow me. After some zigzagging with Max and changing half a dozen street-cars we reached the apartment where he and Millie ("Puck") lived. Both of them expressed the greatest anxiety about my safety, Max insisting that it was insanity to have come to Chicago. The situation, he said, was a repetition of 1887; the press and the police were thirsty for blood. "It's *your* blood they want," he repeated, while he and Millie implored me to leave the country.

I was determined to remain in Chicago. I realized that I could not stay at their home, nor with any other foreign comrades. I had, however, American friends who were not known as anarchists. Max notified Mr. and Mrs. N., who I knew were very fond of me, of my presence and they came at once. They also were worried about me, but they thought I would be safe with them. It was to be only for two days, as I was planning to give myself up to the police as quickly as possible.

Mr. N., the son of a wealthy preacher, lived in a fashionable neighborhood. "Imagine anybody believing I would shelter Emma Goldman!" he said when we had arrived in his house. Late in the afternoon, on Monday, when Mr. N. returned from his office, he informed me that there was a chance to get five thousand dollars from the Chicago *Tribune* for a scoop on an interview. "Fine!" I replied. "We shall need money to fight my case." We agreed that Mr. N. should bring the newspaper representative to his apartment the next morning, and then the three of us would ride down to police headquarters together. In the evening Max and Millie arrived. I had never before seen my friends in such a state of nervous excitement. Max reiterated that I must get away, else I was putting my head in the noose. "If you go to the police, you will never come out alive," he warned me. "It will be the same as with Albert Parsons. You must let us get you over to Canada."

Millie took me aside. "Since Friday," she said, "Max has not slept or taken food. He walks the floor all night and keeps on saying: 'Emma is lost; they will kill her.' " She begged me to soothe Max by promising him that I would escape to Canada, even if I did not intend doing so. I consented and asked Max to make the necessary arrangements to get me away. Overjoyed, he clasped me in his arms. We arranged for Max and Millie to come the next morning with an outfit of clothes to disguise me.

I spent the greater part of the night tearing up letters and papers and destroying what was likely to involve my friends. All preparations completed, I went to sleep. In the morning Mrs. N. left for her office, while her husband went to the Chicago *Tribune*. We agreed that if anyone called, I was to pretend to be the maid.

II.

About nine o'clock, while taking a bath, I heard a sound as if someone were scratching on the window-sill. I paid no attention to it at first. I finished my bath leisurely and began to dress. Then came a crash of glass. I threw my kimono over me and went into the dining-room to investigate. A man was clutching the window-sill with one hand while holding a gun in the other. We were on the third floor and there was no fire-escape. I called out: "Look out, you'll break your neck!"

"Why the hell don't you open the door? Are you deaf?"

He swung through the window and was in the room. I walked over to the entrance and unlocked it. Twelve men, led by a giant, crowded into the apartment. The leader grabbed me by the arm, bellowing: "Who are you?"

"I not speak English—Swedish servant-girl."

He released his hold and ordered his men to search the place. Turning to me, he yelled: "Stand back! We're looking for Emma Goldman." Then he held up a photograph to me. "See this? We want this woman. Where is she?"

I pointed my finger at the picture and said: "This woman I not see here. This woman big—you look in those small boxes will not find her—she too big."

"Oh, shut up!" he bawled. "You can't tell what them anarchists will do."

After they had searched the house, turning everything

upside down, the giant walked over to the book-shelves. "Hell, this is a reg'lar preacher's house," he remarked. "Look at them books. I don't think Emma Goldman would be here." They were about to leave when one of the detectives suddenly called: "Here, Captain Schuettler, what about this?" It was my fountain-pen, a gift from a friend, with my name on it. I had overlooked it. "By golly, that's a find!" cried the captain. "She must have been here and she may come back." He ordered two of his men to remain behind.

I saw that the game was up. There was no sign of Mr. N. or the *Tribune* man, and it could serve no purpose to keep the farce up longer.

"I am Emma Goldman," I announced.

For a moment Schuettler and his men stood there as if petrified. Then the captain roared: "Well, I'll be damned! You're the shrewdest crook I ever met! Take her, quick!"

When I stepped into the cab waiting at the curb, I saw N. approaching in company of the *Tribune* man. It was too late for the scoop, and I did not want my host recognized. I pretended not to see them.

I had often heard of the third degree used by the police in various American cities to extort confessions, but I myself had never been subjected to it. I had been arrested a number of times since 1893; no violence, however, had ever been practised on me. On the day of my arrest, which was September 10, I was kept at police headquarters in a stifling room and grilled to exhaustion from 10:30 A.M. till 7 P.M. At least fifty detectives passed me, each shaking his fist in my face and threatening me with the direst things. One yelled: "You was with Czolgosz in Buffalo! I saw you myself, right in front of Convention Hall. Better confess, d'you hear?" Another: "Look here, Goldman, I seen you with that son of a b - - - - at the fair! Don't you lie now—I seen you, I tell you!" Again: "You've faked enough—you keep this up and sure's you're born you'll get the chair.

Your lover has confessed. He said it was your speech made him shoot the President." I knew they were lying; I knew I had not been with Czolgosz except for a few minutes in Cleveland on May 5, and for half an hour in Chicago on July 12. Schuettler was most ferocious. His massive bulk towered above me, bellowing: "If you don't confess, you'll go the way of those bastard Haymarket anarchists."

I reiterated the story I had told them when first brought to police headquarters, explaining where I had been and with whom. But they would not believe me and kept on bullying and abusing me. My head throbbed, my throat and lips felt parched. A large pitcher of water stood on the table before me, but every time I stretched out my hand for it, a detective would say: "You can drink all you want, but first answer me. When were you with Czolgosz the day he shot the President?" The torture continued for hours. Finally I was taken to the Harrison street police-station and locked in a barred enclosure, exposed to view from every side.

Presently the matron came to inquire if I wanted supper. "No, but water," I said, "and something for my head." She returned with a tin pitcher of tepid water which I gulped down. She could give me nothing for my head except a cold compress. It proved very soothing, and I soon fell asleep.

I woke up with a burning sensation. A plain-clothes man held a reflector in front of me, close to my eyes. I leaped up and pushed him away with all my strength, crying: "You're burning my eyes!" "We'll burn more before we get through with you!" he retorted. With short intermissions this was repeated during three nights. On the third night several detectives entered my cell. "We've got the right dope on you now," they announced. "It was you who financed Czolgosz and you got the money from Dr. Kaplan in Buffalo. We have him all right, and he's confessed everything. Now what you got to say?"

"Nothing more than I have already said," I repeated. "I know nothing about the act."

Since my arrest I had had no word from my friends, nor had anyone come to see me. I realized that I was being kept *incommunicado*. I did get letters, however, most of them unsigned. "You damn bitch of an anarchist," one of them read, "I wish I could get at you. I would tear your heart out and feed it to my dog." "Murderous Emma Goldman," another wrote, "you will burn in hell-fire for your treachery to our country." A third cheerfully promised: "We will cut your tongue out, soak your carcass in oil, and burn you alive."

On the fifth day after my arrest I received a wire. It was from Ed, promising the backing of his firm. "Do not hesitate to use our name. We stand by you to the last." I was glad of the assurance, because it relieved me of the need of keeping silent about my movements on business for Ed's house.

The same evening Chief of Police O'Neill of Chicago came to my cell. He informed me that he would like to have a quiet talk with me. "I have no wish to bully or coerce you," he said. "Perhaps I can help you."

"It would indeed be a strange experience to have help from a chief of police," I replied, "but I am quite willing to answer your questions."

He asked me to give him a detailed account of my movements from May 5, when I had first met Czolgosz, until the day of my arrest in Chicago. I gave him the requested information, but without mentioning my visit to Sasha or the names of the comrades who had been my hosts. As there was no longer any need of shielding Dr. Kaplan, the Isaaks, or Hippolyte, I was in a position to give practically a complete account. When I concluded—what I said being taken down in shorthand—Chief O'Neill remarked: "Unless you're a very clever actress, you are certainly innocent. I think you are innocent, and I am going to do my part to help you out." I was too amazed to thank him; I had never before heard such a tone from a police officer. At the same time I was skeptical of the success of his efforts, even if he should try to do something for me.

Immediately following my conference with the chief I became aware of a decided change in my treatment. My cell door was left unlocked day and night, and I was told by the matron that I could stay in the large room, use the rocking-chair and the table there, order my own food and papers, receive and send out mail. I began at once to lead the life of a society lady, receiving callers all day long, mostly news-paper people who came not so much for interviews as to talk, smoke, and relate funny stories. Others, again, came out of curiosity. Some women reporters brought gifts of books and toilet articles. Most attentive was Katherine Leckie of the Hearst papers. She possessed a better intellect than Nelly Bly, who used to visit me in the Tombs in 1893, and had a much finer social feeling. A strong and ardent feminist, she was at the same time devoted to the cause of labor. Katherine Leckie was the first to take my story of the third degree. She became so outraged at hearing it that she undertook to canvass the various women's organizations in order to induce them to take the matter up.

One day a representative of the *Arbeiter Zeitung* was announced. With joy I saw Max, who whispered to me that he could secure admission only in that capacity. He in-formed me that he had received a letter from Ed with the news that Hearst had sent a representative to Justus Schwab, whose saloon was then one of the most celebrated meeting places for radicals in New York, with an offer of twenty thousand dollars if I would come to New York and give him an exclusive interview. The money would be deposited in a bank acceptable to Justus and Ed. Both of them were convinced, Max said, that Hearst would spend any amount to railroad me. "He needs it to whitewash him-self of the charge of having incited Czolgosz to shoot McKinley," he explained.

The Republican papers of the country had been carrying

front-page stories connecting Hearst with Czolgosz, because
all through the McKinley administration the Hearst press
had violently attacked the President. One of the newspapers
had cartooned the publisher standing behind Czolgosz,
handing him a match to light the fuse of a bomb. Now
Hearst was among the loudest of those demanding the extermination of the anarchists.

"Twenty thousand dollars!" I exclaimed. "What a pity
Ed's letter arrived too late! I certainly would have accepted
the proposal. Think of the fight we could have made and
the propaganda!"

"It is well you still keep your sense of humor," Max
remarked, "but I am happy the letter came too late. Your
situation is serious enough without Mr. Hearst to make it
worse."

Another visitor was a lawyer from Clarence Darrow's
office. He had come to warn me that I was hurting my case
by my persistent defence of Czolgosz; the man was crazy
and I should admit it. "No prominent attorney will accept
your defence if you ally yourself with the assassin of the
President," he assured me. "In fact, you stand in imminent
danger of being held as an accessory to the crime."

I demanded to know why Mr. Darrow himself did not
come if he was so concerned, but his representative was
evasive. He continued to paint my case in sinister colors.
My chances of escape were few at best, it seemed, too few
for me to allow any sentimentality to aggravate it. Czolgosz
was insane, the man insisted; everybody could see it, and,
besides, he was a bad sort to have involved me, a coward
hiding behind a woman's skirts. His talk was repugnant to
me. I informed him that I was not willing to swear away the
reason, character, or life of a defenceless human being and
that I wanted no assistance from his chief.

The country was in a panic. Judging by the press, I was
sure that it was the people of the United States and not
Czolgosz that had gone mad. Not since 1887 had there

been evidenced such lust for blood, such savagery of vengeance. "Anarchists must be exterminated!" the papers raved. "They should be dumped into the sea; there is no place for the vultures under our flag. Emma Goldman has been allowed to ply her trade of murder too long. She should be forced to share the fate of her dupes."

It was a repetition of the dark Chicago days. Fourteen years, years of painful growth, yet fascinating and fruitful years. And now the end! The end? I was only thirty-two and there was yet so much, so very much, undone. And the boy in Buffalo—his life had scarce begun. What was his life, I wondered; what the forces that drove him to this doom? "I did it for the working people," he was reported to have said. The people! Sasha also had tried to do something for the people in his attempt on Frick's life; and our brave Chicago martyrs, and the others in every land and time. But the people are asleep; they remain indifferent. They forge their own chains and do the bidding of their masters to crucify their Christs.

III.

Buffalo was pressing for my extradition, but Chicago asked for authentic data on the case. I had already been given several hearings in court, and on each occasion the district attorney from Buffalo had presented much circumstantial evidence to induce the State of Illinois to surrender me. But Illinois demanded direct proofs. There was a hitch somewhere. I thought it likely that Chief of Police O'Neill was behind the matter.

The chief's attitude toward me had changed the behavior of every officer in the Harrison street police-station. The matron and the two policemen assigned to watch my cell began to lavish attentions on me. The officer on night duty now often appeared with his arms full of parcels, containing fruit, candy, and drinks stronger than grape-juice. "From a friend who keeps a saloon round the corner," he would say, "an admirer of yours." A matron presented me with flowers from the same unknown. One day she brought me the message that he was going to send a grand supper for the coming Sunday.

"Who is the man and why should he admire me?" I inquired.

"Well, we're all Democrats, and McKinley is a Republican," she replied.

"You don't mean you're glad McKinley was shot?" I exclaimed.

"Not glad exactly, but not sorry, neither," she said. "We have to pretend, you know, but we're none of us excited about it."

"I didn't want McKinley killed," I told her.

"We know that," she smiled, "but you're standing up for the boy."

I wondered how many more people in America were pretending the same kind of sympathy with the stricken President as my friends in the station-house.

Buffalo failed to produce evidence to justify my extradition. Chicago was getting weary of the game of hide-and-seek. The authorities would not turn me over to Buffalo, yet at the same time they did not feel like letting me go entirely free. By way of compromise I was put under twenty-thousand-dollar bail. The Isaak group had been put under fifteen-thousand-dollar bail. I knew that it would be almost impossible for our people to raise a total of thirty-five thousand dollars within a few days. I insisted on the others' being bailed out first. Thereupon I was transferred to the Cook county jail.

The night before my transfer was Sunday. My saloon-keeper admirer kept his word; he sent over a huge tray filled with numerous goodies: a big turkey, with all the trimmings, including wine and flowers. A note came with it informing me that he was willing to put up five thousand dollars toward my bail.

"A strange saloon-keeper!" I remarked.

"Not at all," the matron replied. "He's the ward heeler and he hates the Republicans worse than the Devil."

I invited her, my two policemen, and several other officers present to join me in the celebration. They assured me that nothing like it had ever before happened to them—a prisoner playing host to her keepers. "You mean a dangerous anarchist having as guests the guardians of law and order," I corrected. When everybody had left, I noticed that my day watchman lingered behind. I inquired whether he had been changed to night duty. "No," he replied, "I just wanted to tell you that you are not the first anarchist I've been assigned to watch. I was on duty when Parsons and his comrades were in here."

Peculiar and inexplicable the ways of life, intricate the chain of events! Here I was, the spiritual child of those men, imprisoned in the city that had taken their lives, in the same jail, even under the guardianship of the very man who had kept watch in their silent hours. Tomorrow I should be taken to the Cook county jail, within whose walls Parsons, Spies, Engel, and Fischer had been hanged. Strange, indeed, the complex forces that had bound me to those martyrs through all my socially conscious years! And now events were bringing me nearer and nearer—perhaps to a similar end?

The newspapers had published rumors about mobs ready to attack the Harrison street station and planning violence to Emma Goldman before she could be taken to the Cook county jail. Monday morning, flanked by a heavily armed guard, I was led out of the station-house. There were not a dozen people in sight, mostly curiosity-seekers. As usual, the press had deliberately tried to incite a riot.

Ahead of me were two handcuffed prisoners roughly

hustled about by the officers. When we reached the patrol wagon, surrounded by more police, their guns ready for action, I found myself close to the two men. Their features could not be distinguished: their heads were bound up in bandages, leaving only their eyes free. As they stepped to the patrol wagon a policeman hit one of them on the head with his club, at the same time pushing the other prisoner violently into the wagon. They fell over each other, one of them shrieking with pain. I got in next, then turned to the officer. "You brute," I said, "how dare you beat that helpless fellow?" The next thing I knew, I was sent reeling to the floor. He had landed his fist on my jaw, knocking out a tooth and covering my face with blood. Then he pulled me up, shoved me into the seat, and yelled: "Another word from you, you damned anarchist, and I'll break every bone in your body!"

I arrived at the office of the county jail with my waist and skirt covered with blood, my face aching fearfully. No one showed the slightest interest or bothered to ask how I came to be in such a battered condition. They did not even give me water to wash up. For two hours I was kept in a room in the middle of which stood a long table. Finally a woman arrived who informed me that I would have to be searched. "All right, go ahead," I said. "Strip and get on the table," she ordered. I had been repeatedly searched, but I had never before been offered such an insult.

"You'll have to kill me first, or get your keepers to put me on the table by force," I declared. "You'll never get me to do it otherwise."

She hurried out, and I remained alone. After a long wait another woman came in and led me upstairs, where the matron of the tier took charge of me. She was the first to inquire what was the matter with me. After assigning me to a cell she brought a hot-water bottle and suggested that I lie down and get some rest.

The following afternoon Katherine Leckie visited me. I

was taken into a room provided with a double wire screen. It was semi-dark, but as soon as Katherine saw me, she cried: "What on God's earth has happened to you? Your face is all twisted!" No mirror, not even of the smallest size, being allowed in the jail, I was not aware how I looked, though my eyes and lips felt queer to the touch. I told Katherine of my encounter with the policeman's fist. She left swearing vengeance and promising to return after seeing Chief O'Neill.

Toward evening she came back to let me know that the chief had assured her the officer would be punished if I would identify him among the guards of the transport. I refused. I had hardly looked at the man's face and I was not sure I could recognize him. Moreover, I told Katherine, much to her disappointment, that the dismissal of the officer would not restore my tooth; neither would it do away with police brutality. "It is the system I am fighting, my dear Katherine, not the particular offender," I said. But she was not convinced; she wanted something done to arouse popular indignation against such savagery. "Dismissing wouldn't be enough," she persisted. "He should be tried for assault."

Poor Katherine was not aware that I knew she could do nothing. She was not even in a position to speak through her own paper: her story about the third degree had been suppressed. She promptly replied by resigning; she would no longer be connected with such a cowardly journal, she had told the editor. Yet not a word had she breathed to me of her trouble. I learned the story from a reporter of another Chicago daily.

IV.

One evening, while engrossed in a book, I was surprised by several detectives and reporters. "The President has just died," they announced. "How do you feel about it? Aren't you sorry?"

"Is it possible," I asked, "that in the entire United States only the President passed away on this day? Surely many others have also died at the same time, perhaps in poverty and destitution, leaving helpless dependents behind. Why do you expect me to feel more regret over the death of McKinley than of the rest?"

The pencils went flying. "My compassion has always been with the living," I continued. "The dead no longer need it. No doubt that is the reason why you all feel so sympathetic to the dead. You know that you'll never be called upon to make good your protestations."

"Damned good copy," a young reporter exclaimed, "but I think you're crazy."

I was glad when they left. My thoughts were with the boy in Buffalo, whose fate was now sealed. What tortures of mind and body were still to be his before he would be allowed to breathe his last! How would he meet the supreme moment? "I did it for the people," he had said. I paced my cell trying to analyse the probable motives that had decided his purpose.

Suddenly a thought flitted through my mind—that notice by Isaak in *Free Society*!—the charge of "spy" against Nieman because he had "asked suspicious questions and tried to get into the anarchist ranks." I had written Isaak at the time, demanding proofs for the outrageous accusation. As a result of my protest *Free Society* printed a retraction to the effect that a mistake had been made. It had relieved me and I had given the matter no further thought.

Now the whole situation appeared in a new light, clear and terrible. Czolgosz must have read the charge; it must have hurt him to the quick to be so cruelly misjudged by the very people to whom he had come for inspiration. I recalled his eagerness to secure the right kind of books. It was apparent that he had sought in anarchism a solution of the wrongs he saw everywhere about him. No doubt it was that which had induced him to call on me and later on the

Isaaks. Instead of finding help the poor youth saw himself attacked. Was it that experience, fearfully wounding his spirit, that had led to his act? There must also have been other causes, but perhaps his great urge had been to prove that he was sincere, that he felt with the oppressed, that he was no spy.

But why had he chosen the President rather than some more direct representative of the system of economic oppression and misery? Was it because he saw in McKinley the willing tool of Wall Street and of the new American imperialism that flowered under his administration? One of its first steps had been the annexation of the Philippines, an act of treachery to the people whom America had pledged to set free during the Spanish War. McKinley also typified a hostile and reactionary attitude to labor: he had repeatedly sided with the masters by sending troops into strike regions. All these circumstances, I felt, must have exerted a decisive influence upon poor Leon.

Throughout the night thoughts of the unfortunate boy kept crowding in my mind. In vain I sought to divest myself of the harassing reflections by reading. The dawning day still found me pacing my cell, Leon's beautiful face, pale and haunted, before me.

Again I was taken to court for a hearing and again the Buffalo authorities failed to produce evidence to connect me with Czolgosz's act. The Buffalo representative and the Chicago judge sitting on the case kept up a verbal fight for two hours, at the end of which Buffalo was robbed of its prey. I was set free.

Ever since my arrest the press of the country had been continually denouncing me as the instigator of Czolgosz's act, but after my discharge the newspapers published only a few lines in an inconspicuous corner to the effect that "after a month's detention Emma Goldman was found not to have been in complicity with the assassin of President McKinley."

Upon my release I was met by Max, Hippolyte, and other

friends, with whom I went to the Isaak home. The charges against the comrades arrested in the Chicago raids had also been dismissed. Everyone was in high spirits over my escape from an apparently fatal situation.

"We can be grateful to whatever gods watch over you, Emma," said Isaak, "that you were arrested here and not in New York."

"The gods in this case must have been Chief of Police O'Neill," I said laughingly.

"Chief O'Neill!" my friends exclaimed. "What did he have to do with it?"

I told them about my interview with him and his promise of help. Jonathan Crane, a journalist friend of ours present, broke out into uproarious laughter. "You are more naïve than I should have expected, Emma Goldman," he said. "It wasn't you O'Neill cared a damn about! It was his own schemes. Being on the *Tribune,* I happen to know the inside story of the feud in the police department." Crane then related the efforts of Chief O'Neill to put several captains in the penitentiary for perjury and bribery. "Nothing could have come more opportunely for those blackguards than the cry of anarchy," he explained. "They seized upon it as the police did in 1887; it was their chance to pose as saviors of the country and incidentally to whitewash themselves. But it wasn't to O'Neill's interest to let those birds pose as heroes and get back into the department. That's why he worked for you. He's a shrewd Irishman. Just the same, we may be glad that the quarrel brought us back our Emma."

I asked my friends their opinion as to how the idea of connecting my name with Czolgosz had originated. "I refuse to believe that the boy made any kind of a confession or involved me in any way," I stated. "I cannot think that he was capable of inventing something which he must have known might mean my death. I'm convinced that no one with such a frank face could be so craven. It must have come from some other source."

"It did!" Hippolyte declared emphatically. "The whole dastardly story was started by a *Daily News* reporter who used to hang round here pretending to sympathize with our ideas. Late in the afternoon of September 6 he came to the house. He wanted to know all about a certain Czolgosz or Nieman. Had we associated with him? Was he an anarchist? And so forth. Well, you know what I think of reporters—I wouldn't give him any information. But unfortunately Isaak did."

"What was there to hide?" Isaak interrupted. "Everybody about here knew that we had met the man through Emma, and that he used to visit us. Besides, how was I to know that the reporter was going to fabricate such a lying story?"

V.

I urged the Chicago comrades to consider what could be done for the boy in the Buffalo jail. We could not save his life, but we could at least try to explain his act to the world and we should attempt to communicate with him, so that he might feel that he was not forsaken by us. Max doubted the possibility of reaching Czolgosz. He had received a note from a comrade in Buffalo informing him that no one was permitted to see Leon. I suggested that we secure an attorney. Without legal aid Czolgosz would be gagged and railroaded, as Sasha had been in the Frick case.

Isaak advised that a lawyer be engaged in the State of New York, and I decided to leave immediately for the East. My friends argued that it would be folly to do so; I should surely be arrested the moment I reached the city, and turned over to Buffalo, my fate sealed. But it was unthinkable to me to leave Czolgosz to his doom without making an effort in his behalf. No considerations of personal safety should influence us in the matter, I told my friends, adding that I would remain in Chicago for the public meeting that must be organized to explain our attitude toward Czolgosz and his *Attentat*.

On the evening of the meeting one could not get within a block of Brand's Hall, where it was to be held. Strong detachments of police were dispersing the people by force. We tried to hire another hall, but the police had terrorized the hall-keepers. Our efforts to hold a meeting being frustrated, I resolved to state my position in *Free Society*.

"Leon Czolgosz and other men of his type," I wrote in my article, entitled, "The Tragedy of Buffalo,"

> far from being depraved creatures of low instincts are in reality supersensitive beings unable to bear up under too great social stress. They are driven to some violent expression, even at the sacrifice of their own lives, because they cannot supinely witness the misery and suffering of their fellows. The blame for such acts must be laid at the door of those who are responsible for the injustice and inhumanity which dominate the world.

After pointing out the social causes for such acts as that of Czolgosz, I concluded:

> As I write, my thoughts wander to the young man with the girlish face about to be put to death, pacing his cell, followed by cruel eyes:
>
> > "Who watch him when he tries to weep
> > And when he tries to pray,
> > Who watch him lest himself should rob
> > The prison of its prey."
>
> My heart goes out to him in deep sympathy, as it goes out to all the victims of oppression and misery, to the martyrs past and future that die, the forerunners of a better and nobler life.

I turned the article over to Isaak, who promised to have it set up at once.

The police and the press were continuing their hunt for anarchists throughout the country. Meetings were broken up and innocent people arrested. In various places persons suspected of being anarchists were subjected to violence. In Pittsburgh our good friend Harry Gordon was dragged out into the street and nearly lynched. A rope already around his neck, he was saved at the last moment by some by-standers who were touched by the pleading of Mrs. Gordon and her two children. In New York the office of the *Freie Arbeiter Stimme* was attacked by a mob, the furniture demolished, and the type destroyed.

In no case did the police interfere with the doings of the patriotic ruffians. Johann Most was arrested for an article in the *Freiheit* reproducing an essay on political violence by Karl Heinzen, the famous '48 revolutionist, then dead many years. Most was out on bail awaiting his trial. The German comrades in Chicago arranged an affair to raise funds for his defence and invited me to speak. I gladly consented.

Returning to the Isaak home after the meeting, I found the proofs of my article. Looking them over, I was surprised by a paragraph that changed the entire meaning of my statement. It was, I was sure, no other than Isaak, the editor, who was responsible for the change. I confronted him, demanding an explanation. He readily admitted that he had written the little paragraph, "to tone down the article," he explained, "in order to save *Free Society*."

"And incidentally your skin!" I retorted hotly. "For years you've been denouncing people as cowards who could not meet a dangerous situation. Now that you yourself are face to face with one, you draw in your horns. At least you should have asked my permission to make the change."

It required a long discussion to alter Isaak's attitude. He saw that my view was sustained by the rest of the group—his son Abe, Hippolyte, and several others—whereupon he declared that he renounced all responsibility in the matter. My article finally appeared in its original form. Nothing happened to *Free Society*. But my faith in Isaak was shaken.

On my way back to New York I stopped off in Rochester. Arriving in the evening, I walked to my sister Helena's place in order to avoid recognition. A policeman was stationed at the house, but he did not know me. Everyone gasped when I made my appearance.

"How did you get by?" Helena cried. "Didn't you see the officer at the door?"

"Indeed I saw him, but he evidently didn't see me," I laughed. "Don't you folks worry about any policeman; better give me a bath," I cried lightly. My nonchalance dispelled the family's nervous tension. Everybody laughed and Helena clung to me in unchanged love.

All through my incarceration my family had been very devoted to me. They had sent me telegrams and letters, offering money for my defence and any other help I might need. Not a word had they written about the persecution they had been subjected to on my account. They had been pestered to distraction by reporters and kept under surveillance by the authorities. My father had been ostracized by his neighbors and had lost many customers at his little furniture store. At the same time he had also been excommunicated from the synagogue.

My sister Lena, though in poor health, had also been given no peace. She had been terrorized by the police ordering her daughter Stella to appear at headquarters, where they had kept the child the whole day, plying her with questions about her aunt Emma Goldman. Stella had bravely refused to answer, defiantly proclaiming her pride and faith in her *Tante* Emma. Her courage, combined with her youth and beauty, had won general admiration, Helena said.

Even more cruel had been the teachers and pupils of the public school. "Your aunt Emma Goldman is a murderess," they had taunted our children. School was turned to a hideous nightmare for them. My nephews Saxe and Harry had suffered most. Harry's grief over the violent death of his hero was more real than with most of the adults in the country. He deeply felt the disgrace that his own mother's sister should be charged with responsibility for it. Worse yet, his schoolmates denounced him as an anarchist and criminal. The persecution aggravated his misery and completely alienated him from me.

Saxe's unhappiness, on the other hand, resulted from his strong feeling of loyalty to me. His mother and Aunt Helena loved Emma and they had told him she was innocent. They must know better than his schoolmates. Their boisterous aggressiveness had always repelled him; now more than ever he avoided them. My unexpected appearance and outwitting the officer on guard must have quickened Saxe's imagination and increased his admiration for me. His flushed face and shining eyes were eloquent of his emotion. He hovered near me all evening.

It was balm to my bruised spirit to find such a haven of love and peace in the circle of my family. Even my sister Lena, who had often in the past disapproved of my life, now showed warmest affection. Brother Herman and his gentle wife lavished attentions upon me. The imminent danger I had faced, which still threatened me, had served to establish a bond between my family and me stronger than we had ever felt before. I wanted to prolong my happy stay in Rochester to recuperate from the ordeal of Chicago. But the thought of Czolgosz tormented me. I knew that in New York I could make some effort in his behalf.

At the Grand Central Station I was met by my brother Yegor and the two chums who had spent that wonderful month with us in Rochester long before the Czolgosz misery. Yegor looked distressed; he had tried hard to find a place for me, but had failed. No one would rent even a furnished room to Emma Goldman. Our friends who happened to have a vacant room would not run the risk of my staying with them for fear of being evicted. One of the boys offered to let me have his room for a few nights. "No need

to worry," I comforted Yegor. "I am taken care of for the
present, and in the meantime I will find an apartment."

After a long search for a flat I realized that my brother
had not been exaggerating. No one would have me. I went
to see a young prostitute I had once nursed. "Sure, kid, stay
right here!" she welcomed me. "I'm tickled to death to have
you. I'll bunk with a girl friend for a while."

VI.

The encouraging telegram I had received in Chicago from
Ed had been followed by a number of letters assuring me
that I could count on him for whatever I might need:
money, help and advice, and, above all, his friendship. It
was good to know that Ed remained so staunch. When we
met upon my return to New York, he offered me the use of
his apartment while he and his family would be staying with
friends. "You won't find much changed in my place," he
remarked, "all your things are intact in the room that is my
sanctum, where I often dream of our life together." I
thanked him, but I could not accept his generous proposal.
He was too tactful to press the matter, except to inform me
that his firm owed me several hundred dollars in commission.

"I need the money badly," I confided to Ed, "to send
somebody to Buffalo to see Czolgosz. Possibly something
can be done for him. We also ought to organize a mass
meeting at once." He stared at me in bewilderment.

"My dear," he said, shaking his head, "you are evidently
not aware of the panic in the city. No hall in New York can
be had and no one except yourself would be willing to speak
for Czolgosz."

"But no one is expected to eulogize his act!" I argued.
"Surely there must be a few people in the radical ranks who
are capable of sympathy for a doomed human being."

"Capable perhaps," he said doubtfully, "but not brave enough to voice it at this time."

"You may be right," I admitted, "but I intend to make sure of it."

A trusted person was dispatched to Buffalo, but he soon returned without having been able to visit Czolgosz. He reported that no one was permitted to see him. A sympathetic guard had disclosed to our messenger that Leon had repeatedly been beaten into unconsciousness. His physical appearance was such that no outsider was admitted, and for the same reason he could not be taken to court. My friend further reported that, notwithstanding all the torture, Czolgosz had made no confession whatever and had involved no one in his act. A note had been sent in to Leon through the friendly guard.

I learned that an effort had been made in Buffalo to obtain an attorney for Czolgosz, but no one would accept his defence. That made me even more determined to raise my voice in behalf of the poor unfortunate, denied and forsaken by everyone. Before long, however, I became convinced that Ed had been right. No one among the English-speaking radical groups could be induced to participate in a meeting to discuss the act of Leon Czolgosz. Many were willing to protest against my arrest, to condemn the third degree and the treatment I had received. But they would have nothing to do with the Buffalo case. Czolgosz was not an anarchist, his deed had done the movement an irreparable injury, our American comrades insisted.

Most of the Jewish anarchists, even, expressed similar views. Yanofsky, editor of the *Freie Arbeiter Stimme,* went still further. He kept up a campaign against Czolgosz, also denouncing me as an irresponsible person and declaring that he would never again speak from the same platform with me. The only ones who had not lost their heads were of the Latin groups, the Italian, Spanish, and French anarchists.

Their publications had reprinted my article on Czolgosz that had appeared in *Free Society*. They wrote sympathetically of Leon, interpreting his act as a direct result of the increasing imperialism and reaction in this country. The Latin comrades were anxious to help with anything I might suggest, and it was a great comfort to know that at least some anarchists had preserved their judgment and courage in the madhouse of fury and cowardice. Unfortunately, the foreign groups could not reach the American public.

In desperation I clung to the hope that by perseverance and appeals I should be able to rally some public-spirited Americans to express ordinary human sympathy for Leon Czolgosz, even if they felt that they must repudiate his act. Every day brought more disappointment and heartache. I was compelled to face the fact that I had been fighting against an epidemic of abject fear that could not be overcome.

The tragedy in Buffalo was nearing its end. Leon Czolgosz, still ill from the maltreatment he had endured, his face disfigured and head bandaged, was supported in court by two policemen. In its all-embracing justice and mercy the Buffalo court had assigned two lawyers to his defence. What if they did declare publicly that they were sorry to have to plead the case of such a depraved criminal as the assassin of "our beloved" President? They would do their duty just the same! They would see to it that the rights of the defendant were protected in court.

The last act was staged in Auburn prison. It was early dawn, October 29, 1901. The condemned man sat strapped to the electric chair. The executioner stood with his hand on the switch, awaiting the signal. A warden, impelled by Christian mercy, makes a last effort to save the sinner's soul, to induce him to confess. Tenderly he says: "Leon, my boy, why do you shield that bad woman, Emma Goldman? She is not your friend. She has denounced you as a loafer, too lazy to work. She said you had always begged money from her. Emma Goldman has betrayed you, Leon. Why should you shield her?"

Breathless silence, seconds of endless time. It fills the death chamber, creeps into the hearts of the spectators. At last a muffled sound, an almost inaudible voice from under the black mask.

"It doesn't matter what Emma Goldman has said about me. She had nothing to do with my act. I did it alone. I did it for the American people."

A silence more terrible than the first. A sizzling sound— the smell of burnt flesh—a final agonized twitch of life.

Outrage at San Diego

. . . San Diego, California, had always enjoyed considerable freedom of speech. Anarchists, socialists, I.W.W. men, as well as religious sects, had been in the habit of speaking out of doors to large crowds. Then the city fathers of San Diego passed an ordinance doing away with the old custom. The anarchists and I.W.W.'s initiated a free-speech fight, with the result that eighty-four men and women were thrown into jail. Among them was E. E. Kirk, who had defended me in San Francisco in 1909; Mrs. Laura Emerson, a well-known woman rebel; and Jack Whyte, one of the most intelligent I.W.W. boys in California.

When I arrived with Ben [Reitman] in Los Angeles in April [1912], San Diego was in the grip of a veritable civil war. The patriots, known as Vigilantes, had converted the city into a battle-field. They beat, clubbed, and killed men and women who still believed in their constitutional rights. Hundreds of them had come to San Diego from every part of the United States to participate in the campaign. They travelled in box cars, on the bumpers, on the roofs of trains, every moment in danger of their lives, yet sustained by the holy quest for freedom of speech, for which their comrades were already filling the jails.

The Vigilantes raided the I.W.W. headquarters, broke up the furniture, and arrested a large number of men found there. They were taken out to Sorrento to a spot where a flag-pole had been erected. There the I.W.W.'s were forced to kneel, kiss the flag, and sing the national anthem. As an incentive to quicker action one of the Vigilantes would slap them on the back, which was the signal for a general beating. After these proceedings the men were loaded into automobiles and sent to San Onofre, near the county line, placed in a cattle-pen with armed guards over them, and kept without food or drink for eighteen hours. The following morning they were taken out in groups of five and compelled to run the gauntlet. As they passed between the double line of Vigilantes, they were belaboured with clubs and blackjacks. Then the flag-kissing episode was repeated, after which they were told to "hike" up the track and never come back. They reached Los Angeles after a tramp of several days, sore, hungry, penniless, and in deplorable physical condition.

In this struggle, in which the local police were on the side of the Vigilantes, several I.W.W. men lost their lives. The most brutal murder was that of Joseph Mikolasek, who died on May 7. He was one of the many rebels who had attempted to fill the gap caused by the arrest of their speakers. When he ascended the platform, he was assaulted by the police. With difficulty he dragged himself to the socialist headquarters and thence home. He was followed by detectives, who attacked him in his house. One officer fired and severely wounded him. In self-defence Mikolasek had picked up an ax, but his body was riddled with bullets before he had a chance to lift it against his assailants.

On every tour to the Coast I had lectured in San Diego. This time we were also planning meetings there after the

close of our Los Angeles engagements. Reports from San
Diego and the arrival of scores of wounded Vigilante victims decided us to go at once. Especially after the killing of
Mikolasek we felt it imperative to take up the free-speech
fight waged there. First, however, it was necessary to organize relief for the destitute boys who had escaped their
tormentors and had reached us alive. With the help of a
group of women we organized a feeding-station at the
I.W.W. headquarters. We raised funds at my meetings and
collected clothing and food-stuffs from sympathetic store-
keepers.

San Diego was not content with the murder of Mikolasek; it would not permit him even to be buried in the city.
We therefore had his body shipped to Los Angeles, and
prepared a public demonstration in his honour. Joseph
Mikolasek had been obscure and unknown in life, but he
grew to country-wide stature in his death. Even the police
of the city were impressed by the size, dignity, and grief of
the masses that followed his remains to the crematorium.

Some comrades in San Diego had undertaken to arrange
a meeting, and I chose a subject which seemed to express
the situation best—Henrik Ibsen's *An Enemy of the People*.

On our arrival we found a dense crowd at the station. It
did not occur to me that the reception was intended for us; I
thought that some State official was being expected. We
were to be met by our friends Mr. and Mrs. E. E. Kirk, but
they were nowhere to be seen, and Ben suggested that we
go to the U.S. Grant Hotel. We passed unobserved and got
into the hotel autobus. It was hot and stuffy inside and we
climbed up on top. We had barely taken our seats when
someone shouted: "Here she is, here's the Goldman
woman!" At once the cry was taken up by the crowd. Fash-
ionably dressed women stood up in their cars screaming:
"We want that anarchist murderess!" In an instant there

was a rush for the autobus, hands reaching up to pull me down. With unusual presence of mind, the chauffeur started the car at full speed, scattering the crowd in all directions.

At the hotel we met with no objections. We registered and were shown to our rooms. Everything seemed normal. Mr. and Mrs. Kirk called to see us, and we quietly discussed final arrangements for our meeting. In the afternoon the head clerk came to announce that the Vigilantes had insisted on looking over the hotel register to secure the number of our rooms; he would therefore have to transfer us to another part of the house. We were taken to the top floor and assigned to a large suite. Later on, Mr. Holmes, the hotel manager, paid us a visit. We were perfectly safe under his roof, he assured us, but he could not permit us to go down for our meals or leave our rooms. He would have to keep us locked in. I protested that the U.S. Grant Hotel was not a prison. He replied that he could not keep us incarcerated against our will, but that, as long as we remained the guests of the house, we should have to submit to his arrangement for our safety. "The Vigilantes are in an ugly mood," he warned us; "they are determined not to let you speak and to drive you both out of town." He urged us to leave of our own account and volunteered to escort us. He was a kindly man and we appreciated his offer, but we had to refuse it.

Mr. Holmes had barely left when I was called on the telephone. The speaker said that his name was Edwards, that he was at the head of the local Conservatory of Music, and that he had just read in the papers that our hall-keeper had backed out. He offered us the recital hall of the conservatory. "San Diego still seems to have some brave men," I said to the mysterious person at the other end of the telephone, and I invited him to come to see me to talk over his plan. Before long a fine-looking man of about twenty-seven called. In the course of our conversation I pointed out to

him that I might cause him trouble by speaking in his place.
He replied that he did not mind; he was an anarchist in art
and he believed in free speech. If I were willing to take a
chance, so was he. We decided to await developments.

Towards evening a bedlam of auto horns and whistles
filled the street. "The Vigilantes!" Ben cried. There was a
knock at the door, and Mr. Holmes came in, accompanied
by two other men. I was wanted downstairs by the city
authorities, they informed me. Ben sensed danger and insisted that I ask them to send the visitors up. It seemed
timid to me. It was early evening and we were in the principal hotel of the city. What could happen to us? I went
with Mr. Holmes, Ben accompanying us. Downstairs we
were ushered into a room where we found seven men standing in a semicircle. We were asked to sit down and wait for
the Chief of Police, who arrived before long. "Please come
with me," he addressed me; "the Mayor and other officials
are awaiting you next door." We got up to follow, but,
turning to Ben, the Chief said: "You are not wanted,
doctor. Better wait here."

I entered a room filled with men. The window-blinds
were partly drawn, but the large electric street light in front
disclosed an agitated mass below. The Mayor approached
me. "You hear that mob," he said, indicating the street;
"they mean business. They want to get you and Reitman
out of the hotel, even if they have to take you by force. We
cannot guarantee anything. If you consent to leave, we will
give you protection and get you safely out of town."

"That's very nice of you," I replied, "but why don't you
disperse the crowd? Why don't you use the same measures
against these people that you have against the free-speech
fighters? Your ordinance makes it a crime to gather in the
business districts. Hundreds of I.W.W.'s, anarchists, socialists, and trade-union men have been clubbed and arrested,
and some even killed, for this offence. Yet you allow the
Vigilante mob to congregate in the busiest part of the town

and obstruct traffic. All you have to do is to disperse these
law-breakers."

"We can't do it," he said abruptly; "these people are in a
dangerous mood, and your presence makes things worse."

"Very well, then, let me speak to the crowd," I suggested.
"I could do it from a window here. I have faced infuriated
men before and I have always been able to pacify them."

The Mayor refused.

"I have never accepted protection from the police," I
then said, "and I do not intend to do so now. I charge all of
you men here with being in league with the Vigilantes."

Thereupon the officials declared that matters would have
to take their course, and that I should have only myself to
blame if anything happened.

The interview at an end, I went to call Ben. The room I
had left him in was locked. I became alarmed and pounded
on the door. There was no answer. The noise I made
brought a hotel clerk. He unlocked the door, but no one
was there. I ran back to the other room and met the Chief,
who was just coming out.

"Where is Reitman?" I demanded. "What have you done
with him? If any harm comes to him, you will pay for it if I
have to do it with my own hands."

"How should I know?" he replied gruffly.

Mr. Holmes was not in his office, and no one would tell
me what had become of Ben Reitman. In consternation I
returned to my room. Ben did not appear. In dismay I
paced the floor, unable to decide what steps to take or
whom to approach to help me find Ben. I could not call any
person I knew in the city without endangering his safety,
least of all Mr. Kirk; he was already under indictment in
connexion with the free-speech fight. It had been brave of
him and his wife to meet us; it was sure to aggravate his
situation. The circumstance that the Kirks did not return as
they had promised proved that they were being kept away.

I felt helpless. Time dragged on, and at midnight I dozed

off from sheer fatigue. I dreamed of Ben, bound and gagged, his hands groping for me. I struggled to reach him and woke up with a scream, bathed in sweat. There were voices and loud knocking at my door. When I opened, the house detective and another man stepped in. Reitman was safe, they told me. I looked at them in a daze, hardly grasping their meaning. Ben had been taken out by the Vigilantes, they explained, but no harm had come to him. They had only put him on a train for Los Angeles. I did not believe the detective, but the other man looked honest. He reiterated that he had been given absolute assurance that Reitman was safe.

Mr. Holmes came in. He corroborated the man and begged me to consent to leave. There was no object in my remaining any longer in town, he urged. I would not be allowed to lecture and I was only endangering his own position. He hoped I would not take undue advantage because I was a woman. If I remained, the Vigilantes would drive me out of town anyhow.

Mr. Holmes seemed genuinely concerned. I knew there was no chance of holding a meeting. Now that Ben was safe, there was no sense in harassing Mr. Holmes any further. I consented to leave, planning to take the Owl, the 2:45 A.M. train, for Los Angeles. I called for a taxi and drove to the station. The town was asleep, the streets deserted.

I had just purchased my ticket and was walking towards the Pullman car when I caught the sound of approaching autos—the fearful sound I had first heard at the station and later at the hotel. The Vigilantes, of course.

"Hurry, hurry!" someone cried; "get in quick!"

Before I had time to make another step, I was picked up, carried to the train, and literally thrown into the compartment. The blinds were pulled down and I was locked in. The Vigilantes had arrived and were rushing up and down the platform, shouting and trying to board the train. The crew was on guard, refusing to let them on. There was mad yelling and cursing—hideous and terrifying moments till at last the train pulled out.

We stopped at innumerable stations. Each time I peered out eagerly in the hope that Ben might be waiting to join me. But there was no sign of him. When I reached my apartment in Los Angeles, he was not there. The U.S. Grant Hotel men had lied in order to get me out of town!

"He's dead! He's dead!" I cried in anguish. "They've killed my boy!"

In vain I strove to drive the terrible thought away. I called up the Los Angeles *Herald* and the San Francisco *Bulletin* to inform them about Ben's disappearance. Both papers were unequivocal in their condemnation of the Vigilante reign of terror. The guiding spirit of the *Bulletin* was Mr. Fremont Older, perhaps the only man on a capitalist paper brave enough to plead labour's cause. He had made a valiant fight for the McNamaras. Mr. Older's enlightened humanity had created on the Coast a new attitude towards the social offender. Since the San Diego fight he had kept up a fearless attack on the Vigilantes. Mr. Older and the editor of the *Herald* promised to do their utmost to unearth Ben.

At ten o'clock I was called on the long-distance phone. A strange voice informed me that Dr. Reitman was boarding the train for Los Angeles and that he would arrive in the late afternoon. "His friends should bring a stretcher to the station." "Is he alive?" I shouted into the receiver. "Are you telling the truth? Is he alive?" I listened breathlessly, but there was no response.

Two hours dragged on as if the day would never pass. The wait at the station was more excruciating still. At last the train pulled in. Ben lay in a rear car, all huddled up. He was in blue overalls, his face deathly pale, a terrified look in

his eyes. His hat was gone, and his hair was sticky with tar.
At the sight of me he cried: "Oh, Mommy, I'm with you at
last! Take me away, take me home!"

The newspaper men besieged him with questions, but he
was too exhausted to speak. I begged them to leave him
alone and to call later at my apartment.

While helping him to undress, I was horrified to see that
his body was a mass of bruises covered with blotches of tar.
The letters I.W.W. were burned into his flesh. Ben could
not speak; only his eyes tried to convey what he had passed
through. After partaking of some nourishment and sleeping
several hours, he regained a little strength. In the presence
of a number of friends and reporters he told us what had
happened to him.

"When Emma and the hotel manager left the office to go
into another room," Ben related, "I remained alone with
seven men. As soon as the door was closed, they drew out
revolvers. 'If you utter a sound or make a move, we'll kill
you,' they threatened. Then they gathered around me. One
man grabbed my right arm, another the left; a third took
hold of the front of my coat, another of the back, and I was
led out into the corridor, down the elevator to the ground
floor of the hotel, and out into the street past a uniformed
policeman, and then thrown into an automobile. When the
mob saw me, they set up a howl. The auto went slowly
down the main street and was joined by another one containing several persons who looked like business men. This
was about half past ten in the evening. The twenty-mile ride
was frightful. As soon as we got out of town, they began
kicking and beating me. They took turns at pulling my long
hair and they stuck their fingers into my eyes and nose. 'We
could tear your guts out,' they said, 'but we promised the
Chief of Police not to kill you. We are responsible men,
property-owners, and the police are on our side.' When we
reached the county line, the auto stopped at a deserted spot.
The men formed a ring and told me to undress. They tore

my clothes off. They knocked me down, and when I lay naked on the ground, they kicked and beat me until I was almost insensible. With a lighted cigar they burned the letters I.W.W. on my buttocks; then they poured a can of tar over my head and, in the absence of feathers, rubbed sage-brush on my body. One of them attempted to push a cane into my rectum. Another twisted my testicles. They forced me to kiss the flag and sing *The Star-Spangled Banner*. When they tired of the fun, they gave me my underwear for fear we should meet any women. They also gave me back my vest, in order that I might carry my money, railroad ticket, and watch. The rest of my clothes they kept. I was ordered to make a speech, and then they commanded me to run the gauntlet. The Vigilantes lined up, and as I ran past them, each one gave me a blow or a kick. Then they let me go."

Ben's case was but one of many since the struggle in San Diego had begun, but it helped to focus greater attention on the scene of savagery. . . .

Prisons: A Social Crime and Failure

In 1849 Feodor Dostoyevsky wrote on the wall of his prison cell the following story of "The Priest and the Devil":

" 'Hello, you little fat father!' the devil said to the priest. 'What made you lie so to those poor, misled people? What tortures of hell did you depict? Don't you know they are already suffering the tortures of hell in their earthly lives? Don't you know that you and the authorities of the State are my representatives on earth? It is you that make them suffer the pains of hell with which you threaten them. Don't you know this? Well, then, come with me!'

"The devil grabbed the priest by the collar, lifted him high in the air, and carried him to a factory, to an iron foundry. He saw the workmen there running and hurrying to and fro, and toiling in the scorching heat. Very soon the thick, heavy air and the heat are too much for the priest. With tears in his eyes, he pleads with the devil: 'Let me go! Let me leave this hell!'

" 'Oh, my dear friend, I must show you many more places.' The devil gets hold of him again and drags him off to a farm. There he sees workmen threshing the grain. The dust and heat are insufferable. The overseer carries a knout, and unmercifully beats anyone who falls to the ground overcome by hard toil or hunger.

"Next the priest is taken to the huts where these same workers live with their families—dirty, cold, smoky, ill-smelling holes. The devil grins. He points out the poverty and hardships which are at home here.

"'Well, isn't this enough?' he asks. And it seems as if even he, the devil, pities the people. The pious servant of God can hardly bear it. With uplifted hands he begs: 'Let me go away from here. Yes, yes! This is hell on earth!'

"'Well, then, you see. And you still promise them another hell. You torment them, torture them to death mentally when they are already all but dead physically! Come on! I will show you one more hell—one more, the very worst.'

"He took him to a prison and showed him a dungeon, with its foul air and the many human forms, robbed of all health and energy, lying on the floor, covered with vermin that were devouring their poor, naked, emaciated bodies.

"'Take off your silken clothes,' said the devil to the priest, 'put on your ankles heavy chains such as these unfortunates wear; lie down on the cold and filthy floor—and then talk to them about a hell that still awaits them!'

"'No, no!' answered the priest, 'I cannot think of anything more dreadful than this. I entreat you, let me go away from here!'

"'Yes, this is hell. There can be no worse hell than this. Did you not know it? Did you not know that these men and women whom you are frightening with the picture of a hell hereafter—did you not know that they are in hell right here, before they die?' "

This was written fifty years ago in dark Russia, on the wall of one of the most horrible prisons. Yet who can deny that the same applies with equal force to the present time, even to American prisons?

With all our boasted reforms, our great social changes, and our far-reaching discoveries, human beings continue to be sent to the worst of hells, wherein they are outraged, degraded and tortured, that society may be "protected" from the phantoms of its own making.

Prison, a social protection? What monstrous mind ever conceived such an idea? Just as well say that health can be promoted by a widespread contagion.

After eighteen months of horror in an English prison, Oscar Wilde gave to the world his great masterpiece, *The Ballad of Reading Gaol:*

> The vilest deeds, like poison weeds,
>   Bloom well in prison air;
> It is only what is good in Man
>   That wastes and withers there.
> Pale Anguish keeps the heavy gate,
>   And the Warder is Despair.

Society goes on perpetuating this poisonous air, not realizing that out of it can come naught but the most poisonous results.

We are spending at the present $3,500,000 per day, $1,000,095,000 per year, to maintain prison institutions, and that in a democratic country—a sum almost as large as the combined output of wheat, valued at $750,000,000, and the output of coal, valued at $350,000,000. Professor Bushnell of Washington, D. C., estimates the cost of prisons at $6,000,000,000 annually, and Dr. G. Frank Lydston, an eminent American writer on crime, gives $5,000,000,000 annually as a reasonable figure. Such unheard-of expenditure for the purpose of maintaining vast armies of human beings caged up like wild beasts!*

Yet crimes are on the increase. Thus we learn that in America there are four and a half times as many crimes to

* *Crime and Criminals.* W. C. Owen.

every million population today as there were twenty years ago.

The most horrible aspect is that our national crime is murder, not robbery, embezzlement, or rape, as in the South. London is five times as large as Chicago, yet there are one hundred and eighteen murders annually in the latter city, while only twenty in London. Nor is Chicago the leading city in crime, since it is only seventh on the list, which is headed by four Southern cities, and San Francisco and Los Angeles. In view of such a terrible condition of affairs, it seems ridiculous to prate of the protection society derives from its prisons.

The average mind is slow in grasping a truth, but when the most thoroughly organized, centralized institution, maintained at an excessive national expense, has proven a complete social failure, the dullest must begin to question its right to exist. The time is past when we can be content with our social fabric merely because it is "ordained by divine right," or by the majesty of the law.

The widespread prison investigations, agitation and education during the last few years are conclusive proof that men are learning to dig deep into the very bottom of society, down to the causes of the terrible discrepancy between social and individual life.

Why, then, are prisons a social crime and a failure? To answer this vital question it behooves us to seek the nature and cause of crimes, the methods employed in coping with them, and the effects these methods produce in ridding society of the curse and horror of crimes.

First, as to the *nature* of crime:

Havelock Ellis divides crime into four phases, the political, the passional, the insane, and the occasional. He says that the political criminal is the victim of an attempt of a more or less despotic government to preserve its own stability. He is not necessarily guilty of an unsocial offense; he simply tries to overturn a certain political order which may

itself be anti-social. This truth is recognized all over the
world, except in America where the foolish notion still
prevails that in a Democracy there is no place for political
criminals. Yet John Brown was a political criminal; so were
the Chicago Anarchists; so is every striker. Consequently,
says Havelock Ellis, the political criminal of our time or
place may be the hero, martyr, saint of another age. Lombroso calls the political criminal the true precursor of the
progressive movement of humanity.

"The criminal by passion is usually a man of wholesome
birth and honest life, who under the stress of some great,
unmerited wrong has wrought justice for himself."*

Mr. Hugh C. Weir, in *The Menace of the Police,* cites the
case of Jim Flaherty, a criminal by passion, who, instead of
being saved by society, is turned into a drunkard and a
recidivist, with a ruined and poverty-stricken family as the
result.

A more pathetic type is Archie, the victim in Brand
Whitlock's novel, *The Turn of the Balance,* the greatest
American exposé of crime in the making. Archie, even
more than Flaherty, was driven to crime and death by the
cruel inhumanity of his surroundings, and by the unscrupulous hounding of the machinery of the law. Archie and
Flaherty are but the types of many thousands, demonstrating how the legal aspects of crime, and the methods of
dealing with it, help to create the disease which is undermining our entire social life.

"The insane criminal really can no more be considered a
criminal than a child, since he is mentally in the same condition as an infant or an animal."†

The law already recognizes that, but only in rare cases of
a very flagrant nature, or when the culprit's wealth permits
the luxury of criminal insanity. It has become quite fashionable to be the victim of paranoia. But on the whole the

* *The Criminal,* Havelock Ellis.
† *The Criminal.*

"sovereignty of justice" still continues to punish criminally insane with the whole severity of its power. Thus Mr. Ellis quotes from Dr. Richter's statistics showing that in Germany one hundred and six madmen, out of one hundred and forty-four criminally insane, were condemned to severe punishment.

The occasional criminal "represents by far the largest class of our prison population, hence is the greatest menace to social well-being." What is the cause that compels a vast army of the human family to take to crime, to prefer the hideous life within prison walls to the life outside? Certainly that cause must be an iron master, who leaves its victims no avenue of escape, for the most depraved human being loves liberty.

This terrific force is conditioned in our cruel social and economic arrangement. I do not mean to deny the biologic, physiologic, or psychologic factors in creating crime; but there is hardly an advanced criminologist who will not concede that the social and economic influences are the most relentless, the most poisonous germs of crime. Granted even that there are innate criminal tendencies, it is none the less true that these tendencies find rich nutrition in our social environment.

There is close relation, says Havelock Ellis, between crimes against the person and the price of alcohol, between crimes against property and the price of wheat. He quotes Quetelet and Lacassagne, the former looking upon society as the preparer of crime, and the criminals as instruments that execute them. The latter finds that "the social environment is the cultivation medium of criminality; that the criminal is the microbe, an element which only becomes important when it finds the medium which causes it to ferment; *every society has the criminals it deserves.*"*

The most "prosperous" industrial period makes it impos-

* *The Criminal.*

sible for the worker to earn enough to keep up health and
vigor. And as prosperity is, at best, an imaginary condition,
thousands of people are constantly added to the host of the
unemployed. From East to West, from South to North, this
vast army tramps in search of work or food, and all they
find is the workhouse or the slums. Those who have a spark
of self-respect left prefer open defiance, prefer crime to the
emaciated, degraded position of poverty.

Edward Carpenter estimates that five-sixths of indictable
crimes consist in some violation of property rights; but that
is too low a figure. A thorough investigation would prove
that nine crimes out of ten could be traced, directly or indirectly, to our economic and social iniquities, to our system
of remorseless exploitation and robbery. There is no criminal so stupid but recognizes this terrible fact, though he
may not be able to account for it.

A collection of criminal philosophy, which Havelock
Ellis, Lombroso, and other eminent men have compiled,
shows that the criminal feels only too keenly that it is society that drives him to crime. A Milanese thief said to
Lombroso: "I do not rob, I merely take from the rich their
superfluities; besides, do not advocates and merchants
rob?" A murderer wrote: "Knowing that three-fourths of
the social virtues are cowardly vices, I thought an open
assault on a rich man would be less ignoble than the
cautious combination of fraud." Another wrote: "I am imprisoned for stealing a half dozen eggs. Ministers who rob
millions are honored. Poor Italy!" An educated convict said
to Mr. Davitt: "The laws of society are framed for the purpose of securing the wealth of the world to power and cal-
culation, thereby depriving the larger portion of mankind
of its rights and chances. Why should they punish me for
taking by somewhat similar means from those who have
taken more than they had a right to?" The same man
added: "Religion robs the soul of its independence; patriotism is the stupid worship of the world for which the well-

being and the peace of the inhabitants were sacrificed by those who profit by it, while the laws of the land, in restraining natural desires, were waging war on the manifest spirit of the law of our beings. Compared with this," he concluded, "thieving is an honorable pursuit."*

Verily, there is greater truth in this philosophy than in all the law-and-moral books of society.

The economic, political, moral, and physical factors being the microbes of crime, how does society meet the situation?

The methods of coping with crime have no doubt undergone several changes, but mainly in a theoretic sense. In practice, society has retained the primitive motive in dealing with the offender; that is, revenge. It has also adopted the theologic idea; namely, punishment; while the legal and "civilized" methods consist of deterrence or terror, and reform. We shall presently see that all four modes have failed utterly, and that we are today no nearer a solution than in the dark ages.

The natural impulse of the primitive man to strike back, to avenge a wrong, is out of date. Instead, the civilized man, stripped of courage and daring, has delegated to an organized machinery the duty of avenging his wrongs, in the foolish belief that the State is justified in doing what he no longer has the manhood or consistency to do. The "majesty of the law" is a reasoning thing; it would not stoop to primitive instincts. Its mission is of a "higher" nature. True, it is still steeped in the theologic muddle, which proclaims punishment as a means of purification, or the vicarious atonement of sin. But legally and socially the statute exercises punishment, not merely as an infliction of pain upon the offender, but also for its terrifying effect upon others.

* *The Criminal.*

What is the real basis of punishment, however? The notion of a free will, the idea that man is at all times a free agent for good or evil; if he chooses the latter, he must be made to pay the price. Although this theory has long been exploded, and thrown upon the dustheap, it continues to be applied daily by the entire machinery of government, turning it into the most cruel and brutal tormentor of human life. The only reason for its continuance is the still more cruel notion that the greater the terror punishment spreads, the more certain its preventative effect.

Society is using the most drastic methods in dealing with the social offender. Why do they not deter? Although in America a man is supposed to be considered innocent until proven guilty, the instruments of law, the police, carry on a reign of terror, making indiscriminate arrests, beating, clubbing, bullying people, using the barbarous method of the "third degree," subjecting their unfortunate victims to the foul air of the station house, and the still fouler language of its guardians. Yet crimes are rapidly multiplying, and society is paying the price. On the other hand, it is an open secret that when the unfortunate citizen has been given the full "mercy" of the law, and for the sake of safety is hidden in the worst of hells, his real Calvary begins. Robbed of his rights as a human being, degraded to a mere automaton without will or feeling, dependent entirely upon the mercy of brutal keepers, he daily goes through a process of dehumanization, compared with which savage revenge was mere child's play.

There is not a single penal institution or reformatory in the United States where men are not tortured "to be made good," by means of the black-jack, the club, the strait-jacket, the water-cure, the "humming bird" (an electrical contrivance run along the human body), the solitary, the bull-ring, and starvation diet. In these institutions his will is broken, his soul degraded, his spirit subdued by the deadly monotony and routine of prison life. In Ohio, Illinois,

Pennsylvania, Missouri, and in the South, these horrors have become so flagrant as to reach the outside world, while in most other prisons the same Christian methods still prevail. But prison walls rarely allow the agonized shrieks of the victims to escape—prison walls are thick, they dull the sound. Society might with greater immunity abolish all prisons at once, than to hope for protection from these twentieth-century chambers of horrors.

Year after year the gates of prison hells return to the world an emaciated, deformed, will-less, ship-wrecked crew of humanity, with the Cain mark on their foreheads, their hopes crushed, all their natural inclinations thwarted. With nothing but hunger and inhumanity to greet them, these victims soon sink back into crime as the only possibility of existence. It is not at all an unusual thing to find men and women who have spent half their lives—nay, almost their entire existence—in prison. I know a woman on Blackwell's Island, who had been in and out thirty-eight times; and through a friend I learn that a young boy of seventeen, whom he had nursed and cared for in the Pittsburgh penitentiary, had never known the meaning of liberty. From the reformatory to the penitentiary had been the path of this boy's life, until, broken in body, he died a victim of social revenge. These personal experiences are substantiated by extensive data giving overwhelming proof of the utter futility of prisons as a means of deterrence or reform.

Well-meaning persons are now working for a new departure in the prison question—reclamation, to restore once more to the prisoner the possibility of becoming a human being. Commendable as this is, I fear it is impossible to hope for good results from pouring good wine into a musty bottle. Nothing short of a complete reconstruction of society will deliver mankind from the cancer of crime. Still, if the dull edge of our social conscience would be sharpened, the penal institutions might be given a new coat of varnish. But the first step to be taken is the renovation of the social consciousness, which is in a rather dilapidated condition. It is sadly in need to be awakened to the fact that crime is a question of degree, that we all have the rudiments of crime in us, more or less, according to our mental, physical, and social environment; and that the individual criminal is merely a reflex of the tendencies of the aggregate.

With the social consciousness wakened, the average individual may learn to refuse the "honor" of being the bloodhound of the law. He may cease to persecute, despise, and mistrust the social offender, and give him a chance to live and breathe among his fellows. Institutions are, of course, harder to reach. They are cold, impenetrable, and cruel; still, with the social consciousness quickened, it might be possible to free the prison victims from the brutality of prison officials, guards, and keepers. Public opinion is a powerful weapon; keepers of human prey, even, are afraid of it. They may be taught a little humanity, especially if they realize that their jobs depend upon it.

But the most important step is to demand for the prisoner the right to work while in prison, with some monetary recompense that would enable him to lay aside a little for the day of his release, the beginning of a new life.

It is almost ridiculous to hope much from present society when we consider that workingmen, wage-slaves themselves, object to convict labor. I shall not go into the cruelty of this objection, but merely consider the impracticability of it. To begin with, the opposition so far raised by organized labor has been directed against windmills. Prisoners have always worked; only the State has been their exploiter, even as the individual employer has been the robber of organized labor. The States have either set the convicts to work for the government, or they have farmed convict labor to private individuals. Twenty-nine of the States pursue the latter plan. The Federal government and seventeen States have discarded it, as have the leading nations of Europe, since it leads to hideous overworking and abuse of prisoners, and to endless graft.

"Rhode Island, the State dominated by Aldrich, offers perhaps the worst example. Under a five-year contract, dated July 7th, 1906, and renewable for five years more at the option of private contractors, the labor of the inmates of the Rhode Island Penitentiary and the Providence County Jail is sold to the Reliance-Sterling Mfg. Co. at the rate of a trifle less than 25 cents a day per man. This Company is really a gigantic Prison Labor Trust, for it also leases the convict labor of Connecticut, Michigan, Indiana, Nebraska, and South Dakota penitentiaries, and the reformatories of New Jersey, Indiana, Illinois, and Wisconsin, eleven establishments in all.

"The enormity of the graft under the Rhode Island contract may be estimated from the fact that this same Company pays 62½ cents a day in Nebraska for the convict's labor, and that Tennessee, for example, gets $1.10 a day for a convict's work from the Gray-Dudley Hardware Co.; Missouri gets 70 cents a day from the Star Overall Mfg. Co.; West Virginia 65 cents a day from the Kraft Mfg. Co., and Maryland 55 cents a day from Oppenheim, Oberndorf & Co., shirt manufacturers. The very difference in prices points to enormous graft. For example, the Reliance-Sterling Mfg. Co. manufactures shirts, the cost by free labor being not less than $1.20 per dozen, while it pays Rhode Island thirty cents a dozen. Furthermore, the State charges this Trust no rent for the use of its huge factory, charges nothing for power, heat, light, or even drainage, and exacts no taxes. What graft!"*

It is estimated that more than twelve million dollars' worth of workingmen's shirts and overalls is produced annually in this country by prison labor. It is a woman's

* Quoted from the publications of the National Committee on Prison Labor.

industry, and the first reflection that arises is that an immense amount of free female labor is thus displaced. The second consideration is that male convicts, who should be learning trades that would give them some chance of being self-supporting after their release, are kept at this work at which they can not possibly make a dollar. This is the more serious when we consider that much of this labor is done in reformatories, which so loudly profess to be training their inmates to become useful citizens.

The third, and most important, consideration is that the enormous profits thus wrung from convict labor are a constant incentive to the contractors to exact from their unhappy victims tasks altogether beyond their strength, and to punish them cruelly when their work does not come up to the excessive demands made.

Another word on the condemnation of convicts to tasks at which they cannot hope to make a living after release. Indiana, for example, is a State that has made a great splurge over being in the front rank of modern penological improvements. Yet, according to the report rendered in 1908 by the training school of its "reformatory," 135 were engaged in the manufacture of chains, 207 in that of shirts, and 255 in the foundry—a total of 597 in three occupations. But at this so-called reformatory 59 occupations were represented by the inmates, 39 of which were connected with country pursuits. Indiana, like other States, professes to be training the inmates of her reformatory to occupations by which they will be able to make their living when released. She actually sets them to work making chains, shirts, and brooms, the latter for the benefit of the Louisville Fancy Grocery Co. Broom-making is a trade largely monopolized by the blind, shirt-making is done by women, and there is only one free chain-factory in the State, and at that a released convict can not hope to get employment. The whole thing is a cruel farce.

If, then, the States can be instrumental in robbing their helpless victims of such tremendous profits, is it not high time for organized labor to stop its idle howl, and to insist on decent remuneration for the convict, even as labor organizations claim for themselves? In that way working-men would kill the germ which makes of the prisoner an enemy to the interests of labor. I have said elsewhere that thousands of convicts, incompetent and without a trade, without means of subsistence, are yearly turned back into the social fold. These men and women must live, for even an ex-convict has needs. Prison life has made them anti-social beings, and the rigidly closed doors that meet them on their release are not likely to decrease their bitterness. The inevitable result is that they form a favorable nucleus out of which scabs, blacklegs, detectives, and policemen are drawn, only too willing to do the master's bidding. Thus organized labor, by its foolish opposition to work in prison, defeats its own ends. It helps to create poisonous fumes that stifle every attempt for economic betterment. If the working-man wants to avoid these effects he should *insist* on the right of the convict to work, he should meet him as a brother, take him into his organization, and *with his aid turn against the system which grinds them both.*

Last, but not least, is the growing realization of the barbarity and the inadequacy of the definite sentence. Those who believe in, and earnestly aim at, a change are fast coming to the conclusion that man must be given an opportunity to make good. And how is he to do it with ten, fifteen, or twenty years' imprisonment before him? The hope of liberty and of opportunity is the only incentive to life, especially the prisoner's life. Society has sinned so long against him—it ought at least to leave him that. I am not very sanguine that it will, or that any real change in that direction can take place until the conditions that breed both the prisoner and the jailer will be forever abolished.

Out of his mouth a red, red rose!
Out of his heart a white!
For who can say by what strange way
Christ brings his will to light,
Since the barren staff the pilgrim bore
Bloomed in the great Pope's sight.

Preparedness: The
Road to Universal Slaughter

Ever since the beginning of the European conflagration, the whole human race almost has fallen into the deathly grip of the war anesthesis, overcome by the mad teeming fumes of a blood soaked chloroform, which has obscured its vision and paralyzed its heart. Indeed, with the exception of some savage tribes, who know nothing of Christian religion or of brotherly love, and who also know nothing of dreadnaughts, submarines, munition manufacture and war loans, the rest of the race is under this terrible narcosis. The human mind seems to be conscious of but one thing, murderous speculation. Our whole civilization, our entire culture is concentrated in the mad demand for the most perfected weapons of slaughter.

Ammunition! Ammunition! O, Lord, thou who rulest heaven and earth, thou God of love, of mercy and of justice, provide us with enough ammunition to destroy our enemy. Such is the prayer which is ascending daily to the Christian heaven. Just like cattle, panic-stricken in the face of fire, throw themselves into the very flames, so all of the European people have fallen over each other into the devouring flames of the furies of war, and America, pushed to the very brink by unscrupulous politicians, by ranting demagogues, and by military sharks, is preparing for the same terrible feat.

In the face of this approaching disaster, it behooves men and women not yet overcome by the war madness to raise their voice of protest, to call the attention of the people to the crime and outrage which are about to be perpetrated upon them.

America is essentially the melting pot. No national unit composing it is in a position to boast of superior race purity, particular historic mission, or higher culture. Yet the jingoes and war speculators are filling the air with the sentimental slogan of hypocritical nationalism, "America for Americans," "America first, last, and all the time." This cry has caught the popular fancy from one end of the country to another. In order to maintain America, military preparedness must be engaged in at once. A billion dollars of the people's sweat and blood is to be expended for dreadnaughts and submarines for the army and the navy, all to protect this precious America.

The pathos of it all is that the America which is to be protected by a huge military force is not the America of the people, but that of the privileged class; the class which robs and exploits the masses, and controls their lives from the cradle to the grave. No less pathetic is it that so few people realize that preparedness never leads to peace, but that it is indeed the road to universal slaughter.

With the cunning methods used by the scheming diplomats and military cliques of Germany to saddle the masses with Prussian militarism, the American military ring with its Roosevelts, its Garrisons, its Daniels, and lastly its Wilsons, are moving the very heavens to place the militaristic heel upon the necks of the American people, and, if successful, will hurl America into the storm of blood and tears now devastating the countries of Europe.

Forty years ago Germany proclaimed the slogan: "Germany above everything. Germany for the Germans, first, last and always. We want peace; therefore we must prepare for war. Only a well armed and thoroughly prepared nation can maintain peace, can command respect, can be sure of its national integrity." And Germany continued to prepare, thereby forcing the other nations to do the same. The terrible European war is only the culminating fruition of the hydra-headed gospel, military preparedness.

Since the war began, miles of paper and oceans of ink have been used to prove the barbarity, the cruelty, the oppression of Prussian militarism. Conservatives and radicals alike are giving their support to the Allies for no other reason than to help crush that militarism, in the presence of which, they say, there can be no peace or progress in Europe. But though America grows fat on the manufacture of munitions and war loans to the Allies to help crush Prussians the same cry is now being raised in America which, if carried into national action, would build up an American militarism far more terrible than German or Prussian militarism could ever be, and that because nowhere in the world has capitalism become so brazen in its greed and nowhere is the state so ready to kneel at the feet of capital.

Like a plague, the mad spirit is sweeping the country, infesting the clearest heads and staunchest hearts with the deathly germ of militarism. National security leagues, with cannon as their emblem of protection, naval leagues with women in their lead have sprung up all over the country, women who boast of representing the gentler sex, women who in pain and danger bring forth life and yet are ready to dedicate it to the Moloch War. Americanization societies with well known liberals as members, they who but yesterday decried the patriotic clap-trap of to-day, are now lending themselves to befog the minds of the people and to help build up the same destructive institutions in America which they are directly and indirectly helping to pull down in Germany—militarism, the destroyer of youth, the raper of women, the annihilator of the best in the race, the very mower of life.

Even Woodrow Wilson, who not so long ago indulged in the phrase "A nation too proud to fight," who in the beginning of the war ordered prayers for peace, who in his proclamations spoke of the necessity of watchful waiting, even he has been whipped into line. He has now joined his worthy colleagues in the jingo movement, echoing their clamor for preparedness and their howl of "America for Americans." The difference between Wilson and Roosevelt is this: Roosevelt, a born bully, uses the club; Wilson, the historian, the college professor, wears the smooth polished university mask, but underneath it he, like Roosevelt, has but one aim, to serve the big interests, to add to those who are growing phenomenally rich by the manufacture of military supplies.

Woodrow Wilson, in his address before the Daughters of the American Revolution, gave his case away when he said, "I would rather be beaten than ostracized." To stand out against the Bethlehem, du Pont, Baldwin, Remington, Winchester metallic cartridges and the rest of the armament ring means political ostracism and death. Wilson knows that; therefore he betrays his original position, goes back on the bombast of "too proud to fight" and howls as loudly as any other cheap politician for preparedness and national glory, the silly pledge the navy league women intend to impose upon every school child: "I pledge myself to do all in my power to further the interests of my country, to uphold its institutions and to maintain the honor of its name and its flag. As I owe everything in life to my country, I consecrate my heart, mind and body to its service and promise to work for its advancement and security in times of peace and to shrink from no sacrifices or privation in its cause should I be called upon to act in its defence for the freedom, peace and happiness of our people."

To uphold the institutions of our country—that's it—the institutions which protect and sustain a handful of people in the robbery and plunder of the masses, the institutions which drain the blood of the native as well as of the foreigner, and turn it into wealth and power; the institutions which rob the alien of whatever originality he brings with him and in return gives him cheap Americanism, whose glory consists in mediocrity and arrogance.

The very proclaimers of "America first" have long before this betrayed the fundamental principles of real Americanism, of the kind of Americanism that Jefferson had in mind when he said that the best government is that which governs least; the kind of America that David Thoreau worked for when he proclaimed that the best government is the one that doesn't govern at all; or the other truly great Americans who aimed to make of this country a haven of refuge, who hoped that all the disinherited and oppressed people in coming to these shores would give character, quality and meaning to the country. That is not the America of the politician and munition speculators. Their America is powerfully portrayed in the idea of a young New York Sculptor; a hard cruel hand with long, lean, merciless fingers, crushing in over the heart of the immigrant, squeezing out its blood in order to coin dollars out of it and give the foreigner instead blighted hopes and stunted aspirations.

No doubt Woodrow Wilson has reason to defend these institutions. But what an ideal to hold out to the young generation! How is a military drilled and trained people to defend freedom, peace and happiness? This is what Major General O'Ryan has to say of an efficiently trained generation: "The soldier must be so trained that he becomes a mere automaton; he must be so trained that it will destroy his initiative; he must be so trained that he is turned into a machine. The soldier must be forced into the military noose; he must be jacked up; he must be ruled by his superiors with pistol in hand."

This was not said by a Prussian Junker; not by a German barbarian; not by Treitschke or Bernhardi, but by an American Major General. And he is right. You cannot conduct war with equals; you cannot have militarism with free born men; you must have slaves, automatons, machines, obedient disciplined creatures, who will move, act, shoot and kill at the command of their superiors. That is preparedness, and nothing else.

It has been reported that among the speakers before the Navy League was Samuel Gompers. If that is true, it signalizes the greatest outrage upon labor at the hands of its own leaders. Preparedness is not directed only against the external enemy; it aims much more at the internal enemy. It concerns that element of labor which has learned not to hope for anything from our institutions, that awakened part of the working people which has realized that the war of classes underlies all wars among nations, and that if war is justified at all it is the war against economic dependence and political slavery, the two dominant issues involved in the struggle of the classes.

Already militarism has been acting its bloody part in every economic conflict, with the approval and support of the state. Where was the protest of Washington when "our men, women and children" were killed in Ludlow? Where was that high sounding outraged protest contained in the note to Germany? Or is there any difference in killing "our men, women and children" in Ludlow or on the high seas? Yes, indeed. The men, women and children at Ludlow were working people, belonging to the disinherited of the earth, foreigners who had to be given a taste of the glories of Americanism, while the passengers of the *Lusitania* represented wealth and station—therein lies the difference.

Preparedness, therefore, will only add to the power of the

privileged few and help them to subdue, to enslave and crush labor. Surely Gompers must know that, and if he joins the howl of the military clique, he must stand condemned as a traitor to the cause of labor.

Just as it is with all the other institutions in our confused life, which were supposedly created for the good of the people and have accomplished the very reverse, so it will be with preparedness. Supposedly, America is to prepare for peace; but in reality it will be the cause of war. It always has been thus—all through bloodstained history, and it will continue until nation will refuse to fight against nation, and until the people of the world will stop preparing for slaughter. Preparedness is like the seed of a poisonous plant; placed in the soil, it will bear poisonous fruit. The European mass destruction is the fruit of that poisonous seed. It is imperative that the American workers realize this before they are driven by the jingoes into the madness that is forever haunted by the spectre of danger and invasion; they must know that to prepare for peace means to invite war, means to unloose the furies of death over land and seas.

That which has driven the masses of Europe into the trenches and to the battlefields is not their inner longing for war; it must be traced to the cut-throat competition for military equipment, for more efficient armies, for larger warships, for more powerful cannon. You cannot build up a standing army and then throw it back into a box like tin soldiers. Armies equipped to the teeth with weapons, with highly developed instruments of murder and backed by their military interests, have their own dynamic functions. We have but to examine into the nature of militarism to realize the truism of this contention.

Militarism consumes the strongest and most productive elements of each nation. Militarism swallows the largest part of the national revenue. Almost nothing is spent on education, art, literature and science compared with the amount devoted to militarism in times of peace, while in

times of war everything else is set at naught; all life stag-
nates, all effort is curtailed; the very sweat and blood of the
masses are used to feed this insatiable monster—militarism.
Under such circumstances, it must become more arrogant,
more aggressive, more bloated with its own importance. If
for no other reason, it is out of surplus energy that militarism must act to remain alive; therefore it will seek an
enemy or create one artificially. In this civilized purpose and
method, militarism is sustained by the state, protected by
the laws of the land, fostered by the home and the school,
and glorified by public opinion. In other words, the function
of militarism is to kill. It cannot live except through murder.

But the most dominant factor of military preparedness
and the one which inevitably leads to war, is the creation of
group interests, which consciously and deliberately work
for the increase of armament whose purposes are furthered
by creating the war hysteria. This group interest embraces
all those engaged in the manufacture and sale of munitions
and in military equipment for personal gain and profit. For
instance, the family Krupp, which owns the largest cannon
munition plant in the world; its sinister influence in Germany, and in fact in many other countries, extends to the
press, the school, the church and to statesmen of highest
rank. Shortly before the war, Carl Liebknecht, the one
brave public man in Germany now, brought to the attention
of the Reichstag that the family Krupp had in its employ
officials of the highest military position, not only in Germany, but in France and in other countries. Everywhere its
emissaries have been at work, systematically inciting national hatreds and antagonisms. The same investigation
brought to light an international war supply trust who care
not a hang for patriotism, or for love of the people, but who
use both to incite war and to pocket millions of profits out
of the terrible bargain.

It is not at all unlikely that the history of the present war
will trace its origin to this international murder trust. But is

it always necessary for one generation to wade through oceans of blood and heap up mountains of human sacrifice that the next generation may learn a grain of truth from it all? Can we of to-day not profit by the cause which led to the European war, can we not learn that it was preparedness, thorough and efficient preparedness on the part of Germany and the other countries for military aggrandizement and material gain; above all can we not realize that preparedness in America must and will lead to the same result, the same barbarity, the same senseless sacrifice of life? Is America to follow suit, is it to be turned over to the American Krupps, the American military cliques? It almost seems so when one hears the jingo howls of the press, the blood and thunder tirades of bully Roosevelt, the sentimental twaddle of our college-bred President.

The more reason for those who still have a spark of libertarianism and humanity left to cry out against this great crime, against the outrage now being prepared and imposed upon the American people. It is not enough to claim being neutral; a neutrality which sheds crocodile tears with one eye and keeps the other riveted upon the profits from war supplies and war loans is not neutrality. It is a hypocritical cloak to cover the country's crimes. Nor is it enough to join the bourgeois pacifists, who proclaim peace among the nations, while helping to perpetuate the war among the classes, a war which in reality is at the bottom of all other wars.

It is this war of the classes that we must concentrate upon, and in that connection the war against false values, against evil institutions, against all social atrocities. Those who appreciate the urgent need of co-operating in great struggles must oppose military preparedness imposed by the state and capitalism for the destruction of the masses. They must organize the preparedness of the masses for the overthrow of both capitalism and the state. Industrial and economic preparedness is what the workers need. That

alone leads to revolution at the bottom as against mass
destruction from on top. That alone leads to true internationalism of labor against Kaiserdom, Kingdom, diploma-
cies, military cliques and bureaucracy. That alone will give
the people the means to take their children out of the slums,
out of the sweat shops and the cotton mills. That alone will
enable them to inculcate in the coming generation a new
ideal of brotherhood, to rear them in play and song and
beauty; to bring up men and women, not automatons. That
alone will enable woman to become the real mother of the
race, who will give to the world creative men, and not
soldiers who destroy. That alone leads to economic and
social freedom, and does away with all wars, all crimes, and
all injustice.

Address to the Jury

President Woodrow Wilson, in order to "make the world safe for democracy," asked Congress to declare war on Germany in April 1917. In May, Goldman and Berkman, who had been steadily campaigning against American participation in the war, stepped up their campaign. When President Wilson signed a Draft Bill setting June 4, 1917, as Registration Day for all twenty-one- to thirty-year-old men, Goldman and Berkman composed a No-Conscription Manifesto of which they distributed 100,000 copies, founded a No-Conscription League with branches in many cities,[1] and organized a series of antiwar rallies. At one of

---

[1] The platform of the league, as summarized by Goldman in the June 1917 issue of *Mother Earth*, was as follows:

> We oppose conscription because we are internationalists, anti-militarists, and opposed to all wars waged by capitalist governments.
>
> We will fight for what we choose to fight for. We will never fight simply because we are ordered to fight.
>
> We believe that the militarization of America is an evil that far outweighs, in its anti-social and anti-libertarian effects, any good that may come from America's participation in the war.
>
> We will resist conscription by every means in our power, and we will sustain those who, for similar reasons, refuse to be conscripted.

*their rallies, a supporter was arrested, convicted of con-
spiracy, and sentenced to two years in prison for doing
nothing more than handing out announcements of Goldman's coming Registration Day rally. It was inevitable that
the government would stop Goldman and Berkman too.*

*On June 15, 1917, shortly after the Draft Bill had
become law, the joint offices of Goldman's* Mother Earth
and Berkman's labor sheet, The Blast, *were raided and
ransacked by federal marshals, the contents confiscated,
and the two editors arrested.*

*Their trial commenced on June 27, Goldman's forty-
eighth birthday. On the street below the courtroom, a re-
cruiting station had been set up, assisted by a military band
that periodically played* The Star-Spangled Banner. *Whenever the music drifted up through the window, everyone in
the courtroom was ordered, on pain of ejection, to stand.
The defendants, however, resolutely remained seated.*

*Acting as their own attorneys, Goldman and Berkman
had to defend themselves not only against the specific
charge of conspiring "to induce persons not to register," but
also against prosecution claims that they had "advocated
violence" in their publications and speeches, even though,
as the judge eventually said, the testimony "about violence
was not germane to the case." The prosecution even tried to
show that the anarchists' antiwar campaign waged in*
Mother Earth *and* Blast *had been financed by "German
money," a charge it was easy for the defendants to disprove.*

*In her defense Goldman read into the record portions of
her essays, and called many celebrated radical witnesses.
Berkman handled the question of how he and Goldman—
never secret revolutionaries—could have been guilty of
"conspiracy," when their position was known to "a hundred
million people." ("Every conspiracy is by its very nature
secret; a case can hardly be supposed where men concert
together for crime and advertise their purpose to the
world," wrote Supreme Court Justice John M. Harlan in*

1957—forty years too late to help Goldman and Berkman.)

After deliberating for thirty-nine minutes, the jury declared both defendants guilty. The judge sentenced each of them to the maximum two years in prison, imposed the maximum $10,000 fines, and recommended that they be deported when their sentences were up.

Editor's note

GENTLEMEN OF THE JURY:

As in the case of my co-defendant, Alexander Berkman, this is also the first time in my life I have ever addressed a jury. I once had occasion to speak to three judges.

On the day after our arrest it was given out by the U. S. Marshal and the District Attorney's office that the "big fish" of the No-Conscription activities had been caught, and that there would be no more trouble-makers and disturbers to interfere with the highly democratic effort of the Government to conscript its young manhood for the European slaughter. What a pity that the faithful servants of the Government, personified in the U. S. Marshal and the District Attorney, should have used such a weak and flimsy net for their big catch. The moment the anglers pulled their heavily laden net ashore, it broke, and all the labor was so much wasted energy.

The methods employed by Marshal McCarthy and his hosts of heroic warriors were sensational enough to satisfy the famous circus men, Barnum & Bailey. A dozen or more heroes dashing up two flights of stairs, prepared to stake their lives for their country, only to discover the two dangerous disturbers and trouble-makers, Alexander Berkman and Emma Goldman, in their separate offices, quietly at work at their desks, wielding not a sword, nor a gun or a bomb, but merely their pens! Verily, it required courage to catch such big fish.

To be sure, two officers equipped with a warrant would
have sufficed to carry out the business of arresting the defendants Alexander Berkman and Emma Goldman. Even the
police know that neither of them is in the habit of running
away or hiding under the bed. But the farce-comedy had to
be properly staged if the Marshal and the District Attorney
were to earn immortality. Hence the sensational arrest;
hence, also, the raid upon the offices of *The Blast, Mother
Earth* and the No-Conscription League.

In their zeal to save the country from the trouble-makers,
the Marshal and his helpers did not even consider it necessary to produce a search warrant. After all, what matters a
mere scrap of paper when one is called upon to raid the
offices of Anarchists! Of what consequence is the sanctity of
property, the right of privacy, to officials in their dealings
with Anarchists! In our day of military training for battle,
an Anarchist office is an appropriate camping ground.
Would the gentlemen who came with Marshal McCarthy
have dared to go into the offices of Morgan, or Rockefeller,
or of any of those men without a search warrant? They
never showed us the search warrant, although we asked
them for it. Nevertheless, they turned our office into a battlefield, so that when they were through with it, it looked
like invaded Belgium, with the only difference that the in-
vaders were not Prussian barbarians but good American
patriots bent on making New York safe for democracy.

The stage having been appropriately set for the three-act
comedy, and the first act successfully played by carrying off
the villains in a madly dashing automobile—which broke
every traffic regulation and barely escaped crushing every
one in its way—the second act proved even more ludicrous.
Fifty thousand dollars bail was demanded, and real estate
refused when offered by a man whose property is rated at
three hundred thousand dollars, and that after the District
Attorney had considered and, in fact, promised to accept
the property for one of the defendants, Alexander Berk-

man, thus breaking every right guaranteed even to the most heinous criminal.

Finally the third act, played by the Government in this court during the last week. The pity of it is that the prosecution knows so little of dramatic construction, else it would have equipped itself with better dramatic material to sustain the continuity of the play. As it was, the third act fell flat, utterly, and presents the question, Why such a tempest in a teapot?

Gentlemen of the jury, my comrade and co-defendant having carefully and thoroughly gone into the evidence presented by the prosecution, and having demonstrated its entire failure to prove the charge of conspiracy or any overt acts to carry out that conspiracy, I shall not impose upon your patience by going over the same ground, except to emphasize a few points. To charge people with having conspired to do something which they have been engaged in doing most of their lives, namely their campaign against war, militarism and conscription as contrary to the best interests of humanity, is an insult to human intelligence.

And how was that charge proven? By the fact that *Mother Earth* and *The Blast* were printed by the same printer and bound in the same bindery. By the further evidence that the same expressman had delivered the two publications! And by the still more illuminating fact that on June 2nd *Mother Earth* and *The Blast* were given to a reporter at his request, if you please, and gratis.

Gentlemen of the jury, you saw the reporter who testified to this overt act. Did any one of you receive the impression that the man was of conscriptable age, and if not, in what possible way is the giving of *Mother Earth* to a reporter for news purposes proof demonstrating the overt act?

It was brought out by our witnesses that the *Mother Earth* magazine has been published for twelve years; that it was never held up, and that it has always gone through the U. S. mail as second-class mail matter. It was further proven that the magazine appeared each month about the first or second, and that it was sold or given away at the office to whoever wanted a copy. Where, then, is the overt act?

Just as the prosecution has utterly failed to prove the charge of conspiracy, so has it also failed to prove the overt act by the flimsy testimony that *Mother Earth* was given to a reporter. The same holds good regarding *The Blast*.

Gentlemen of the jury, the District Attorney must have learned from the reporters the gist of the numerous interviews which they had with us. Why did he not examine them as to whether or not we had counseled young men not to register? That would have been a more direct way of getting at the facts. In the case of the reporter from the New York *Times*, there can be no doubt that the man would have been only too happy to accommodate the District Attorney with the required information. A man who disregards every principle of decency and ethics of his profession as a newspaper man, by turning material given him as news over to the District Attorney, would have been glad to oblige a friend. Why did Mr. Content neglect such a golden opportunity? Was it not because the reporter of the *Times*, like all the other reporters, must have told the District Attorney that the two defendants stated, on each and every occasion, they would not tell people not to register?

Perhaps the *Times* reporter refused to go to the extent of perjuring himself. Patrolmen and detectives are not so timid in such matters. Hence Mr. Randolph and Mr. Cadell, to rescue the situation. Imagine employing tenth-rate stenographers to report the very important speeches of dangerous trouble-makers! What lack of forethought and efficiency on the part of the District Attorney! But even these two members of the police department failed to prove by their notes that we advised people not to register. But since they had to produce something incriminating against Anarchists, they conveniently resorted to the old standby, always credited to us, "We believe in violence and we will use violence."

Assuming, gentlemen of the jury, that this sentence was really used at the meeting of May 18th, it would still fail to prove the indictment which charges conspiracy and overt acts to carry out the conspiracy. And that is all we are charged with. Not violence, not Anarchism. I will go further and say, that had the indictment been for the advocacy of violence, you gentlemen of the jury, would still have to render a verdict of "Not Guilty," since the mere belief in a thing or even the announcement that you would carry out that belief can not possibly constitute a crime.

However, I wish to say emphatically that no such expression as "We believe in violence and we will use violence" was uttered at the meeting of May 18th, or at any other meeting. I could not have employed such a phrase, as there was no occasion for it. If for no other reason, it is because I want my lectures and speeches to be coherent and logical. The sentence credited to me is neither.

I have read to you my position toward political violence from a lengthy essay called "The Psychology of Political Violence."

But to make that position clearer and simpler, I wish to say that I am a social student. It is my mission in life to ascertain the cause of our social evils and of our social difficulties. As a student of social wrongs it is my aim to diagnose a wrong. To simply condemn the man who has committed an act of political violence, in order to save my skin, would be as unpardonable as it would be on the part of the physician, who is called to diagnose a case, to condemn the patient because the patient has tuberculosis, cancer, or some other disease. The honest, earnest, sincere physician does not only prescribe medicine, he tries to find out the cause of the disease. And if the patient is at all capable as to means, the doctor will say to him, "Get out of this putrid air, get out of the factory, get out of the place where your lungs are being infected." He will not merely give him medicine. He will tell him the cause of the disease. And that is precisely my position in regard to acts of violence. That is what I have said on every platform. I have attempted to explain the cause and the reason for acts of political violence.

It is organized violence on top which creates individual violence at the bottom. It is the accumulated indignation against organized wrong, organized crime, organized injustice which drives the political offender to his act. To condemn him means to be blind to the causes which make him. I can no more do it, nor have I the right to, than the physician who were to condemn the patient for his disease. You and I and all of us who remain indifferent to the crimes of poverty, of war, of human degradation, are equally responsible for the act committed by the political offender. May I therefore be permitted to say, in the words of a great teacher: "He who is without sin among you, let him cast the first stone." Does that mean advocating violence? You might as well accuse Jesus of advocating prostitution, because He took the part of the prostitute, Mary Magdalene.

Gentlemen of the jury, the meeting of the 18th of May was called primarily for the purpose of voicing the position of the conscientious objector and to point out the evils of conscription. Now, who and what is the conscientious objector? Is he really a shirker, a slacker, or a coward? To call him that is to be guilty of dense ignorance of the forces which impel men and women to stand out against the whole world like a glittering lone star upon a dark horizon. The conscientious objector is impelled by what President Wilson in his speech of Feb. 3, 1917, called "the righteous passion for justice upon which all war, all structure of family, State and of mankind must rest as the ultimate base of our existence and our liberty." The righteous passion for justice which can never express itself in human slaughter—that is the force which makes the conscientious objector. Poor indeed is the country which fails to recognize the importance of that new type of humanity as the "ultimate base of our existence and liberty." It will find itself barren of that which makes for character and quality in its people.

The meeting of May 18th was held before the Draft Bill had actually gone into effect. The President signed it late in the evening of the 18th. Whatever was said at that meeting, even if I had counseled young men not to register, that meeting cannot serve as proof of an overt act. Why, then, has the Prosecuting Attorney dwelt so much, at such length, and with such pains on that meeting, and so little on the other meetings held on the eve of registration and after? Is it not because the District Attorney knew that we had no stenographic notes of that meeting? He knew it because he was approached by Mr. Weinberger and other friends for a copy of the transcript, which request he refused. Evidently, the District Attorney felt safe to use the notes of a patrolman and a detective, knowing that they would swear to anything their superiors wanted. I never like to accuse anyone—I wouldn't go so far as my co-defendant, Mr. Berkman, in saying that the District Attorney doctored the document; I don't know whether he did or not. But I do know that Patrolman Randolph and Detective Cadell doctored the notes, for the simple reason that I didn't say those things. But though we could not produce our own stenographic notes, we have been able to prove by men and women of unimpeachable character and high intelligence that the notes of Randolph are utterly false. We have also proven beyond a reasonable doubt, and Mr. Content did not dare question our proof, that at the Hunts' Point Palace, held on the eve of registration, I expressly stated that I cannot and will not tell people not to register. We have further proven that this was my definite stand, which was explained in my statement sent from Springfield and read at the meeting of May 23rd.

When we go through the entire testimony given on behalf of the prosecution, I insist that there is not one single point to sustain the indictment for conspiracy or to prove the overt acts we are supposed to have committed. But we were even compelled to bring a man eighty years of age to the witness stand in order to stop, if possible, any intention to drag in the question of German money. It is true, and I appreciate it, that Mr. Content said he had no knowledge of it. But, gentlemen of the jury, somebody from the District Attorney's office or someone from the Marshal's office must have given out the statement that a bank receipt for $2,400 was found in my office and must have told the newspapers the fake story of German money. As if we would ever touch German money, or Russian money, or American money coming from the ruling class, to advance our ideas! But in order to forestall any suspicion, any insinuation, in order to stand clear before you, we were compelled to bring an old man here to inform you that he has been a radical all his life, that he is interested in our ideas, and that he is the man who contributed the money for radical purposes and for the work of Miss Goldman.

Gentlemen of the jury, you will be told by the Court, I am sure, that when you render a verdict you must be convinced beyond a reasonable doubt; that you must not assume that we are guilty before we are proven guilty; and that it is your duty to assume that we are innocent. And yet, as a matter of fact, the burden of proof has been laid upon us. We had to bring witnesses. If we had had time we could have brought fifty more witnesses, each corroborating the others. Some of those people have no relation with us. Some are writers, poets, contributors to the most conventional magazines. Is it likely that they would swear to something in our favor if it were not the truth? Therefore I insist, as did my co-defendant Alexander Berkman, that the prosecution has made a very poor showing in proving the conspiracy or any overt act.

Gentlemen of the jury, we have been in public life for twenty-seven years. We have been haled into court, in and out of season—we have never denied our position. Even the police know that Emma Goldman and Alexander Berkman are not shirkers. You have had occasion during this trial to convince yourselves that we do not deny. We have gladly and proudly claimed responsibility, not only for what we ourselves have said and written, but even for things written by others and with which we did not agree. Is it plausible, then, that we would go through the ordeal, trouble and expense of a lengthy trial to escape responsibility in this instance? A thousand times no! But we refuse to be tried on a trumped-up charge, or to be convicted by perjured testimony, merely because we are Anarchists and hated by the class whom we have openly fought for many years.

Gentlemen, during our examination of talesmen, when we asked whether you would be prejudiced against us if it were proven that we propagated ideas and opinions contrary to those held by the majority, you were instructed by the Court to say, "If they are within the law." But what the Court did not tell you is, that no new faith—not even the most humane and peaceable—has ever been considered "within the law" by those who were in power. The history of human growth is at the same time the history of every new idea heralding the approach of a brighter dawn, and the brighter dawn has always been considered illegal, outside of the law.

Gentlemen of the jury, most of you, I take it, are believers in the teachings of Jesus. Bear in mind that he was put to death by those who considered his views as being against the law. I also take it that you are proud of your Americanism. Remember that those who fought and bled for your liberties were in their time considered as being against the law, as dangerous disturbers and troublemakers. They not only preached violence, but they carried

out their ideas by throwing tea into the Boston harbor.
They said that "Resistance to tyranny is obedience to God."
They wrote a dangerous document called the Declaration
of Independence. A document which continues to be dangerous to this day, and for the circulation of which a young
man was sentenced to ninety days prison in a New York
Court, only the other day. They were the Anarchists of
their time—they were never within the law.

Your Government is allied with the French Republic.
Need I call your attention to the historic fact that the great
upheaval in France was brought about by extra-legal
means? The Dantes, the Robespierres, the Marats, the
Herberts, aye even the man who is responsible for the most
stirring revolutionary music, the Marseillaise (which unfortunately has deteriorated into a war tune), even Camille
Desmoulins, were never within the law. But for those great
pioneers and rebels, France would have continued under
the yoke of the idle Louis XVI, to whom the sport of shooting jack rabbits was more important than the destiny of the
people of France.

Ah, gentlemen, on the very day when we were being
tried for conspiracy and overt acts, your city officials and
representatives welcomed with music and festivities the
Russian Commission. Are you aware of the fact that nearly
all of the members of that Commission have only recently
been released from exile? The ideas they propagated were
never within the law. For nearly a hundred years, from
1825 to 1917, the Tree of Liberty in Russia was watered by
the blood of her martyrs. No greater heroism, no nobler
lives had ever been dedicated to humanity. Not one of them
worked within the law. I could continue to enumerate
almost endlessly the hosts of men and women in every land
and in every period whose ideas and ideals redeemed the
world because they were not within the law.

Never can a new idea move within the law. It matters not
whether that idea pertains to political and social changes or

to any other domain of human thought and expression—to science, literature, music; in fact, everything that makes for freedom and joy and beauty must refuse to move within the law. How can it be otherwise? The law is stationary, fixed, mechanical, "a chariot wheel" which grinds all alike without regard to time, place and condition, without ever taking into account cause and effect, without ever going into the complexity of the human soul.

Progress knows nothing of fixity. It cannot be pressed into a definite mould. It cannot bow to the dictum, "I have ruled," "I am the regulating finger of God." Progress is ever renewing, ever becoming, ever changing—*never is it within the law*.

If that be crime, we are criminals even like Jesus, Socrates, Galileo, Bruno, John Brown and scores of others. We are in good company, among those whom Havelock Ellis, the greatest living psychologist, describes as the political criminals recognized by the whole civilized world, except America, as men and women who out of deep love for humanity, out of a passionate reverence for liberty and an all-absorbing devotion to an ideal are ready to pay for their faith even with their blood. We cannot do otherwise if we are to be true to ourselves—we know that the political criminal is the precursor of human progress—the political criminal of to-day must needs be the hero, the martyr and the saint of the new age.

But, says the Prosecuting Attorney, the press and the unthinking rabble, in high and low station, "that is a dangerous doctrine and unpatriotic at this time." No doubt it is. But are we to be held responsible for something which is as unchangeable and unalienable as the very stars hanging in the heavens unto time and all eternity?

Gentlemen of the jury, we respect your patriotism. We would not, if we could, have you change its meaning for yourself. But may there not be different kinds of patriotism as there are different kinds of liberty? I for one cannot believe that love of one's country must needs consist in blindness to its social faults, in deafness to its social discords, in inarticulation of its social wrongs. Neither can I believe that the mere accident of birth in a certain country or the mere scrap of a citizen's paper constitutes the love of country.

I know many people—I am one of them—who were not born here, nor have they applied for citizenship, and who yet love America with deeper passion and greater intensity than many natives whose patriotism manifests itself by pulling, kicking, and insulting those who do not rise when the national anthem is played. Our patriotism is that of the man who loves a woman with open eyes. He is enchanted by her beauty, yet he sees her faults. So we, too, who know America, love her beauty, her richness, her great possibilities; we love her mountains, her canyons, her forests, her Niagara, and her deserts—above all do we love the people that have produced her wealth, her artists who have created beauty, her great apostles who dream and work for liberty—but with the same passionate emotion we hate her superficiality, her cant, her corruption, her mad, unscrupulous worship at the altar of the Golden Calf.

We say that if America has entered the war to make the world safe for democracy, she must first make democracy safe in America. How else is the world to take America seriously, when democracy at home is daily being outraged, free speech suppressed, peaceable assemblies broken up by overbearing and brutal gangsters in uniform; when free press is curtailed and every independent opinion gagged. Verily, poor as we are in democracy, how can we give of it to the world? We further say that a democracy conceived in the military servitude of the masses, in their economic enslavement, and nurtured in their tears and blood, is not democracy at all. It is despotism—the cumulative result of a chain of abuses which, according to that dangerous document, the Declaration of Independence, the people have the right to overthrow.

The District Attorney has dragged in our Manifesto, and he has emphasized the passage, "Resist conscription." Gentlemen of the jury, please remember that that is not the charge against us. But admitting that the Manifesto contains the expression, "Resist conscription," may I ask you, is there only *one kind* of resistance? Is there only the resistance which means the gun, the bayonet, the bomb or flying machine? Is there not another kind of resistance? May not the people simply fold their hands and declare, "We will not fight when we do not believe in the necessity of war"? May not the people who believe in the repeal of the Conscription Law, because it is unconstitutional, express their opposition in word and by pen, in meetings and in other ways? What right has the District Attorney to interpret that particular passage to suit himself? Moreover, gentlemen of the jury, I insist that the indictment against us does not refer to conscription. We are charged with a conspiracy against registration. And in no way or manner has the prosecution proven that we are guilty of conspiracy or that we have committed an overt act.

Gentlemen of the jury, you are not called upon to accept our views, to approve of them or to justify them. You are not even called upon to decide whether our views are within or against the law. You are called upon to decide whether the prosecution has proven that the defendants Emma Goldman and Alexander Berkman have conspired to urge people not to register. And whether their speeches and writings represent overt acts.

Whatever your verdict, gentlemen, it cannot possibly affect the rising tide of discontent in this country against war which, despite all boasts, is a war for conquest and military power. Neither can it affect the ever increasing opposition to conscription which is a military and industrial yoke placed upon the necks of the American people. Least of all will your verdict affect those to whom human life is sacred, and who will not become a party to the world slaughter. Your verdict can only add to the opinion of the world as to whether or not justice and liberty are a living force in this country or a mere shadow of the past.

Your verdict may, of course, affect us temporarily, in a physical sense—it can have no effect whatever upon our spirit. For even if we were convicted and found guilty and the penalty were that we be placed against a wall and shot dead, I should nevertheless cry out with the great Luther: "Here I am and here I stand and I cannot do otherwise."

And gentlemen, in conclusion let me tell you that my co-defendant, Mr. Berkman, was right when he said the eyes of America are upon you. They are upon you not because of sympathy for us or agreement with Anarchism. They are upon you because it must be decided sooner or later whether we are justified in telling people that we will give them democracy in Europe, when we have no democracy here? Shall free speech and free assemblage, shall criticism and opinion—which even the espionage bill did not include —be destroyed? Shall it be a shadow of the past, the great historic American past? Shall it be trampled underfoot by any detective, or policeman, anyone who decides upon it? Or shall free speech and free press and free assemblage continue to be the heritage of the American people?

Gentlemen of the jury, whatever your verdict will be, as far as we are concerned, nothing will be changed. I have held ideas all my life. I have publicly held my ideas for twenty-seven years. Nothing on earth would ever make me change my ideas except one thing; and that is, if you will prove to me that our position is wrong, untenable, or lacking in historic fact. But never would I change my ideas because I am found guilty. I may remind you of two great Americans, undoubtedly not unknown to you, gentlemen of the jury; Ralph Waldo Emerson and Henry David Thoreau.

When Thoreau was placed in prison for refusing to pay taxes, he was visited by Ralph Waldo Emerson and Emerson said: "David, what are you doing in jail?" and Thoreau replied: "Ralph, what are you doing outside, when honest people are in jail for their ideals?" Gentlemen of the jury, I do not wish to influence you. I do not wish to appeal to your passions. I do not wish to influence you by the fact that I am a woman. I have no such desires and no such designs. I take it that you are sincere enough and honest enough and brave enough to render a verdict according to your convictions, beyond the shadow of a reasonable doubt.

Please forget that we are Anarchists. Forget that it is claimed that we propagated violence. Forget that something appeared in *Mother Earth* when I was thousands of miles away, three years ago. Forget all that, and merely consider the evidence. Have we been engaged in a conspiracy? has that conspiracy been proven? have we committed overt acts? have those overt acts been proven? We for the defense say they have not been proven. And therefore your verdict must be not guilty.

But whatever your decision, the struggle must go on. We are but the atoms in the incessant human struggle towards the light that shines in the darkness—the Ideal of economic, political and spiritual liberation of mankind!

PART FOUR

TWO REVOLUTIONS
AND A SUMMARY

PREFACE TO PART FOUR

"One can't make an omelette without breaking eggs," people said in defense of the excesses of the Russian revolution. The poet Panaït Istrati is reported by Victor Serge to have replied: "All right, I can see the broken eggs. Now where's this omelette of yours?"

Learning of the Bolshevik revolution in 1917, Emma Goldman had extolled it all over America as "the promise and hope of the world." She was not even particularly sorry to be deported there two years later. For the sake of the revolution, she shelved her longstanding quarrel with Marxist groups, all of whom had seemed to her either "aggressively centralistic" or else stuck "in the muddy waters of parliamentarianism."

By the time she left Russia in December 1921, having spent two years in agonizing examination of the situation there, she too was convinced it was mainly a mess of broken eggs. The State, even the socialist State, and the revolution seemed to her "incompatible and mutually destructive." She set down her experiences and conclusions in a book entitled by her "My Two Years in Russia," but changed by her publisher without her permission to *My Disillusionment in Russia*.[1] The skillfully drawn narrative of her two-year sojourn ends with an afterword, which

---

[1] The American edition was published by Doubleday, Page Co. in 1923 without the final twelve chapters. Subsequently Doubleday, Page Co. published the missing section separately as *My Further Disillusionment in Russia* (1924). Both parts were published together in the 1925 British edition, and were reissued in the United States in a single-volume Apollo Edition by Thomas Y. Crowell in 1970.

Goldman called "the most vital part" of the book. That afterword is reprinted here. In it Goldman draws her distressing conclusions about Bolshevism and the relation of State to revolution, of means to ends.

A decade later the predominant criticism of Soviet Russia held that Bolshevik excesses represented communism-in-practice; on the basis of it, many former radicals abandoned their revolutionary goals. In contrast, Goldman's leftwing critique argued that Bolshevism was not communism at all, but rather the most ruthless sort of State capitalism, discrediting not the revolution but the State. This view is set forth in her article, "There Is No Communism in Russia," published in the *American Mercury,* Vol. XXXIV, in April 1935.

A year later, after the Spanish anarchists had joined the Popular Front to fight fascism in Spain, Goldman was called to Spain to participate. Pessimistic about the fate of a world turning to the right, and depressed over Berkman's suicide, she little suspected that she would find in Barcelona her cherished anarchist revolution come to life. When she did, she was jubilant.

George Orwell described the 1936–1937 Barcelona scene[2] in *Homage to Catalonia:*

> The aspect of Barcelona was something startling and overwhelming. It was the first time that I had ever been in a town where the working class was in the saddle. Practically every building of any size had been seized by the workers and was draped with red flags or with the red and black flag of the Anarchists. . . . There was a belief in the revolution and the future, a feeling of having suddenly emerged into an era of equality and freedom. Human beings were trying to behave as human beings and not as cogs in the capitalist machine. In the barbers' shops were Anarchist notices (the barbers were mostly Anarchists) solemnly explaining that barbers were no longer slaves. In the streets were colored posters appealing to prostitutes to stop being prostitutes.

[2] George Orwell, *Homage to Catalonia,* Boston, Beacon Paperback Ed., 1955, pp. 4–6.

And the Aragon scene:[3]

> I had dropped more or less by chance into the only community
> of any size in Western Europe where political consciousness and
> disbelief in capitalism were more normal than their opposites.
> Up here in Aragon one was among tens of thousands of people,
> mainly, though not entirely, of working-class origin, all living
> at the same level and mingling on terms of equality. In theory
> it was perfect equality and even in practice it was not far from
> it. . . . Many of the normal motives of civilized life—snob-
> bishness, money grubbing, fear of the boss, etc.—had simply
> ceased to exist. The ordinary class-division of society had disap-
> peared to an extent that is almost unthinkable in the money-
> tainted air of England: there was no one there except the
> peasants and ourselves, and no one owned anyone else as his
> master.

The many years of uncompromising anarchist agitation in Spain
had evidently paid off. "Your revolution," Goldman told a rally
of revolutionary Libertarian Youth, "will destroy forever [the
notion] that anarchism stands for chaos." The powerful anarchist
CNT–FAI (Confederación Nacional del Trabajo and the Feder-
ación Anarquista Iberia), which alone represented a half-million
workers in 1936, assigned her the job of running their propaganda effort in England.

Before 1937 was out, the situation in Spain had vastly
changed. Originally, anarchists, communists, left and right
socialists, and republican liberals all fought side by side in their
own militias in a Popular Front to defend the republic against
the insurrectionary forces of army, church, and nobility, led by
General Francisco Franco and his cohorts. But irreconcilable
divisions in the Popular Front soon developed over the form the
revolution should take. On the one side there were anarchists
and left socialists, standing for workers' control; on the other
were right socialists, liberals, and Moscow-directed communists,
standing for State control and militarization (i.e., absorbing the
various militias into a hierarchical army, and if necessary in-

[3] *Ibid.*, pp. 103–4.

stituting a draft). And in addition, there were the Republicans, who wanted no revolution at all. The CNT–FAI faced the terrible dilemma of whether to support the coalition government (increasingly communist-dominated, after arms began coming in from Russia), thus strengthening the very parties and institutions that wished to destroy anarchism, or to oppose the government as anarchist principles demanded, at the risk of destroying antifascist unity. They had to choose between sacrificing the anarchist revolution to the war, or the war to the anarchist revolution. Choosing at last to concentrate on winning the war, they traded their revolutionary spirit for the spirit of compromise and joined the Popular Front government, accepting posts in four ministries. From that time on, Goldman pointed out, they were working for their enemies. Before long, the communists, in control of the government, were openly sabotaging anarchist agricultural and factory collectives, refusing arms to anarchist soldiers at the front, and eventually, in May 1937, shooting anarchists in the streets.

Goldman did not approve the anarchist compromises, which looked to her like another mess of broken eggs. Writing in July 1937 in *Spain and the World,* she said:

> From the moment leaders of the CNT–FAI entered into ministries and submitted to the conditions imposed upon them by Soviet Russia in return for some arms, I foresaw the inevitable price our comrades will have to pay. . . . The Anarchist participation in the Government and the concessions made to Russia have resulted in almost irreparable harm to the Revolution.[4]

But she understood the anarchists' painful dilemma, and for the sake of the omelette never faltered in her support of them. To her friend Ethel Mannin she wrote:

> Having come close to the insurmountable difficulties confronting the CNT–FAI I can understand better the concessions they

[4] Quoted by Ethel Mannin in *Women and the Revolution,* New York, Dutton, 1939, p. 184.

have made. . . . I cannot reconcile myself to some of them, but I realize that when one is in a burning house one does not consider one's possessions, one tries to jump to safety.[5]

Her address to the International Working Men's Association Congress, which met in Paris late in 1937, deals with these very problems. The text (undated), from the New York Public Library's Manuscript Division, is a portrait of Emma's dilemmas. At the congress, Goldman was attacked from the left as an apologist for the CNT–FAI compromises, and from the right as a critic of them; and though she had always before maintained an extreme left position, her total sympathy with the Spanish anarchist effort led her for once to muster all compassion in support of the Spanish anarchist decisions.[6] It's a pity she didn't live to write a book on her experiences in Spain, as she did on her experiences in Russia.

The final selection, "Was My Life Worth Living?" was published in *Harper's Magazine,* Vol. CLXX, in December 1934, between the two revolutions. It comes last because in many ways it is the most contemporary. In it Goldman reaffirms the anarchist faith that guided her all her life and relegated her, by the time of the writing, to the fringe of politics. Prefacing the piece, the editors of *Harper's* wrote:

It is strange what time does to political causes. A generation ago it seemed to many American conservatives as if the opinions which Emma Goldman was expressing might sweep the world. Now she fights almost alone for what seems to be a lost cause; contemporary radicals are overwhelmingly opposed to her; more than that, her devotion to liberty and her detestation of government interference might be regarded as placing her anomalously in the same part of the political spectrum as the gentlemen of the Liberty League, only in a more extreme position at its edge. Yet in this article, which might be regarded as her last will and testament, she sticks to her guns. Needless

[5] *Ibid.*

[6] Richard Drinnon, *Rebel in Paradise,* Chicago, University of Chicago Press, 1961, pp. 309–10.

to say, her opinions are not ours. We offer them as an exhibit of valiant consistency, of *really* rugged individualism unaltered by opposition or by advancing age.

Strange indeed what time does to political causes. In this essay, decrying the "whole complex of authority and institutional domination which strangles life," seeing that "the pattern of life has become standardized, routinized, and mechanized like canned food and Sunday sermons," Goldman predicts that the time is coming when centralist solutions to society's problems will be seen to have failed and "Anarchism will be vindicated."

Afterword to
My Disillusionment in Russia

I.

Non-Bolshevik Socialist critics of the Russian failure contend that the Revolution could not have succeeded in Russia because industrial conditions had not reached the necessary climax in that country. They point to Marx, who taught that a social revolution is possible only in countries with a highly developed industrial system and its attendant social antagonisms. They therefore claim that the Russian Revolution could not be a social revolution, and that historically it had to evolve along constitutional, democratic lines, complemented by a growing industry, in order to ripen the country economically for the basic change.

This orthodox Marxian view leaves an important factor out of consideration—a factor perhaps more vital to the possibility and success of a social revolution than even the industrial element. That is the psychology of the masses at a given period. Why is there, for instance, no social revolution in the United States, France, or even in Germany? Surely these countries have reached the industrial development set by Marx as the culminating stage. The truth is that industrial development and sharp social contrasts are of themselves by no means sufficient to give birth to a new society or to call forth a social revolution. The necessary social consciousness, the required mass psychology is missing in such countries as the United States and the others mentioned. That explains why no social revolution has taken place there.

In this regard Russia had the advantage of other more industrialized and "civilized" lands. It is true that Russia was not as advanced industrially as her Western neighbours. But the Russian mass psychology, inspired and intensified by the February Revolution, was ripening at so fast a pace that within a few months the people were ready for such ultra-revolutionary slogans as "All power to the Soviets" and "The land to the peasants, the factories to the workers."

The significance of these slogans should not be underestimated. Expressing in a large degree the instinctive and semi-conscious will of the people, they yet signified the complete social, economic, and industrial re-organization of Russia. What country in Europe or America is prepared to interpret such revolutionary mottoes into life? Yet in Russia, in the months of June and July, 1917, these slogans became popular and were enthusiastically and actively taken up, in the form of direct action, by the bulk of the industrial and agrarian population of more than 150 millions. That was sufficient proof of the "ripeness" of the Russian people for the social revolution.

As to economic "preparedness" in the Marxian sense, it must not be forgotten that Russia is preëminently an agrarian country. Marx's dictum presupposes the industrialization of the peasant and farmer population in every highly developed society, as a step toward social fitness for revolution. But events in Russia, in 1917, demonstrated that revolution does not await this process of industrialization and—what is more important—cannot be made to wait. The Russian peasants began to expropriate the landlords and the workers took possession of the factories without taking cognizance of Marxian dicta.

This popular action, by virtue of its own logic, ushered in the social revolution in Russia, upsetting all Marxian calculations. The psychology of the Slav proved stronger than social-democratic theories.

That psychology involved the passionate yearning for liberty nurtured by a century of revolutionary agitation among all classes of society. The Russian people had fortunately remained politically unsophisticated and untouched by the corruption and confusion created among the proletariat of other countries by "democratic" liberty and self-government. The Russian remained, in this sense, natural and simple, unfamiliar with the subtleties of politics, of parliamentary trickery, and legal makeshifts. On the other hand, his primitive sense of justice and right was strong and vital, without the disintegrating finesse of pseudo-civilization. He knew what he wanted and he did not wait for "historic inevitability" to bring it to him: he employed direct action. The Revolution to him was a fact of life, not a mere theory for discussion.

Thus the social revolution took place in Russia in spite of the industrial backwardness of the country. But to make the Revolution was not enough. It was necessary for it to advance and broaden, to develop into economic and social reconstruction. That phase of the Revolution necessitated fullest play of personal initiative and collective effort. The development and success of the Revolution depended on the broadest exercise of the creative genius of the people, on the coöperation of the intellectual and manual proletariat. Common interest is the *leit motif* of all revolutionary endeavour, especially on its constructive side. This spirit of mutual purpose and solidarity swept Russia with a mighty.

wave in the first days of the October–November Revolution. Inherent in that enthusiasm were forces that could have moved mountains if intelligently guided by exclusive consideration for the well-being of the whole people. The medium for such effective guidance was on hand: the labour organizations and the coöperatives with which Russia was covered as with a network of bridges combining the city with the country; the Soviets which sprang into being responsive to the needs of the Russian people; and, finally, the intelligentsia whose traditions for a century expressed heroic devotion to the cause of Russia's emancipation.

But such a development was by no means within the program of the Bolsheviki. For several months following October they suffered the popular forces to manifest themselves, the people carrying the Revolution into ever-widening channels. But as soon as the Communist Party felt itself sufficiently strong in the government saddle, it began to limit the scope of popular activity. All the succeeding acts of the Bolsheviki, all their following policies, changes of policies, their compromises and retreats, their methods of suppression and persecution, their terrorism and extermination of all other political views—all were but the *means to an end:* the retaining of the State power in the hands of the Communist Party. Indeed, the Bolsheviki themselves (in Russia) made no secret of it. The Communist Party, they contended, is the advance guard of the proletariat, and the dictatorship must rest in its hands. Alas, the Bolsheviki reckoned without their host—without the peasantry, whom neither the *razvyortska,* the Tcheka, nor the wholesale shooting could persuade to support the Bolshevik régime. The peasantry became the rock upon which the best-laid plans and schemes of Lenin were wrecked. But Lenin, a nimble acrobat, was skilled in performing within the narrowest margin. The new economic policy was introduced just in time to ward off the disaster which was slowly but surely overtaking the whole Communist edifice.

II.

The "new economic policy" came as a surprise and a shock to most Communists. They saw in it a reversal of everything that their Party had been proclaiming—a reversal of Communism itself. In protest some of the oldest members of the Party, men who had faced danger and persecution under the old régime while Lenin and Trotsky lived abroad in safety, left the Communist Party embittered and disappointed. The leaders then declared a lockout. They ordered the clearing of the Party ranks of all "doubtful" elements. Everybody suspected of an independent attitude and those who did not accept the new economic policy as the last word in revolutionary wisdom were expelled. Among them were Communists who for years had rendered most devoted service. Some of them, hurt to the quick by the unjust and brutal procedure, and shaken to their depths by the collapse of what they held most high, even resorted to suicide. But the smooth sailing of Lenin's new gospel had to be assured, the gospel of the sanctuary of private property and the freedom of cut-throat competition erected upon the ruins of four years of revolution.

However, Communist indignation over the new economic policy merely indicated the confusion of mind on the part of Lenin's opponents. What else but mental confusion could approve of the numerous acrobatic political stunts of Lenin and yet grow indignant at the final somersault, its logical culmination? The trouble with the devout Communists was that they clung to the Immaculate Conception of the Communist State which by the aid of the Revolution was to redeem the world. But most of the leading Communists never entertained such a delusion. Least of all Lenin.

During my first interview I received the impression that he was a shrewd politician who knew exactly what he was about and that he would stop at nothing to achieve his ends.

After hearing him speak on several occasions and reading his works I became convinced that Lenin had very little concern in the Revolution and that Communism to him was a very remote thing. The centralized political State was Lenin's deity, to which everything else was to be sacrificed. Someone said that Lenin would sacrifice the Revolution to save Russia. Lenin's policies, however, have proven that he was willing to sacrifice both the Revolution and the country; or at least part of the latter, in order to realize his political scheme with what was left of Russia.

Lenin was the most pliable politician in history. He could be an ultra-revolutionary, a compromiser and conservative at the same time. When like a mighty wave the cry swept over Russia. "All power to the Soviets!" Lenin swam with the tide. When the peasants took possession of the land and the workers of the factories, Lenin not only approved of those direct methods but went further. He issued the famous motto, "Rob the robbers," a slogan which served to confuse the minds of the people and caused untold injury to revolutionary idealism. Never before did any real revolutionist interpret social expropriation as the transfer of wealth from one set of individuals to another. Yet that was exactly what Lenin's slogan meant. The indiscriminate and irresponsible raids, the accumulation of the wealth of the former bourgeoisie by the new Soviet bureaucracy, the chicanery practised toward those whose only crime was their former status, were all the results of Lenin's "Rob the robbers" policy. The whole subsequent history of the Revolution is a kaleidoscope of Lenin's compromises and betrayal of his own slogans.

Bolshevik acts and methods since the October days may seem to contradict the new economic policy. But in reality they are links in the chain which was to forge the all-powerful, centralized Government with State Capitalism as its economic expression. Lenin possessed clarity of vision and an iron will. He knew how to make his comrades in Russia and outside of it believe that his scheme was true Socialism and his methods the revolution. No wonder that Lenin felt such contempt for his flock, which he never hesitated to fling into their faces. "Only fools can believe that Communism is possible in Russia now," was Lenin's reply to the opponents of the new economic policy.

As a matter of fact, Lenin was right. True Communism was never attempted in Russia, unless one considers thirty-three categories of pay, different food rations, privileges to some and indifference to the great mass as Communism.

In the early period of the Revolution it was comparatively easy for the Communist Party to possess itself of power. All the revolutionary elements, carried away by the ultra-revolutionary promises of the Bolsheviki, helped the latter to power. Once in possession of the State the Communists began their process of elimination. All the political parties and groups which refused to submit to the new dictatorship had to go. First the Anarchists and Left Social Revolutionists, then the Mensheviki and other opponents from the Right, and finally everybody who dared aspire to an opinion of his own. Similar was the fate of all independent organizations. They were either subordinated to the needs of the new State or destroyed altogether, as were the Soviets, the trade unions and the coöperatives—three great factors for the realization of the hopes of the Revolution.

The Soviets first manifested themselves in the revolution of 1905. They played an important part during that brief but significant period. Though the revolution was crushed, the Soviet idea remained rooted in the minds and hearts of the Russian masses. At the first dawn which illuminated Russia in February, 1917, the Soviets revived again and came into bloom in a very short time. To the people the Soviets by no means represented a curtailment of the spirit of the Revolution. On the contrary, the Revolution was to find its highest, freest practical expression through the Soviets. That was why the Soviets so spontaneously and rapidly spread throughout Russia. The Bolsheviki realized the significance of the popular trend and joined the cry. But once in control of the Government the Communists saw that the Soviets threatened the supremacy of the State. At the same time they could not destroy them arbitrarily without undermining their own prestige at home and abroad as the sponsors of the Soviet system. They began to shear them gradually of their powers and finally to subordinate them to their own needs.

The Russian trade unions were much more amenable to emasculation. Numerically and in point of revolutionary fibre they were still in their childhood. By declaring adherence to the trade unions obligatory the Russian labour organizations gained in physical stature, but mentally they remained in the infant stage. The Communist State became the wet nurse of the trade unions. In return the organizations served as the flunkeys of the State. "A school for Communism," said Lenin in the famous controversy on the functions of the trade unions. Quite right. But an antiquated school where the spirit of the child is fettered and crushed. Nowhere in the world are labour organizations as subservient to the will and the dictates of the State as they are in Bolshevik Russia.

The fate of the coöperatives is too well known to require elucidation. The coöperatives were the most essential link between the city and the country. Their value to the Revolution as a popular and successful medium of exchange and distribution and to the reconstruction of Russia was incalculable. The Bolshevik transformed them into cogs of the Government machine and thereby destroyed their usefulness and efficiency.

III.

It is now clear why the Russian Revolution, as conducted by the Communist Party, was a failure. The political power of the Party, organized and centralized in the State, sought to maintain itself by all means at hand. The central authorities attempted to force the activities of the people into forms corresponding with the purposes of the Party. The sole aim of the latter was to strengthen the State and monopolize all economical, political, and social activities—even all cultural manifestations. The Revolution had an entirely different object, and in its very character it was the negation of authority and centralization. It strove to open ever-larger fields for proletarian expression and to multiply the phases of individual and collective effort. The aims and tendencies of the Revolution were diametrically opposed to those of the ruling political party.

Just as diametrically opposed were the *methods* of the Revolution and of the State. Those of the former were inspired by the spirit of the Revolution itself: that is to say, by emancipation from all oppressive and limiting forces; in short, *by libertarian principles*. The methods of the State, on the contrary—of the Bolshevik State as of every government—were based on *coercion*, which in the course of things necessarily developed into systematic violence, oppression, and terrorism. Thus two opposing tendencies struggled for supremacy: the Bolshevik State against the Revolution. That struggle was a life-and-death struggle. The two tendencies, contradictory in aims and methods, could not work harmoniously: the triumph of the State meant the defeat of the Revolution.

It would be an error to assume that the failure of the Revolution was due entirely to the character of the Bolsheviki. Fundamentally, it was the result of the principles and methods of Bolshevism. It was the authoritarian spirit and principles of the State which stifled the libertarian and liberating aspirations. Were any other political party in control of the government in Russia the result would have been essentially the same. It is not so much the Bolsheviki who killed the Russian Revolution as the Bolshevik idea. It was

Marxism, however modified; in short, fanatical governmentalism. Only this understanding of the underlying forces that crushed the Revolution can present the true lesson of that world-stirring event. The Russian Revolution reflects on a small scale the century-old struggle of the libertarian principle against the authoritarian. For what is progress if not the more general acceptance of the principles of liberty as against those of coercion? The Russian Revolution was a libertarian step defeated by the Bolshevik State, by the temporary victory of the reactionary, the governmental idea.

That victory was due to a number of causes. Most of them have already been dealt with in the preceding chapters. The main cause, however, was not the industrial backwardness of Russia, as claimed by many writers on the subject. That cause was cultural which, though giving the Russian people certain advantages over their more sophisticated neighbours, also had some fatal disadvantages. The Russian was "culturally backward" in the sense of being unspoiled by political and parliamentary corruption. On the other hand, that very condition involved inexperience in the political game and a naïve faith in the miraculous power of the party that talked the loudest and made the most promises. This faith in the power of government served to enslave the Russian people to the Communist Party even before the great masses realized that the yoke had been put around their necks.

The libertarian principle was strong in the initial days of the Revolution, the need for free expression all-absorbing. But when the first wave of enthusiasm receded into the ebb of everyday prosaic life, a firm conviction was needed to keep the fires of liberty burning. There was only a comparative handful in the great vastness of Russia to keep those fires lit—the Anarchists, whose number was small and whose efforts, absolutely suppressed under the Czar, had had no time to bear fruit. The Russian people, to some extent instinctive Anarchists, were yet too unfamiliar with true libertarian principles and methods to apply them effectively to life. Most of the Russian Anarchists themselves were unfortunately still in the meshes of limited group activities and of individualistic endeavour as against the more important social and collective efforts. The Anarchists, the future unbiased historian will admit, have played a very important rôle in the Russian Revolution—a rôle far more significant and fruitful than their comparatively small number would have led one to expect. Yet honesty and sincerity compel me to state that their work would have been of infinitely greater practical value had they been better organized and equipped to guide the released energies of the people toward the re-organization of life on a libertarian foundation.

But the failure of the Anarchists in the Russian Revolution—in the sense just indicated—does by no means argue the defeat of the libertarian idea. On the contrary, the Russian Revolution has demonstrated beyond doubt that the State idea, State Socialism, in all its manifestations (economic, political, social, educational) is entirely and hopelessly bankrupt. Never before in all history has authority, government, the State, proved so inherently static, reactionary, and even counter-revolutionary in effect. In short, the very antithesis of revolution.

It remains true, as it has through all progress, that only the libertarian spirit and method can bring man a step further in his eternal striving for the better, finer and freer life. Applied to the great social upheavals known as revolutions, this tendency is as potent as in the ordinary evolutionary process. The authoritarian method has been a failure all through history and now it has again failed in the Russian Revolution. So far human ingenuity has discovered no other principle except the libertarian, for man has indeed uttered the highest wisdom when he said that liberty is the mother of order, not its daughter. All political tenets and parties notwithstanding, no revolution can be truly and permanently successful unless it puts its emphatic veto upon all tyranny and centralization, and determinedly strives to make the revolution a real revaluation of all economic, social, and cultural values. Not mere substitution of one political party for another in the control of the Government, not the masking of autocracy by proletarian slogans, not the dictatorship of a new class over an old one, not political scene shifting of any kind, but the complete reversal of all these authoritarian principles will alone serve the revolution.

In the economic field this transformation must be in the hands of the industrial masses: the latter have the choice between an industrial State and Anarcho-syndicalism. In the case of the former the menace to the constructive development of the new social structure would be as great as from the political State. It would become a dead weight upon the growth of the new forms of life. For that very reason syndicalism (or industrialism) alone is not, as its exponents claim, sufficient unto itself. It is only when the libertarian spirit permeates the economic organizations of the workers that the manifold creative energies of the people can manifest themselves, and the revolution be safeguarded and defended. Only free initiative and popular participation in the affairs of the revolution can prevent the terrible blunders committed in Russia. For instance, with fuel only a hundred versts [about sixty-six miles] from Petrograd there would have been no necessity for that city to suffer from cold had the workers' economic organizations of Petrograd been free to exercise their initiative for the common good. The peasants of the Ukraine would not have been hampered in the cultivation of their land had they had access to the farm implements stacked up in the warehouses of Kharkov and other industrial centres awaiting orders from Moscow for their distribution. These are characteristic examples of Bolshevik governmentalism and centralization, which should serve as a warning to the workers of Europe and America of the destructive effects of Statism.

The industrial power of the masses, expressed through their libertarian associations—Anarcho-syndicalism—is alone able to organize successfully the economic life and carry on production. On the other hand, the coöperatives, working in harmony with the industrial bodies, serve as the distributing and exchange media between city and country, and at the same time link in fraternal bond the industrial and agrarian masses. A common tie of mutual service and aid is created which is the strongest bulwark of the revolution—far more effective than compulsory labour, the Red Army, or terrorism. In that way alone can revolution act as a leaven to quicken the development of new social forms and inspire the masses to greater achievements.

But libertarian industrial organizations and the coöperatives are not the only media in the interplay of the complex phases of social life. There are the cultural forces which, though closely related to the economic activities, have yet their own functions to perform. In Russia the Communist State became the sole arbiter of all the needs of the social body. The result, as already described, was complete cultural stagnation and the paralysis of all creative endeavour. If such a débacle is to be avoided in the future, the cultural forces, while remaining rooted in the economic soil, must yet retain independent scope and freedom of expression. Not adherence to the dominant political party but devotion to the revolution, knowledge, ability, and—above all—the creative impulse should be the criterion of fitness for cultural work. In Russia this was made impossible almost from the beginning of the October Revolution, by the violent separation of the intelligentsia and the masses. It is true that the original offender in this case was the intelligentsia, especially the technical intelligentsia, which in Russia tenaciously clung—as it does in other countries—to the coat-tails of the bourgeoisie. This element, unable to comprehend the significance of revolutionary events, strove to stem the tide by wholesale sabotage. But in Russia there was also another kind of intelligentsia—one with a glorious revolutionary past of a hundred years. That part of the intelligentsia kept faith with the people, though it could not unreservedly accept the new dictatorship. The fatal error of the Bolsheviki was that they made no distinction between the two elements. They met sabotage with wholesale terror against the intelligentsia as a class, and inaugurated a campaign of hatred more intensive than the persecution of the bourgeoisie itself—a method which created an abyss between the intelligentsia and the proletariat and reared a barrier against constructive work.

Lenin was the first to realize that criminal blunder. He pointed out that it was a grave error to lead the workers to believe that they could build up the industries and engage in cultural work without the aid and coöperation of the intelligentsia. The proletariat had neither the knowledge nor the training for the task, and the intelligentsia had to be restored in the direction of the industrial life. But the recognition of one error never safeguarded Lenin and his Party from immediately committing another. The technical intelligentsia was called back on terms which added disintegration to the antagonism against the régime.

While the workers continued to starve, engineers, industrial experts, and technicians received high salaries, special privileges, and the best rations. They became the pampered employees of the State and the new slave drivers of the masses. The latter, fed for years on the fallacious teachings that muscle alone is necessary for a successful revolution and that only physical labour is productive, and incited by the campaign of hatred which stamped every intellectual a counter-revolutionist and speculator, could not make peace with those they had been taught to scorn and distrust.

Unfortunately Russia is not the only country where this

proletarian attitude against the intelligentsia prevails. Everywhere political demagogues play upon the ignorance of the masses, teach them that education and culture are bourgeois prejudices, that the workers can do without them, and that they alone are able to rebuild society. The Russian Revolution has made it very clear that both brain and muscle are indispensable to the work of social regeneration. Intellectual and physical labour are as closely related in the social body as brain and hand in the human organism. One cannot function without the other.

It is true that most intellectuals consider themselves a class apart from and superior to the workers, but social conditions everywhere are fast demolishing the high pedestal of the intelligentsia. They are made to see that they, too, are proletarians, even more dependent upon the economic master than the manual worker.

Unlike the physical proletarian, who can pick up his tools and tramp the world in search of a change from a galling situation, the intellectual proletarians have their roots more firmly in their particular social environment and cannot so easily change their occupation or mode of living. It is therefore of utmost importance to bring home to the workers the rapid proletarization of the intellectuals and the common tie thus created between them. If the Western world is to profit by the lessons of Russia, the demagogic flattery of the masses and blind antagonism toward the intelligentsia must cease. That does not mean, however, that the toilers should depend entirely upon the intellectual element. On the contrary, the masses must begin right now to prepare and equip themselves for the great task the revolution will put upon them. They should acquire the knowledge and technical skill necessary for managing and directing the intricate mechanism of the industrial and social structure of their respective countries. But even at best the workers will need the coöperation of the professional and cultural elements. Similarly the latter must realize that their

true interests are identical with those of the masses. Once
the two social forces learn to blend into one harmonious
whole, the tragic aspects of the Russian Revolution would
to a great extent be eliminated. No one would be shot because he "once acquired an education." The scientist, the
engineer, the specialist, the investigator, the educator, and
the creative artist, as well as the carpenter, machinist, and
the rest, are all part and parcel of the collective force which
is to shape the revolution into the great architect of the new
social edifice. Not hatred, but unity; not antagonism, but
fellowship; not shooting, but sympathy—that is the lesson
of the great Russian débacle for the intelligentsia as well as
the workers. All must learn the value of mutual aid and
libertarian coöperation. Yet each must be able to remain
independent in his own sphere and in harmony with the
best he can yield to society. Only in that way will productive
labour and educational and cultural endeavour express
themselves in ever newer and richer forms. That is to me
the all-embracing and vital moral taught by the Russian
Revolution.

IV.

In the previous pages I have tried to point out why Bolshevik principles, methods, and tactics failed, and that similar
principles and methods applied in any other country, even
of the highest industrial development, must also fail. I have
further shown that it is not only Bolshevism that failed, but
Marxism itself. That is to say, the STATE IDEA, the *authoritative principle* has been proven bankrupt by the experience
of the Russian Revolution. If I were to sum up my whole
argument in one sentence I should say: The inherent tendency of the State is to concentrate, to narrow, and monopolize all social activities; the nature of revolution is, on
the contrary, to grow, to broaden, and disseminate itself in
ever-wider circles. In other words, the State is institutional

and static; revolution is fluent, dynamic. These two tendencies are incompatible and mutually destructive. The State idea killed the Russian Revolution and it must have the same result in all other revolutions, unless the *libertarian idea prevail*.

Yet I go much further. It is not only Bolshevism, Marxism, and Governmentalism which are fatal to revolution as well as to all vital human progress. The main cause of the defeat of the Russian Revolution lies much deeper. It is to be found in the whole Socialist conception of revolution itself.

The dominant, almost general, idea of revolution—particularly the Socialist idea—is that revolution is a violent change of social conditions through which one social class, the working class, becomes dominant over another class, the capitalist class. It is the conception of a purely physical change, and as such it involves only political scene shifting and institutional rearrangements. Bourgeois dictatorship is replaced by the "dictatorship of the proletariat"—or by that of its "advance guard," the Communist Party; Lenin takes the seat of the Romanovs, the Imperial Cabinet is rechristened Soviet of People's Commissars, Trotsky is appointed Minister of War, and a labourer becomes the Military Governor General of Moscow. That is, in essence, the Bolshevik conception of revolution, as translated into actual practice. And with a few minor alterations it is also the idea of revolution held by all other Socialist parties.

This conception is inherently and fatally false. Revolution is indeed a violent process. But if it is to result only in a change of dictatorship, in a shifting of names and political personalities, then it is hardly worth while. It is surely not worth all the struggle and sacrifice, the stupendous loss in human life and cultural values that result from every revolution. If such a revolution were even to bring greater social well-being (which has not been the case in Russia) then it would also not be worth the terrific price paid: mere improvement can be brought about without bloody revolution. It is not palliatives or reforms that are the real aim and purpose of revolution, as I conceive it.

In my opinion—a thousandfold strengthened by the Russian experience—the great mission of revolution, of the SO-CIAL REVOLUTION, is a *fundamental transvaluation of values*. A transvaluation not only of social, but also of human values. The latter are even preëminent, for they are the basis of all social values. Our institutions and conditions rest upon deep-seated ideas. To change those conditions and at the same time leave the underlying ideas and values intact means only a superficial transformation, one that cannot be permanent or bring real betterment. It is a change of form only, not of substance, as so tragically proven by Russia.

It is at once the great failure and the great tragedy of the Russian Revolution that it attempted (in the leadership of the ruling political party) to change only institutions and conditions, while ignoring entirely the human and social values involved in the Revolution. Worse yet, in its mad passion for power, the Communist State even sought to strengthen and deepen the very ideas and conceptions which the Revolution had come to destroy. It supported and encouraged all the worst anti-social qualities and systematically destroyed the already awakened conception of the new revolutionary values. The sense of justice and equality, the love of liberty and of human brotherhood—these fundamentals of the real regeneration of society—the Communist State suppressed to the point of extermination. Man's instinctive sense of equity was branded as weak sentimentality; human dignity and liberty became a bourgeois superstition; the sanctity of life, which is the very essence of social reconstruction, was condemned as unrevolutionary, almost counter-revolutionary. This fearful perversion of fundamental values bore within itself the seed of destruction. With the conception that the Revolution was only a means of securing political power, it was inevitable that all revolutionary values should be subordinated to the needs of the Socialist State; indeed, exploited to further the security of the newly acquired governmental power. "Reasons of State," masked as the "interests of the Revolution and of the People," became the sole criterion of action, even of feeling. Violence, the tragic inevitability of revolutionary upheavals, became an established custom, a habit, and was presently enthroned as the most powerful and "ideal" institution. Did not Zinoviev himself canonize Dzerzhinsky, the head of the bloody Tcheka, as the "saint of the Revolution"? Were not the greatest public honours paid by the State to Uritsky, the founder and sadistic chief of the Petrograd Tcheka?

This perversion of the ethical values soon crystallized into the all-dominating slogan of the Communist Party: THE END JUSTIFIES ALL MEANS. Similarly in the past the Inquisition and the Jesuits adopted this motto and subordinated to it all morality. It avenged itself upon the Jesuits as it did upon the Russian Revolution. In the wake of this slogan followed lying, deceit, hypocrisy and treachery, murder, open and secret. It should be of utmost interest to students of social psychology that two movements as widely separated in time and ideas as Jesuitism and Bolshevism *reached exactly similar results* in the evolution of the principle that the end justifies all means. The historic parallel, almost entirely ignored so far, contains a most important lesson for all coming revolutions and for the whole future of mankind.

There is no greater fallacy than the belief that aims and purposes are one thing, while methods and tactics are another. This conception is a potent menace to social regeneration. All human experience teaches that methods and means cannot be separated from the ultimate aim. The means employed become, through individual habit and social practice, part and parcel of the final purpose; they influence it, modify it, and presently the aims and means become identical. From the day of my arrival in Russia I felt it, at first vaguely, then ever more consciously and clearly. The great and inspiring aims of the Revolution became so clouded with and obscured by the methods used by the ruling political power that it was hard to distinguish what was temporary means and what final purpose. Psychologically and socially the means necessarily influence and alter the aims. The whole history of man is continuous proof of the maxim that to divest one's methods of ethical concepts means to sink into the depths of utter demoralization. In that lies the real tragedy of the Bolshevik philosophy as applied to the Russian Revolution. May this lesson not be in vain.

No revolution can ever succeed as a factor of liberation unless the MEANS used to further it be identical in spirit and tendency with the PURPOSES to be achieved. Revolution is the negation of the existing, a violent protest against man's inhumanity to man with all the thousand and one slaveries it involves. It is the destroyer of dominant values upon which a complex system of injustice, oppression, and wrong has been built up by ignorance and brutality. It is the herald of NEW VALUES, ushering in a transformation of the basic relations of man to man, and of man to society. It is not a mere reformer, patching up some social evils; not a mere changer of forms and institutions; not only a re-distributor of social well-being. It is all that, yet more, much more. It is, first and foremost, the TRANSVALUATOR, the bearer of *new* values. It is the great TEACHER of the NEW ETHICS, inspiring man with a new concept of life and its manifestations in social relationships. It is the mental and spiritual regenerator.

Its first ethical precept is the identity of means used and aims sought. The ultimate end of all revolutionary social change is to establish the sanctity of human life, the dignity of man, the right of every human being to liberty and well-being. Unless this be the essential aim of revolution, violent social changes would have no justification. For *external* social alterations can be, and have been, accomplished by the normal processes of evolution. Revolution, on the contrary, signifies not mere *external* change, but *internal,* basic, fundamental change. That internal change of concepts and ideas, permeating ever-larger social strata, finally culminates in the violent upheaval known as revolution. Shall that climax reverse the process of transvaluation, turn against it, betray it? That is what happened in Russia. On the contrary, the revolution itself must quicken and further the process of which it is the cumulative expression; its main mission is to inspire it, to carry it to greater heights, give it fullest scope for expression. Only thus is revolution true to itself.

Applied in practice it means that the period of the actual revolution, the so-called transitory stage, must be the introduction, the prelude to the new social conditions. It is the threshold to the NEW LIFE, the new HOUSE OF MAN AND HUMANITY. As such it must be of the spirit of the new life, harmonious with the construction of the new edifice.

To-day is the parent of to-morrow. The present casts its shadow far into the future. That is the law of life, individual and social. Revolution that divests itself of ethical values thereby lays the foundation of injustice, deceit, and oppression for the future society. The *means* used to *prepare* the future become its *cornerstone.* Witness the tragic condition of Russia. The methods of State centralization have paralysed individual initiative and effort; the tyranny of the dictatorship has cowed the people into slavish submission and all but extinguished the fires of liberty; organized terrorism has depraved and brutalized the masses and stifled every idealistic aspiration; institutionalized murder has cheapened human life, and all sense of the dignity of man and the value of life has been eliminated; coercion at every step has made effort bitter, labour a punishment, has turned the whole of existence into a scheme of mutual deceit, and has revived the lowest and most brutal instincts of man. A sorry heritage to begin a new life of freedom and brotherhood.

It cannot be sufficiently emphasized that revolution is in vain unless inspired by its ultimate ideal. Revolutionary methods must be in tune with revolutionary aims. The means used to further the revolution must harmonize with its purposes. In short, the ethical values which the revolution is to establish in the new society must be *initiated* with the revolutionary activities of the so-called transitional period. The latter can serve as a real and dependable bridge to the better life only if built of the same material as the life to be achieved. Revolution is the mirror of the coming day; it is the child that is to be the Man of To-morrow.

There Is No
Communism in Russia

Communism is now on everybody's lips. Some talk of it with the exaggerated enthusiasm of a new convert, others fear and condemn it as a social menace. But I venture to say that neither its admirers—the great majority of them—nor those who denounce it have a very clear idea of what Bolshevik Communism really is.

Speaking generally, Communism is the ideal of human equality and brotherhood. It considers the exploitation of man by man as the source of all slavery and oppression. It holds that economic inequality leads to social injustice and is the enemy of moral and intellectual progress. Communism aims at a society where classes have been abolished as a result of common ownership of the means of production and distribution. It teaches that only in a classless, solidaric commonwealth can man enjoy liberty, peace and well-being.

My purpose is to compare Communism with its application in Soviet Russia, but on closer examination I find it an impossible task. As a matter of fact, there is no Communism in the U.S.S.R. Not a single Communist principle, not a single item of its teaching is being applied by the Communist party there.

To some this statement may appear as entirely false; others may think it vastly exaggerated. Yet I feel sure that an objective examination of conditions in present-day Russia will convince the unprejudiced reader that I speak with entire truth.

It is necessary to consider here, first of all, the fundamental idea underlying the alleged Communism of the Bolsheviki. It is admittedly of a centralized, authoritarian kind. That is, it is based almost exclusively on governmental coercion, on violence. It is not the Communism of voluntary association. It is compulsory State Communism. This must be kept in mind in order to understand the method applied by the Soviet state to carry out such of its plans as may seem to be Communistic.

The first requirement of Communism is the socialization of the land and of the machinery of production and distribution. Socialized land and machinery belong to the people, to be settled upon and used by individuals or groups according to their needs. In Russia land and machinery are not socialized but *nationalized*. The term is a misnomer, of course. In fact, it is entirely devoid of content. In reality there is no such thing as national wealth. A nation is too abstract a term to "own" anything. Ownership may be by an individual, or by a group of individuals; in any case by some quantitatively defined reality. When a certain thing does not belong to an individual or group, it is either nationalized or socialized. If it is nationalized, it belongs to the state; that is, the government has control of it and may dispose of it according to its wishes and views. But when a thing is socialized, every individual has free access to it and may use it without interference from anyone.

In Russia there is no socialization either of land or of production and distribution. Everything is nationalized; it belongs to the government, exactly as does the post-office in

America or the railroad in Germany and other European countries. There is nothing of Communism about it.

No more Communistic than the land and means of production is any other phase of the Soviet economic structure. All sources of existence are owned by the central government; foreign trade is its absolute monopoly; the printing presses belong to the state, and every book and paper issued is a government publication. In short, the entire country and everything in it is the property of the state, as in ancient days it used to be the property of the crown. The few things not yet nationalized, as some old ramshackle houses in Moscow, for instance, or some dingy little stores with a pitiful stock of cosmetics, exist on sufferance only, with the government having the undisputed right to confiscate them at any moment by simple decree.

Such a condition of affairs may be called state capitalism, but it would be fantastic to consider it in any sense Communistic.

II.

Let us now turn to production and consumption, the levers of all existence. Maybe in them we shall find a degree of Communism that will justify us in calling life in Russia Communistic, to some extent at least.

I have already pointed out that the land and the machinery of production are owned by the state. The methods of production and the amounts to be manufactured by every industry in each and every mill, shop and factory are determined by the state, by the central government—by Moscow—through its various organs.

Now, Russia is a country of vast extent, covering about one sixth of the earth's surface. It is peopled by a mixed population of 165,000,000. It consists of a number of large republics, of various races and nationalities, each region having its own particular interests and needs. No doubt, industrial and economic planning is vitally necessary for the well-being of a community. True Communism—economic equality as between man and man and between communities—requires the best and most efficient planning by each community, based upon its local requirements and possibilities. The basis of such planning must be the complete freedom of each community to produce according to its needs and to dispose of its products according to its judgment: to exchange its surplus with other similarly independent communities without let or hindrance by any external authority.

That is the essential politico-economic nature of Communism. It is neither workable nor possible on any other basis. It is necessarily libertarian, Anarchistic.

There is no trace of such Communism—that is to say, of any Communism—in Soviet Russia. In fact, the mere suggestion of such a system is considered criminal there, and any attempt to carry it out is punished by death.

Industrial planning and all the processes of production and distribution are in the hands of the central government. Its Supreme Economic Council is subject only to the authority of the Communist Party. It is entirely independent of the will or wishes of the people comprising the Union of Socialist Soviet Republics. Its work is directed by the policies and decisions of the Kremlin. This explains why Soviet Russia exported vast amounts of wheat and other grain while wide regions in the south and southeast of Russia were stricken with famine, so that more than two million of its people died of starvation (1932–1933).

There were "reasons of state" for it. The euphonious has from time immemorial masked tyranny, exploitation and the determination of every ruler to prolong and perpetuate his rule. Incidentally, I may mention that—in spite of country-wide hunger and lack of the most elemental necessities of life in Russia—the entire First Five-Year Plan aimed at developing that branch of heavy industry which serves, or can be made to serve, *military* purposes.

As with production, so with distribution and every other form of activity. Not only individual cities and towns, but the constituent parts of the Soviet Union are entirely deprived of independent existence. Politically mere vassals of Moscow, their whole economic, social and cultural activity is planned, cut out for them and ruthlessly controlled by the "proletarian dictatorship" in Moscow. More: the life of every locality, of every individual even, in the so-called "Socialist" republics is managed in the very last detail by the "general line" laid down by the "center." In other words, by the Central Committee and Politbureau of the Party, both of them controlled absolutely by one man, Stalin. To call such a dictatorship, this personal autocracy more powerful and absolute than any Czar's, by the name of Communism seems to me the acme of imbecility.

III.

Let us see now how Bolshevik "Communism" affects the lives of the masses and of the individual.

There are naïve people who believe that at least some features of Communism have been introduced into the lives of the Russian people. I wish it were true, for that would be a hopeful sign, a promise of potential development along that line. But the truth is that in no phase of Soviet life, no more in the social than in individual relations, has there ever been any attempt to apply Communist principles in any shape or form. As I have pointed out before, the very suggestion of free, voluntary Communism is taboo in Russia and is regarded as counter-revolutionary and high treason against the infallible Stalin and the holy "Communist" Party.

And here I do not speak of the libertarian, Anarchist Communism. What I assert is that there is not the least sign in Soviet Russia even of authoritarian, State Communism. Let us glance at the actual facts of everyday life there.

The essence of Communism, even of the coercive kind, is the absence of social classes. The introduction of economic equality is its first step. This has been the basis of all Communist philosophies, however they may have differed in other respects. The purpose common to all of them was to secure social justice; and all of them agreed that it was not possible without establishing economic equality. Even Plato, in spite of the intellectual and moral strata in his Republic, provided for absolute economic equality, since the ruling classes were not to enjoy greater rights or privileges than the lowest social unit.

Even at the risk of condemnation for telling the whole truth, I must state unequivocally and unconditionally that the very opposite is the case in Soviet Russia. Bolshevism has not abolished the classes in Russia: it has merely reversed their former relationship. As a matter of fact, it has multiplied the social divisions which existed before the Revolution.

When I arrived in Soviet Russia in January, 1920, I found innumerable economic categories, based on the food rations received from the government. The sailor was getting the best ration, superior in quality, quantity and variety to the food issued to the rest of the population. He was the aristocrat of the Revolution: economically and socially he was universally considered to belong to the new privileged classes. After him came the soldier, the Red Army man, who received a much smaller ration, even less bread. Below the soldier in the scale was the worker in the military industries; then came other workers, subdivided into the skilled, the artisan, the laborer, etc. Each category received a little less bread, fats, sugar, tobacco, and other products (whenever they were to be had at all). Members of the former bourgeoisie, officially abolished as a class and expropriated, were in the last economic category and received practically nothing. Most of them could secure neither work nor lodgings, and it was no one's business how they were to exist, to keep from stealing or from joining the counter-revolutionary armies and robber bands.

The possession of a red card, proving membership in the Communist Party, placed one above all these categories. It entitled its owner to a special ration, enabled him to eat in the Party *stolovaya* (mess-room) and produced, particularly if supported by recommendations from party members higher up, warm underwear, leather boots, a fur coat, or other valuable articles. Prominent party men had their own dining-rooms, to which the ordinary members had no access. In the Smolny, for instance, then the headquarters of the Petrograd government, there were two different dining-rooms, one for Communists in high position, the other for the lesser lights. Zinoviev, then chairman of the Petrograd Soviet and virtual autocrat of the Northern District, and other government heads took their meals at home in the Astoria, formerly the best hotel in the city, turned into the first Soviet House, where they lived with their families.

Later on I found the same situation in Moscow, Kharkov, Kiev, Odessa—everywhere in Soviet Russia.

It was the Bolshevik system of "Communism." What dire effects it had in causing dissatisfaction, resentment and antagonism throughout the country, resulting in industrial and agrarian sabotage, in strikes and revolts—of this further on. It is said that man does not live by bread alone. True, but he cannot live at all without it. To the average man, to the masses in Russia, the different rations established in the country for the liberation of which they had bled, was the symbol of the new régime. It signified to them the great lie of Bolshevism, the broken promises of freedom, for freedom meant to them social justice, economic equality. The instinct of the masses seldom goes wrong; in this case it proved prophetic. What wonder, then, that the universal enthusiasm over the Revolution soon turned into disillusionment and bitterness, to opposition and hatred. How often Russian workers complained to me: "We don't mind working hard and going hungry. It's the injustice which we mind. If the country is poor, if there is little bread, then let us all share that little, but let us share equally. As things are now, it's the same as it used to be; some get more, others less, and some get nothing at all."

The Bolshevik system of privilege and inequality was not long in producing its inevitable results. It created and fostered social antagonisms; it alienated the masses from the Revolution, paralysed their interest in it and their energies, and thus defeated all the purposes of the Revolution.

The same system of privilege and inequality, strengthened and perfected, is in force today.

The Russian Revolution was in the deepest sense a social upheaval: its fundamental tendency was libertarian, its essential aim economic and social equality. Long before the October–November days (1917) the city proletariat began taking possession of the mills, shops and factories, while the peasants expropriated the big estates and turned the land to communal use. The continued development of the Revolution in its Communist direction depended on the unity of the revolutionary forces and the direct, creative initiative of the laboring masses. The people were enthusiastic in the great object before them; they eagerly applied their energies to the work of social reconstruction. Only they who had for centuries borne the heaviest burdens could, through free and systematic effort, find the road to a new, regenerated society.

But Bolshevik dogmas and "Communist" statism proved a fatal handicap to the creative activities of the people. The fundamental characteristic of Bolshevik psychology is distrust of the masses. Their Marxist theories, centering all power in the exclusive hands of their party, quickly resulted in the destruction of revolutionary coöperation, in the arbitrary and ruthless suppression of all other political parties and movements. Bolshevik tactics encompassed the systematic eradication of every sign of dissatisfaction, stifled all criticism and crushed independent opinion, popular initiative and effort. Communist dictatorship, with its extreme mechanical centralization, frustrated the economic and industrial activities of the country. The great masses were deprived of the opportunity to shape the policies of the Revolution or to take part in the administration of their own affairs. The labor unions were governmentalized and turned into mere transmitters of the orders of the state. The people's coöperatives—that vital nerve of active solidarity and mutual help between city and country—were liquidated. The Soviets of peasants and workers were castrated and transformed into obedient committees. The government monopolized every phase of life. A bureaucratic machine was created, appalling in its inefficiency, corruption, brutality. The Revolution was divorced from the people and thus doomed to perish; and over all hung the dreaded sword of Bolshevik terrorism.

That was the "Communism" of the Bolsheviki in the first stages of the Revolution. Everyone knows that it brought the complete paralysis of industry, agriculture and transport. It was the period of "military Communism," of agrarian and industrial conscription, of the razing of peasant villages by Bolshevik artillery—those "constructive" social and economic policies of Bolshevik Communism which resulted in the fearful famine in 1921.

IV.

And today? Has that "Communism" changed its nature? Is it actually different from the "Communism" of 1921? To my regret I must state that, in spite of all widely advertised changes and new economic policies, Bolshevik "Communism" is essentially the same as it was in 1921.

Today the peasantry in Soviet Russia is entirely dispossessed of the land. The *sovkhozi* are government farms on which the peasant works as a hired man, just as the man in the factory. This is known as "industrialization" of agriculture, "transforming the peasant into a proletarian." In the *kolkhoz* the land only nominally belongs to the village. Actually it is owned by the government. The latter can at any moment—and often does—commandeer the *kolkhoz* members for work in other parts of the country or exile whole villages for disobedience. The *kolkhozi* are worked collectively, but the government control of them amounts to expropriation. It taxes them at its own will; it sets whatever price it chooses to pay for grain and other products, and neither the individual peasant nor the village Soviet has any say in the matter. Under the mask of numerous levies and compulsory government loans, it appropriates the products of the *kolkhozi,* and for some actual or pretended offenses punishes them by taking away all their grain.

The fearful famine of 1921 was admittedly due chiefly to the *razverstka,* the ruthless expropriation practiced at the time. It was because of it, and of the rebellion that resulted, that Lenin decided to introduce the NEP—the New Economic Policy which limited state expropriation and enabled the peasant to dispose of some of his surplus for his own benefit. The NEP immediately improved economic conditions throughout the land. The famine of 1932–1933 was due to similar "Communist" methods of the Bolsheviki: to enforced collectivization.

The same result as in 1921 followed. It compelled Stalin to revise his policy somewhat. He realised that the welfare of a country, particularly of one predominantly agricultural as Russia is, depends primarily on the peasantry. The motto was proclaimed: the peasant must be given opportunity to greater "well-being." This "new" policy is admittedly only a breathing spell for the peasant. It has no more of Communism in it than the previous agrarian policies. From the beginning of Bolshevik rule to this day, it has been nothing but expropriation in one form or another, now and then differing in degree but always the same in kind—a continuous process of state robbery of the peasantry, of prohibitions, violence, chicanery and reprisals, exactly as in the worst days of Czarism and the World War. The present policy is but a variation of the "military Communism" of 1920–1921, with more of the military and less of the Communist element in it. Its "equality" is that of a penitentiary; its "freedom" that of a chain gang. No wonder the Bolsheviki declare that liberty is a bourgeois prejudice.

Soviet apologists insist that the old "military Communism" was justified in the initial period of the Revolution in the days of the blockade and military fronts. But more than sixteen years have passed since. There are no more blockades, no more fighting fronts, no more counter-revolution. Soviet Russia has secured the recognition of all the great governments of the world. It emphasizes its good will toward the bourgeois states, solicits their coöperation and is doing a large business with them. In fact, the Soviet government is on terms of friendship even with Mussolini and Hitler, those famous champions of liberty. It is helping capitalism to weather its economic storms by buying millions of dollars' worth of products and opening new markets to it.

This is, in the main, what Soviet Russia has accomplished during seventeen years since the Revolution. But as to Communism—that is another matter. In this regard, the Bolshevik government has followed exactly the same course as before, and worse. It has made some superficial changes politically and economically, but fundamentally it has remained exactly the same state, based on the same principle of violence and coercion and using the same methods of terror and compulsion as in the period of 1920–1921.

There are more classes in Soviet Russia today than in 1917, more than in most other countries in the world. The Bolsheviki have created a vast Soviet bureaucracy, enjoying special privileges and almost unlimited authority over the masses, industrial and agricultural. Above that bureaucracy is the still more privileged class of "responsible comrades," the new Soviet aristocracy. The industrial class is divided and subdivided into numerous gradations. There are the *udarniki,* the shock troops of labor, entitled to various privileges; the "specialists," the artisans, the ordinary workers and laborers. There are the factory "cells," the shop committees, the pioneers, the *komsomoltsi,* the party members, all enjoying material advantages and authority. There is the large class of *lishentsi,* persons deprived of civil rights, the greater number of them also of chance to work, of the right to live in certain places, practically cut off from all means of existence. The notorious "pale" of the Czarist times, which forbade Jews to live in certain parts of the country, has been revived for the entire population by the introduction of the new Soviet passport system. Over and above all these classes is the dreaded G.P.U., secret, powerful and arbitrary, a government within the government. The G.P.U., in its turn, has its own class divisions. It has its own armed forces, its own commercial and industrial establishments, its own laws and regulations, and a vast slave army of convict labor. Aye, even in the Soviet prisons and concentration camps there are various classes with special privileges.

In the field of industry the same kind of "Communism" prevails as in agriculture. A sovietized Taylor system is in vogue throughout Russia, combining a minimum standard of production and piece work—the highest degree of exploitation and human degradation, involving also endless differences in wages and salaries. Payment is made in money, in rations, in reduced charges for rent, lighting, etc., not to speak of the special rewards and premiums for *udarniki.* In short, it is the *wage system* which is in operation in Russia.

Need I emphasize that an economic arrangement based

on the wage system cannot be considered as in any way
related to Communism? It is its antithesis.

V.

All these features are to be found in the present Soviet
system. It is unpardonable naïveté, or still more unpardonable hypocrisy, to pretend—as the Bolshevik apologists
do—that the compulsory labor service in Russia is "the self-
organization of the masses for purposes of production."

Strange to say, I have met seemingly intelligent persons
who claim that by such methods the Bolsheviki "are building Communism." Apparently they believe that building
consists in ruthless destruction, physically and morally, of
the best values of mankind. There are others who pretend
to think that the road to freedom and coöperation leads
through labor slavery and intellectual suppression. According to them, to instill the poison of hatred and envy, of
universal espionage and terror, is the best preparation for
manhood and the fraternal spirit of Communism.

I do not think so. I think that there is nothing more
pernicious than to degrade a human being into a cog of a
soulless machine, turn him into a serf, into a spy or the
victim of a spy. There is nothing more corrupting than
slavery and despotism.

There is a psychology of political absolutism and dictatorship, common to all forms: the means and methods
used to achieve a certain end in the course of time themselves become the end. The ideal of Communism, of Socialism, has long ago ceased to inspire the Bolshevik leaders as
a class. Power and the strengthening of power has become
their sole object. But abject subjection, exploitation and
degradation are developing a new psychology in the great
mass of the people also.

The young generation in Russia is the product of Bol-

shevik principles and methods. It is the result of sixteen
years of official opinions, the only opinions permitted in the
land. Having grown up under the deadly monopoly of ideas
and values, the youth in the U.S.S.R. knows hardly anything about Russia itself. Much less does it know of the
world outside. It consists of blind fanatics, narrow and intolerant, it lacks all ethical perception, it is devoid of the
sense of justice and fairness. To this element is added a
class of climbers and careerists, of self-seekers reared on the
Bolshevik dogma: "The end justifies the means." Yet it
were wrong to deny the exceptions in the ranks of Russia's
youth. There are a goodly number who are deeply sincere,
heroic, idealistic. They see and feel the force of the loudly
professed party ideals. They realize the betrayal of the
masses. They suffer deeply under the cynicism and callous-
ness towards every human emotion. The presence of *kom-
somolszi* in the Soviet political prisons, concentration
camps and exile, and the escapes under most harrowing
difficulties prove that the young generation does not consist
entirely of cringing adherents. No, not all of Russia's youth
has been turned into puppets, obsessed bigots, or worshippers at Stalin's shrine and Lenin's tomb.

Already the dictatorship has become an absolute necessity for the continuation of the régime. For where there are
classes and social inequality, there the state must resort to
force and suppression. The ruthlessness of such a situation
is always in proportion to the bitterness and resentment
imbuing the masses. That is why there is more governmental terrorism in Soviet Russia than anywhere else in the
civilized world today, for Stalin has to conquer and enslave
a stubborn peasantry of a hundred millions. It is popular
hatred of the régime which explains the stupendous industrial sabotage in Russia, the disorganization of the transport
after sixteen years of virtual military management; the terrific famine in the South and Southeast, notwithstanding
favorable natural conditions and in spite of the severest

measures to compel the peasants to sow and reap, in spite even of wholesale extermination and of the deportation of more than a million peasants to forced labor camps.

Bolshevik dictatorship is an absolutism which must constantly be made more relentless in order to survive, calling for the complete suppression of independent opinion and criticism within the party, within even its highest and most exclusive circles. It is a significant feature of this situation that official Bolshevism and its paid and unpaid agents are constantly assuring the world that "all is well in Soviet Russia and getting better." It is of the same quality as Hitler's constant emphasis of how greatly he loves peace while he is feverishly increasing his military strength.

Far from getting better the dictatorship is daily growing more relentless. The latest decree against so-called counter-revolutionists, or traitors to the Soviet State, should convince even some of the most ardent apologists of the wonders performed in Russia. The decree adds strength to the already existing laws against everyone who cannot or will not reverence the infallibility of the holy trinity, Marx, Lenin and Stalin. And it is more drastic and cruel in its effect upon every one deemed a culprit. To be sure, hostages are nothing new in the U.S.S.R. They were already part of the terror when I came to Russia. Peter Kropotkin and Vera Figner had protested in vain against this black spot on the escutcheon of the Russian Revolution. Now, after seventeen years of Bolshevik rule, a new decree was thought necessary. It not only revives the taking of hostages; it even aims at cruel punishment for every adult member of the real or imaginary offender's family. The new decree defines treason to the state as

> any acts committed by citizens of the U.S.S.R. detrimental to the military forces of the U.S.S.R., its independence or the inviolability of its territory, such as espionage, betrayal of military or state secrets, going over to the side of the enemy,

fleeing to a foreign country or flight [this time the word used means airplane flight] to a foreign country.

Traitors have, of course, always been shot. What makes the new decree more terrifying is the remorseless punishment it demands for everyone living with or supporting the hapless victim, whether he knows of the crime or not. He may be imprisoned, or exiled, or even shot. He may lose his civil rights, and he may forfeit everything he owns. In other words, the new decree sets a premium on informers who, to save their own skins, will ingratiate themselves with the G.P.U., will readily turn over the unfortunate kin of the offenders to the Soviet henchmen.

This new decree must forever put to rest any remaining doubts as to the existence of true Communism in Russia. It departs from even the pretense of internationalism and proletarian class interest. The old tune is now changed to a pæan song of the Fatherland, with the ever servile Soviet press loudest in the chorus:

> Defense of the Fatherland is the supreme law of life, and he who raises his hand against the Fatherland, who betrays it, must be destroyed.

Soviet Russia, it must now be obvious, is an absolute despotism politically and the crassest form of state capitalism economically.

Address to the International Working Men's Association Congress

Life imposes strange situations on all of us. For forty-eight years I was considered an extremist in our ranks. One who refused to compromise our ideas or tactics for any purpose whatsoever—one who always insisted that the Anarchist aim and methods must harmonize, or the aim would never be achieved. Yet here I am trying to explain the action of our Spanish comrades to the European opponents, and the criticism of the latter to the comrades of the CNT–FAI. In other words, after a lifetime of an extreme left position I find myself in the center, as it were.

I have seen from the moment of my first arrival in Spain in September 1936 that our comrades in Spain are plunging head foremost into the abyss of compromise that will lead them far away from their revolutionary aim. Subsequent events have proven that those of us who saw the danger ahead were right. The participation of the CNT–FAI in the government, and concessions to the insatiable monster in Moscow, have certainly *not* benefited the Spanish Revolution, or even the anti-Fascist struggle. Yet closer contact with reality in Spain, with the almost insurmountable odds against the aspirations of the CNT–FAI, made me understand their tactics better, and helped me to guard against any dogmatic judgment of our comrades.

I am inclined to believe that the critics in our ranks outside of Spain would be less rigid in their appraisal if they too had come closer to the life-and-death struggle of the CNT–FAI—not that I do not agree with their criticism. I think them 95 per cent right. However, I insist that independent thinking and the right of criticism have ever been our proudest Anarchist boast, indeed, the very bulwark of Anarchism. The trouble with our Spanish comrades is their marked sensitivity to criticism, or even to advice from any comrade outside of Spain. But for that, they would understand that their critics are moved not by villainy, but by their deepest concern for the fate of the CNT–FAI.

The Spanish Anarcho-Syndicalist and Anarchist movements until very recently have held out the most glaring fulfillment of all our dreams and aspirations. I cannot therefore blame those of our comrades who see in the compromises of the Spanish Anarchists a reversal of all they had held high for well nigh seventy years. Naturally some comrades have grown apprehensive and have begun to cry out against the slippery road which the CNT–FAI entered on. I have known these comrades for years. They are among my dearest friends. I know it is their revolutionary integrity which makes them so critical, and not any ulterior motive. If our Spanish comrades could only understand this, they would be less indignant, nor consider their critics their enemies.

Also, I fear that the critics too are very much at fault. They are no less dogmatic than the Spanish comrades. They condemn every step made in Spain unreservedly. In their sectarian attitude they have overlooked the motive element recognised in our time even in capitalist courts. Yet it is a fact that one can never judge human action unless one has discovered the motive back of the action.

When I have pointed this out to our critical comrades they have insisted that Lenin and his group were also moved by the best intentions, "and see what they have made of the Revolution." I fail to see even the remotest similarity. Lenin aimed at a formidable State machine, a deadly dictatorship. From the very beginning, this spelled the death of the Russian Revolution—whereas the CNT–FAI not only aimed at, but actually gave life to, libertarian economic reconstructions. From the very moment they had driven the Fascists and militarists out of Catalonia, this herculean task was never lost sight of. The work achieved, considering the insurmountable obstacles, was extraordinary. Already on my first visit I was amazed to find so many collectives in the large cities and the villages.

I returned to Spain with apprehension because of all the rumours that had reached me after the May events of the destruction of the collectives. It is true that the Lister and Karl Marx Brigades went through Aragon and places in Catalonia like a cyclone, devastating everything in their way; but it is nevertheless the fact that most of the collectives were keeping up as if no harm had come to them. In fact I found the collectives in September and October 1937 in better-organised condition and in better working order— and that, after all, is the most important achievement that must be kept in mind in any appraisal of the mistakes made by our comrades in Spain. Unfortunately, our critical comrades do not seem to see this all-important side of the CNT–FAI. Yet it is this which differentiates them from Lenin and his crowd who, far from even attempting to articulate the Russian Revolution in terms of constructive effort, destroyed everything during the civil war and even many years after.

Strangely enough, the very comrades of the civil war in

Russia who had explained every step of the dictatorship as "revolutionary necessity" are now the most unyielding opponents of the CNT–FAI. "We have learned our lesson from the Russian Revolution," they say. But as no one learns anything from the experience of others, we must, whether we like it or not, give our Spanish comrades a chance to find their bearings through their own experience. Surely our own flesh and blood are entitled to the same patient help and solidarity some of us have given generously to our arch-enemies the Communists.

The CNT–FAI are not so wrong when they insist that the conditioning in Spain is quite different from that which actuated the struggle in Russia. In point of fact the two social upheavals are separate and distinct from each other.

The Russian Revolution came on top of a war-exhausted people, with all the social fabric in Russia disintegrated, the country far removed from outside influences. Whatever dangers it encountered during the civil war came entirely from within the country itself. Even the help given to the interventionists by England, Poland, and France were contributed sparingly. Not that these countries were not ready to crush the Revolution by means of well-equipped armies; but Europe was too sapped. There were neither men nor arms enough to enable the Russian counter-revolutionists to destroy the Revolution and its people.

The revolution in Spain was the result of a military and Fascist conspiracy. The first imperative need that presented itself to the CNT–FAI was to drive out the conspiratorial gang. The Fascist danger had to be met with almost bare hands. In this process the Spanish workers and peasants soon came to see that their enemies were not only Franco and his Moorish hordes. They soon found themselves beseiged by formidable armies and an array of modern arms furnished to Franco by Hitler and Mussolini, with all the imperialist pack playing their sinister underhanded game. In other words, while the Russian Revolution and the civil war were being fought out on Russian soil and by Russians, the Spanish revolution and anti-Fascist war involves all the powers of Europe. It is no exaggeration to say that the Spanish Civil War has spread out far beyond its own confines.

As if that were not enough to force the CNT–FAI to hold themselves up by *any* means, rather than to see the revolution and the masses drowned in the bloodbath prepared for them by Franco and his allies—our comrades had also to contend with the inertia of the international proletariat. Herein lies another tragic difference between the Russian and Spanish revolutions.

The Russian Revolution had met with almost instantaneous response and unstinted support from the workers in every land. This was soon followed by the revolution in Germany, Austria, and Hungary; and the general strike of the British workers who refused to load arms intended for the counter-revolutionists and interventionists. It brought about the mutiny in the Black Sea, and raised the workers everywhere to the highest pitch of enthusiasm and sacrifice.

The Spanish revolution, on the other hand, just because its leaders are Anarchists, immediately became a sore in the eyes not only of the bourgeoisie and the democratic governments, but also of the entire school of Marxists and liberals. In point of truth the Spanish revolution was betrayed by the whole world.

It has been suggested that our comrades in every country have contributed handsomely in men and money to the Spanish struggle, and that they alone should have been appealed to.

Well, comrades, we are members of the same family and we are among ourselves. We therefore need not beat around the bush. The deplorable fact is that there is no Anarchist or Anarcho-Syndicalist movement of any great consequence outside of Spain, and in a smaller degree France, with the exception of Sweden. Whatever Anarchist movements there are in other countries consist of small groups. In all England, for instance, there is no organised movement—only a few groups.

With the most fervent desire to aid the revolution in Spain, our comrades outside of it were neither numerically nor materially strong enough to turn the tide. Thus finding themselves up against a stone wall, the CNT–FAI was forced to descend from its lofty traditional heights to compromise right and left: participation in the government, all sorts of humiliating overtures to Stalin, superhuman tolerance for his henchmen who were openly plotting and conniving against the Spanish revolution.

Of all the unfortunate concessions our people have made, their entry into ministries seemed to me the least offensive. No, I have not changed my attitude toward government as an evil. As all through my life, I still hold that the State is a cold monster, and that it devours everyone within its reach. Did I not know that the Spanish people see in government a mere makeshift, to be kicked overboard at will, that they had never been deluded and corrupted by the parliamentary myth, I should perhaps be more alarmed for the future of the CNT–FAI. But with Franco at the gate of Madrid, I could hardly blame the CNT–FAI for choosing a lesser evil—participation in the government rather than dictatorship, the most deadly evil.

Russia has more than proven the nature of this beast. After twenty years it still thrives on the blood of its makers. Nor is its crushing weight felt in Russia alone. Since Stalin began his invasion of Spain, the march of his henchmen has been leaving death and ruin behind them. Destruction of numerous collectives, the introduction of the Tcheka with its "gentle" methods of treating political opponents, the arrest of thousands of revolutionaries, and the murder in broad daylight of others. All this and more, has Stalin's dictatorship given Spain, when he sold arms to the Spanish people in return for good gold. Innocent of the jesuitical trick of "our beloved comrade" Stalin, the CNT–FAI could not imagine in their wildest dreams the unscrupulous designs hidden behind the seeming solidarity in the offer of arms from Russia.

Their need to meet Franco's military equipment was a matter of life and death. The Spanish people had not a moment to lose if they were not to be crushed. What wonder if they saw in Stalin the saviour of the anti-Fascist war? They have since learned that Stalin helped to make Spain safe against the Fascists so as to make it safer for his own ends.

The critical comrades are not at all wrong when they say that it does not seem worthwhile to sacrifice one ideal in the struggle against Fascism, if it only means to make room for Soviet Communism. I am entirely of their view—that there is no difference between them. My own consolation is that with all their concentrated criminal efforts, Soviet Communism has not taken root in Spain. I know whereof I speak. On my recent visit to Spain I had ample opportunity to convince myself that the Communists have failed utterly to win the sympathies of the masses; quite the contrary. They have never been so hated by the workers and peasants as now.

It is true that the Communists are in the government and have political power—that they use their power to the detriment of the revolution, the anti-Fascist struggle, and the prestige of the CNT–FAI. But strange as it may seem, it is nevertheless no exaggeration when I say that in a moral sense the CNT has gained immeasurably. I give a few proofs.

Since the May events the Madrid circulation of the CNT [paper] has almost doubled, while the two Communist papers in that city have only 26,000. The CNT alone has 100,000 throughout Castile. The same has happened with our paper, *Castilla Libre*. In addition, there is the *Frente Libertario,* with a circulation of 100,000 copies.

A more significant fact is that when the Communists call a meeting it is poorly attended. When the CNT–FAI hold meetings the halls are packed to overflowing. I had one occasion to convince myself of this truth. I went to Allecante with comrade Federica Montseney and although the meeting was held in the forenoon, and rain came down in a downpour, the hall was nevertheless packed to capacity. It is the more surprising that the Communists can lord it over everybody; but it is one of the many contradictions of the situation in Spain.

If our comrades have erred in permitting the Communist invasion it was only because the CNT–FAI are the implacable enemies of Fascism. They were the first, not only in Spain but in the whole world, to repulse Fascism, and they are determined to remain the last on the battlefield, until the beast is slain. This supreme determination sets the CNT-FAI apart in the history of indomitable champions and fighters for freedom the world has ever known. Compared with this, their compromises appear in a less glaring light.

True, the tacit consent to militarization on the part of our Spanish comrades was a violent break with their Anarchist past. But grave as this was, it must also be considered in the light of their utter military inexperience. Not only theirs but ours as well. All of us have talked rather glibly about antimilitarism. In our zeal and loathing of war we have lost sight of modern warfare, of the utter helplessness of untrained and unequipped men face to face with mechanized armies, and armed to their teeth for the battle on land, sea, and air. I still feel the same abhorrence of militarism, its dehumanization, its brutality and its power to turn men into automatons. But my contact with our comrades at the various fronts during my first visit in 1936 convinced me that some training was certainly needed if our militias were not to be sacrificed like newborn children on the altar of war.

While it is true that after July 19 tens of thousands of old and young men volunteered to go to the front—they went with flying colours and the determination to conquer Franco in a short time—they had no previous military training or experience. I saw a great many of the militia when I visited the Durruti and Huesca fronts. They were all inspired by their ideal—by the hatred of Fascism and passionate love of freedom. No doubt that would have carried them a long way if they had had only the Spanish Fascists to face; but when Germany and Italy began pouring in hundreds of thousands of men and masses of war materiel, our militias proved very inadequate indeed. If it was inconsistent on the part of the CNT–FAI to consent to militarisation, it was also inconsistent for us to change our attitude toward war, which some of us had held all our lives. We had always condemned war as serving capitalism and no other purpose; but when we realised that our heroic comrades in Barcelona had to continue the anti-Fascist struggle, we immediately rallied to their support, which was undoubtedly a departure from our previous stand on war. Once we realised that it would be impossible to meet hordes of Fascists armed to the very teeth, we could not escape the next step, which was militarisation. Like so many actions of the CNT–FAI undoubtedly contrary to our philosophy, they were not of their making or choosing. They were imposed upon them by the development of the struggle, which if not brought to a successful end, would exterminate the CNT–FAI, destroy their constructive achievements, and set back Anarchist thought and ideas not only in Spain but in the rest of the world.

Dear comrades, it is not a question of justification of everything the CNT–FAI have been doing. It is merely trying to understand the forces that drove and drive them on. Whether to triumph or defeat will depend a great deal on how much we can awaken the international proletariat to come to the rescue of the struggle in Spain; and unless we can create unity among ourselves, I do not see how we can call upon the workers of the world to unite in their efforts to conquer Fascism and to rescue the Spanish revolution.

Our comrades have a sublime ideal to inspire them; they have great courage and the iron will to conquer Fascism. All that goes a long way to hold up their morale. Airplanes bombarding towns and villages and all the other monster mechanisms cannot be stopped by spiritual values. The greater the pity that our side was not prepared, nor had the physical means to match the inexhaustible supplies streaming into Franco's side.

It is a miracle of miracles that our people are still on deck, more than ever determined to win. I cannot but think that the training our comrades are getting in the military schools will make them fitter to strike, and with greater force. I have been strengthened in this belief by my talks with young comrades in the military schools—with some of them at the Madrid front and with CNT–FAI members occupying high military positions. They all assured me that they had gained much through the military training, and that they feel more competent and surer of themselves to meet the enemy forces. I am not forgetting the danger of militarisation in a prolonged war. If such a calamity should happen, there will not be many of our gallant militias left to return as military ultimatums. I fervently hope that Fascism will be conquered quickly, and that our comrades can return from the front in triumph to where they came from—the collectives, land and industries. For the present there is no danger that they will become cogs in the military wheel.

All these factors directing the course of the CNT–FAI should be taken into consideration by the comrade critics, who after all are far removed from the struggle, hence really not in a position to see the whole tragic drama through the eyes of those who are in the actual struggle.

I do not mean to say that I may not also reach the painful point of disagreement with the CNT–FAI. But until

Fascism is conquered, I would not raise my hand against them. For the present my place is at the side of the Spanish comrades and their great struggle against a whole world.

Comrades, the CNT–FAI are in a burning house; the flames are shooting up through every crevice, coming nearer and nearer to scorch our comrades. At this crucial moment, and with but few people trying to help save our people from the consuming flame, it seems to me a breach of solidarity to pour the acid of your criticism on their burned flesh. As for myself, I cannot join you in this. I know the CNT–FAI have gone far afield from their and our ideology. But that cannot make me forget their glorious revolutionary traditions of seventy years. Their gallant struggle—always haunted, always driven at bay, always in prison and exile. This makes me think that the CNT–FAI have remained fundamentally the same, and that the time is not far off when they will again prove themselves the symbol, the inspirational force, that the Spanish Anarcho-Syndicalists and Anarchists have always been to the rest of the Anarchists in the world.

Since I have been privileged to be in Spain twice—near the comrades, near their splendid constructive labour— since I was able to see their selflessness and determination to build a new life on their soil, my faith in our comrades has deepened into a firm conviction that, whatever their inconsistencies, they will return to first principles. Tested by the fires of the anti-Fascist war and the revolution, the CNT–FAI will emerge unscathed. Therefore I am with them, regardless of everything. A thousand times would I have rather remained in Spain to risk my life in their struggle than returned to the so-called safety in England. But since that could not be, I mean to strain every muscle and every nerve to make known, in as far as my pen and voice can reach, the great moral and organisational force of the CNT–FAI and the valour and heroism of our Spanish comrades.

Was My Life Worth Living?

How much a personal philosophy is a matter of temperament and how much it results from experience is a moot question. Naturally we arrive at conclusions in the light of our experience, through the application of a process we call reasoning to the facts observed in the events of our lives. The child is susceptible to fantasy. At the same time he sees life more truly in some respects than his elders do as he becomes conscious of his surroundings. He has not yet become absorbed by the customs and prejudices which make up the largest part of what passes for thinking. Each child responds differently to his environment. Some become rebels, refusing to be dazzled by social superstitions. They are outraged by every injustice perpetrated upon them or upon others. They grow ever more sensitive to the suffering round them and the restrictions which authority places in their way. Others become rubber stamps, registering every convention and taboo imposed upon them.

I evidently belong to the first category. Since my earliest recollection of my youth in Russia I have rebelled against orthodoxy in every form. I could never bear to witness harshness whether on the part of our parents to us or in their dealings with the servants. I was outraged over the official brutality practiced on the peasants in our neighborhood. I wept bitter tears when the young men were conscripted into the army and torn from homes and hearths. I resented the treatment of our servants, who did the hardest work and yet had to put up with wretched sleeping quarters and the leavings of our table. I was indignant when I discovered that love between young people of Jewish and Gentile origin was considered the crime of crimes, and the birth of an illegitimate child the most depraved immorality.

On coming to America I had the same hopes as have most European immigrants and the same disillusionment, though the latter affected me more keenly and more deeply. The immigrant without money and without connections is not permitted to cherish the comforting illusion that America is a benevolent uncle who assumes a tender and impartial guardianship of nephews and nieces. I soon learned that in a republic there are myriad ways by which the strong, the cunning, the rich can seize power and hold it. I saw the many work for small wages which kept them always on the borderline of want for the few who made huge profits. I saw the courts, the halls of legislation, the press, and the schools —in fact every avenue of education and protection—effectively used as an instrument for the safeguarding of a minority, while the masses were denied every right. I found that the politicians knew how to befog every issue, how to control public opinion and manipulate votes to their own advantage and to that of their financial and industrial allies. This was the picture of democracy I soon discovered on my arrival in the United States. Fundamentally there have been few changes since that time.

This situation, which was a matter of daily experience, was brought home to me with a force that tore away shams and made reality stand out vividly and clearly by an event which occurred shortly after my coming to America. It was the so-called Haymarket riot, which resulted in the trial and conviction of eight men, among them five Anarchists. Their crime was an all-embracing love for their fellow-men and their determination to emancipate the oppressed and disinherited masses. In no way had the State of Illinois succeeded in proving their connection with the bomb that had been thrown at an open-air meeting in Haymarket Square in Chicago. It was their Anarchism which resulted in their conviction and execution on the 11th of November, 1887. This judicial crime left an indelible mark on my mind and heart and sent me forth to acquaint myself with the ideal for which these men had died so heroically. I dedicated myself to their cause.

It requires something more than personal experience to gain a philosophy or point of view from any specific event. It is the quality of our response to the event and our capacity to enter into the lives of others that help us to make their lives and experiences our own. In my own case my convictions have derived and developed from events in the lives of others as well as from my own experience. What I have seen meted out to others by authority and repression, economic and political, transcends anything I myself may have endured.

I have often been asked why I maintained such a non-compromising antagonism to government and in what way I have found myself oppressed by it. In my opinion every individual is hampered by it. It exacts taxes from production. It creates tariffs, which prevent free exchange. It stands ever for the *status quo* and traditional conduct and belief. It comes into private lives and into most intimate personal relations, enabling the superstitious, puritanical, and distorted ones to impose their ignorant prejudice and moral servitudes upon the sensitive, the imaginative, and the free spirits. Government does this by its divorce laws, its moral censorships, and by a thousand petty persecutions of those who are too honest to wear the moral mask of respectability. In addition, government protects the strong at the expense of the weak, provides courts and laws which the rich may scorn and the poor must obey. It enables the predatory rich to make wars to provide foreign markets for the favored ones, with prosperity for the rulers and wholesale death for the ruled. However, it is not only government in the sense of the state which is destructive of every individual value and quality. It is the whole complex of authority and institutional domination which strangles life. It is the superstition, myth, pretense, evasions, and subservience which support authority and institutional domination. It is the reverence for these institutions instilled in the school, the Church, and the home in order that man may believe and obey without protest. Such a process of devitalizing and distorting personalities of the individual and of whole communities may have been a part of historical evolution; but it should be strenuously combated by every honest and independent mind in an age which has any pretense to enlightenment.

It has often been suggested to me that the Constitution of the United States is a sufficient safeguard for the freedom of its citizens. It is obvious that even the freedom it pretends to guarantee is very limited. I have not been impressed with the adequacy of the safeguard. The nations of the world, with centuries of international law behind them, have never hesitated to engage in mass destruction when solemnly pledged to keep the peace; and the legal documents in America have not prevented the United States from doing the same. Those in authority have and always will abuse their power. And the instances when they do not do so are as rare as roses growing on icebergs. Far from the Constitution playing any liberating part in the lives of the American people, it has robbed them of the capacity to rely on their own resources or do their own thinking. Americans are so easily hoodwinked by the sanctity of law and authority. In fact, the pattern of life has become standardized, routinized, and mechanized like canned food and Sunday ser-

mons. The hundred-percenter easily swallows syndicated
information and factory-made ideas and beliefs. He thrives
on the wisdom given him over the radio and cheap magazines by corporations whose philanthropic aim is selling
America out. He accepts the standards of conduct and art
in the same breath with the advertising of chewing gum,
toothpaste, and shoe polish. Even songs are turned out like
buttons or automobile tires—all cast from the same mold.

II.

Yet I do not despair of American life. On the contrary, I
feel that the freshness of the American approach and the
untapped stores of intellectual and emotional energy resi-
dent in the country offer much promise for the future. The
War has left in its wake a confused generation. The madness
and brutality they had seen, the needless cruelty and waste
which had almost wrecked the world made them doubt the
values their elders had given them. Some, knowing nothing
of the world's past, attempted to create new forms of life
and art from the air. Others experimented with decadence
and despair. Many of them, even in revolt, were pathetic.
They were thrust back into submission and futility because
they were lacking in an ideal and were further hampered by
a sense of sin and the burden of dead ideas in which they
could no longer believe.

Of late there has been a new spirit manifested in the
youth which is growing up with the Depression. This spirit is
more purposeful though still confused. It wants to create a
new world, but is not clear as to how it wants to go about it.
For that reason the young generation asks for saviors. It
tends to believe in dictators and to hail each new aspirant
for that honor as a messiah. It wants cut and dried systems
of salvation with a wise minority to direct society on some
one-way road to utopia. It has not yet realized that it must
save itself. The young generation has not yet learned that

the problems confronting them can be solved only by themselves and will have to be settled on the basis of social and economic freedom in co-operation with the struggling masses for the right to the table and joy of life.

As I have already stated, my objection to authority in whatever form has been derived from a much larger social view, rather than from anything I myself may have suffered from it. Government has, of course, interfered with my full expression, as it has with others. Certainly the powers have not spared me. Raids on my lectures during my thirty-five years' activity in the United States were a common occurrence, followed by innumerable arrests and three convictions to terms of imprisonment. This was followed by the annulment of my citizenship and my deportation. The hand of authority was forever interfering with my life. If I have none the less expressed myself, it was in spite of every curtailment and difficulty put in my path and not because of them. In that I was by no means alone. The whole world has given heroic figures to humanity, who in the face of persecution and obloquy have lived and fought for their right and the right of mankind to free and unstinted expression. America has the distinction of having contributed a large quota of native-born children who have most assuredly not lagged behind. Walt Whitman, Henry David Thoreau, Voltairine de Cleyre, one of America's great Anarchists, Moses Harman, the pioneer of woman's emancipation from sexual bondage, Horace Traubel, sweet singer of liberty, and quite an array of other brave souls have expressed themselves in keeping with their vision of a new social order based on freedom from every form of coercion. True, the price they had to pay was high. They were deprived of most of the comforts society offers to ability and talent, but denies when they will not be subservient. But whatever the price, their lives were enriched beyond the common lot. I, too, feel enriched beyond measure. But that is due to the discovery of Anarchism, which more than anything else has strengthened my conviction that authority stultifies human development, while full freedom assures it.

I consider Anarchism the most beautiful and practical philosophy that has yet been thought of in its application to individual expression and the relation it establishes between the individual and society. Moreover, I am certain that Anarchism is too vital and too close to human nature ever to die. It is my conviction that dictatorship, whether to the right or to the left, can never work—that it never has worked, and that time will prove this again, as it has been proved before. When the failure of modern dictatorship and authoritarian philosophies becomes more apparent and the realization of failure more general, Anarchism will be vindicated. Considered from this point, a recrudescence of Anarchist ideas in the near future is very probable. When this occurs and takes effect, I believe that humanity will at last leave the maze in which it is now lost and will start on the path to sane living and regeneration through freedom.

There are many who deny the possibility of such regeneration on the ground that human nature cannot change. Those who insist that human nature remains the same at all times have learned nothing and forgotten nothing. They certainly have not the faintest idea of the tremendous strides that have been made in sociology and psychology, proving beyond a shadow of a doubt that human nature is plastic and can be changed. Human nature is by no means a fixed quantity. Rather, it is fluid and responsive to new conditions. If, for instance, the so-called instinct of self-preservation were as fundamental as it is supposed to be, wars would have been eliminated long ago, as would all dangerous and hazardous occupations.

Right here I want to point out that there would not be such great changes required as is commonly supposed to insure the success of a new social order, as conceived by Anarchists. I feel that our present equipment would be adequate if the artificial oppressions and inequalities and the organized force and violence supporting them were removed.

Again it is argued that if human nature can be changed, would not the love of liberty be trained out of the human heart? Love of freedom is a universal trait, and no tyranny has thus far succeeded in eradicating it. Some of the modern dictators might try it, and in fact are trying it with every means of cruelty at their command. Even if they should last long enough to carry on such a project—which is hardly conceivable—there are other difficulties. For one thing, the people whom the dictators are attempting to train would have to be cut off from every tradition in their history that might suggest to them the benefits of freedom. They would also have to isolate them from contact with any other people from whom they could get libertarian ideas. The very fact, however, that a person has a consciousness of self, of being different from others, creates a desire to act freely. The craving for liberty and self-expression is a very fundamental and dominant trait.

As is usual when people are trying to get rid of uncomfortable facts, I have often encountered the statement that the average man does not want liberty; that the love for it exists in very few; that the American people, for instance, simply do not care for it. That the American people are not wholly lacking in the desire for freedom was proved by their resistance to the late Prohibition Law, which was so effective that even the politicians finally responded to popular demand and repealed the amendment. If the American masses had been as determined in dealing with more important issues, much more might have been accomplished. It is true, however, that the American people are just beginning to be ready for advanced ideas. This is due to the historical evolution of the country. The rise of capitalism and a very powerful state are, after all, recent in the United States. Many still foolishly believe themselves back in the pioneer tradition when success was easy, opportunities more plentiful than now, and the economic position of the individual was not likely to become static and hopeless.

It is true, none the less, that the average American is still steeped in these traditions, convinced that prosperity will yet return. But because a number of people lack individuality and the capacity for independent thinking I cannot admit that for this reason society must have a special nursery to regenerate them. I would insist that liberty, real liberty, a freer and more flexible society, is the only medium for the development of the best potentialities of the individual.

I will grant that some individuals grow to great stature in revolt against existing conditions. I am only too aware of the fact that my own development was largely in revolt. But I consider it absurd to argue from this fact that social evils should be perpetrated to make revolt against them necessary. Such an argument would be a repetition of the old religious idea of purification. For one thing it is lacking in imagination to suppose that one who shows qualities above the ordinary could have developed only in one way. The person who under this system has developed along the lines of revolt might readily in a different social situation have developed as an artist, scientist, or in any other creative and intellectual capacity.

III.

Now I do not claim that the triumph of my ideas would eliminate all possible problems from the life of man for all time. What I do believe is that the removal of the present artificial obstacles to progress would clear the ground for new conquests and joy of life. Nature and our own complexes are apt to continue to provide us with enough pain and struggle. Why then maintain the needless suffering imposed by our present social structure, on the mythical grounds that our characters are thus strengthened, when broken hearts and crushed lives about us every day give the lie to such a notion?

Most of the worry about the softening of human character under freedom comes from prosperous people. It would be difficult to convince the starving man that plenty to eat would ruin his character. As for individual development in the society to which I look forward, I feel that with freedom and abundance unguessed springs of individual initiative would be released. Human curiosity and interest in the world could be trusted to develop individuals in every conceivable line of effort.

Of course those steeped in the present find it impossible to realize that gain as an incentive could be replaced by another force that would motivate people to give the best that is in them. To be sure, profit and gain are strong factors in our present system. They have to be. Even the rich feel a sense of insecurity. That is, they want to protect what they have and to strengthen themselves. The gain and profit motives, however, are tied up with more fundamental motives. When a man provides himself with clothes and shelter, if he is the moneymaker type, he continues to work to establish his status—to give himself prestige of the sort admired in the eyes of his fellow-men. Under different and more just conditions of life these more fundamental motives could be put to special uses, and the profit motive, which is only their manifestation, will pass away. Even to-day the scientist, inventor, poet, and artist are not primarily moved by the consideration of gain or profit. The urge to create is the first and most impelling force in their lives. If this urge is lacking in the mass of workers it is not at all surprising, for their occupation is deadly routine. Without any relation to their lives or needs, their work is done in the most appalling surroundings, at the behest of those who have the power of life and death over the masses. Why then should they be impelled to give of themselves more than is absolutely necessary to eke out their miserable existence?

In art, science, literature, and in departments of life which we believe to be somewhat removed from our daily living we are hospitable to research, experiment, and innovation. Yet, so great is our traditional reverence for authority that an irrational fear arises in most people when experiment is suggested to them. Surely there is even greater reason for experiment in the social field than in the scientific. It is to be hoped, therefore, that humanity or some portion of it will be given the opportunity in the not too distant future to try its fortune living and developing under an application of freedom corresponding to the early stages of an anarchistic society. The belief in freedom assumes that human beings can co-operate. They do it even now to a surprising extent, or organized society would be impossible. If the devices by which men can harm one another, such as private property, are removed and if the worship of authority can be discarded, co-operation will be spontaneous and inevitable, and the individual will find it his highest calling to contribute to the enrichment of social well-being.

Anarchism alone stresses the importance of the individual, his possibilities and needs in a free society. Instead of telling him that he must fall down and worship before institutions, live and die for abstractions, break his heart and stunt his life for taboos, Anarchism insists that the center of gravity in society is the individual—that he must think for himself, act freely, and live fully. The aim of Anarchism is that every individual in the world shall be able to do so. If he is to develop freely and fully, he must be relieved from the interference and oppression of others. Freedom is, therefore, the cornerstone of the Anarchist philosophy. Of course, this has nothing in common with a much boasted "rugged individualism." Such predatory individualism is really flabby, not rugged. At the least danger to its safety it runs to cover of the state and wails for protection of armies, navies, or whatever devices for strangulation it has at its command. Their "rugged individualism" is simply one of the many pretenses the ruling class makes to unbridled business and political extortion.

Regardless of the present trend toward the strong-armed man, the totalitarian states, or the dictatorship from the left, my ideas have remained unshaken. In fact, they have been strengthened by my personal experience and the world events through the years. I see no reason to change, as I do not believe that the tendency of dictatorship can ever successfully solve our social problems. As in the past so I do now insist that freedom is the soul of progress and essential to every phase of life. I consider this as near a law of social evolution as anything we can postulate. My faith is in the individual and in the capacity of free individuals for united endeavor.

The fact that the Anarchist movement for which I have striven so long is to a certain extent in abeyance and overshadowed by philosophies of authority and coercion affects me with concern, but not with despair. It seems to me a point of special significance that many countries decline to admit Anarchists. All governments hold the view that while parties of the right and left may advocate social changes, still they cling to the idea of government and authority. Anarchism alone breaks with both and propagates uncompromising rebellion. In the long run, therefore, it is Anarchism which is considered deadlier to the present régime than all other social theories that are now clamoring for power.

Considered from this angle, I think my life and my work have been successful. What is generally regarded as success —acquisition of wealth, the capture of power or social prestige—I consider the most dismal failures. I hold when it is said of a man that he has arrived, it means that he is finished—his development has stopped at that point. I have always striven to remain in a state of flux and continued growth, and not to petrify in a niche of self-satisfaction. If I had my life to live over again, like anyone else, I should wish to alter minor details. But in any of my more important actions and attitudes I would repeat my life as I have lived it. Certainly I should work for Anarchism with the same devotion and confidence in its ultimate triumph.

Index

ABOUT THE EDITOR

ALIX KATES SHULMAN grew up in Cleveland, Ohio.
After graduating from Western Reserve University
there, she moved to New York City, where she studied
philosophy at Columbia and mathematics at New York
University.

An active feminist, she now lives in Manhattan with
her husband and two children. Her essays on anarchist women and other feminist subjects have appeared
in Women's Liberation journals and anthologies. She
is the author of *Memoirs of an Ex-Prom Queen,* a
novel; *To The Barricades,* a biography of Emma
Goldman; and several books for children.

VINTAGE BELLES—LETTRES

VINTAGE CRITICISM,
LITERATURE, MUSIC, AND ART

VINTAGE POLITICAL SCIENCE
AND SOCIAL CRITICISM